I0824761

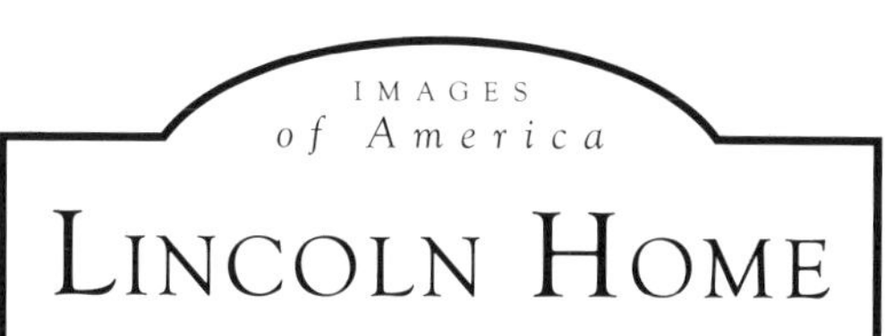
IMAGES
of America
LINCOLN HOME

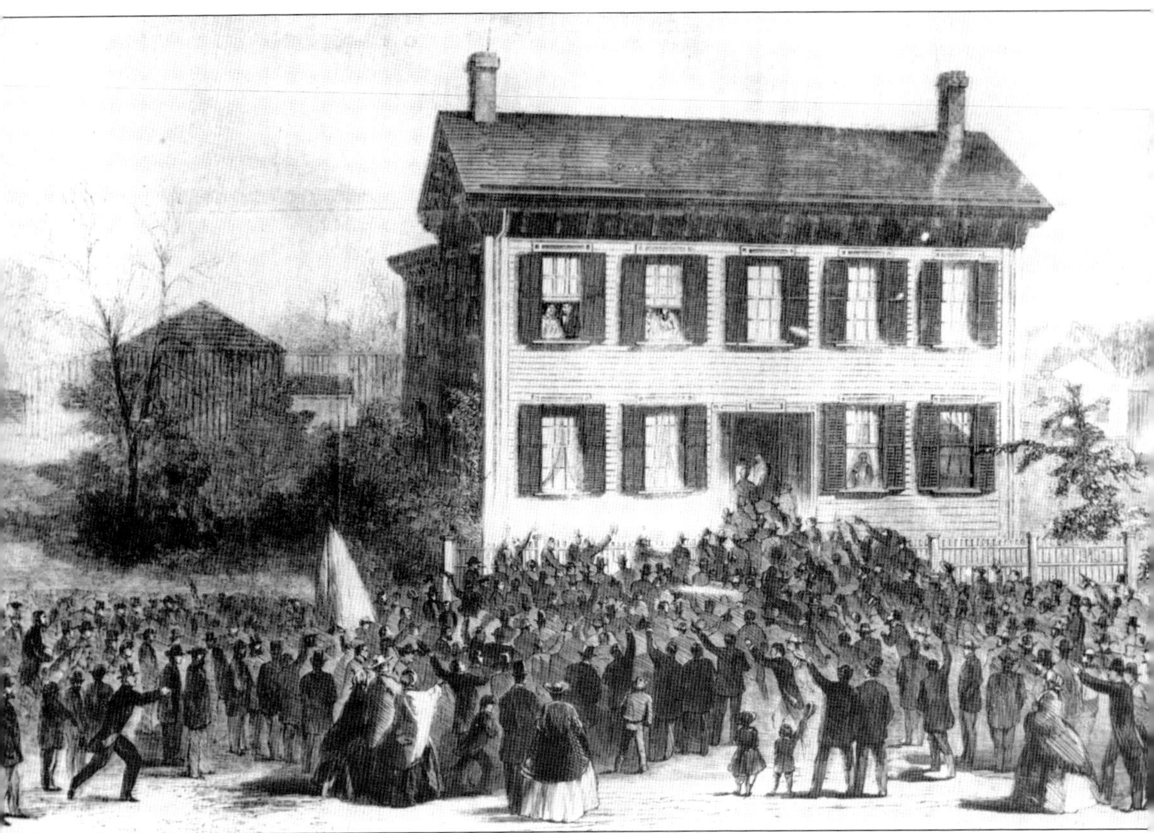

Enthusiastic supporters gathered outside of Abraham Lincoln's home on the morning of November 7, 1860, to celebrate his election to the presidency the day before. Abraham and Mary Lincoln can be seen looking out of Lincoln's bedroom window at the upper left. (Author's collection.)

On the Cover: This 1905 image shows tourists in a buggy passing in front of the Lincoln Home, while three boys stare at the camera from the other side of the horse. The Lincoln Elm stands in the foreground (it would be destroyed in a storm the following year). A sign near the front door reads "Lincoln Residence" and provides the hours of operation. (Abraham Lincoln Presidential Library and Museum.)

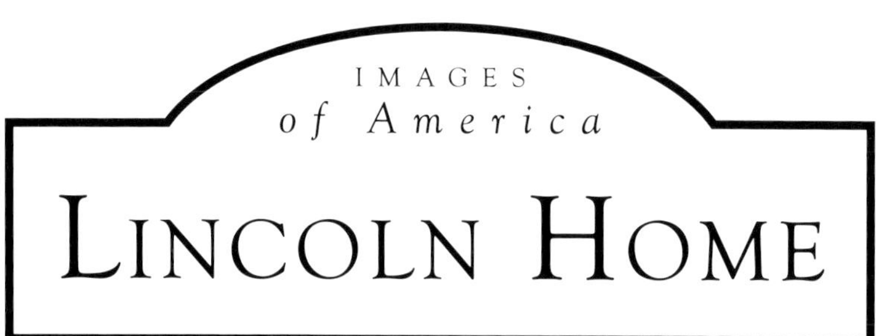

Jonathan W. White

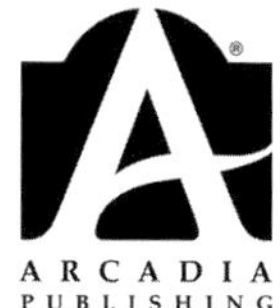

ISBN 9781-4671-6336-1

Published by Arcadia Publishing
Charleston, South Carolina

Printed in the United States of America

Library of Congress Control Number: 2026934318

For all general information, please contact Arcadia Publishing:
Telephone 843-853-2070
Fax 843-853-0044
E-mail sales@arcadiapublishing.com

Visit us on the Internet at www.arcadiapublishing.com

For my parents, Bill and Eileen White,
who instilled in me a love of history.

And for Lauren, Charlotte, and Clara,
who go with me to all the Lincoln sites.

Contents

Acknowledgments

I thank the many people who helped make this book a reality. First, I thank Amy Devaisher, store manager at the Lincoln Home National Historic Site, for her enthusiastic support of this book and my other works on Lincoln.

Many people and institutions helped me collect images for this book. I thank Stephanie Martin and Kim McNutt of the Sangamon Valley Collection (SVC) at the Lincoln Library in Springfield; Sylvia Frank Rodrigue, Linda Buhman, and Kristine Priddy of SIU Press; Donna Stewart of the Coles County Genealogical Society; John Popolis of Lincoln Home National Historic Site (LIHO); Daniel Worthington of the Papers of Abraham Lincoln; Kelsey Wise and Matthew Deihl of the Abraham Lincoln Presidential Library and Museum (ALPLM); Zoe Cheek of the Lyman & Merrie Wood Museum of Springfield History in Massachusetts (WMSH Archives); Olga Tsapina of the Huntington Library (HL); Sandra Fritz of the Office of the Illinois Secretary of State (ILSOS); Michael Lynch and Alexandria Olson of Lincoln Memorial University (LMU); the Portrait Collection of the Church of Jesus Christ of Latter-day Saints (LDS); the Mary Todd Lincoln House and the University of Kentucky Special Collections (MTL); and John Lupton of the Illinois Supreme Court Historic Preservation Commission. Kevin Whaley of the Indiana State Museum and Jessie Cortesi and Abbie Meek of the Rolland Center for Lincoln Research at the Allen County Public Library provided images from the Lincoln Financial Foundation Collection (LFFC). Any photographs credited as LFA are from the Lincoln Family Album at the Rolland Center. I especially thank Stephanie Martin, Jessie Cortesi, John Popolis, and Matthew Deihl for going above and beyond in helping me track down images.

Several private families and collectors also generously shared images. I thank Heather Cornelius, who made scans from the George Buss Collection (GBC); Chris and Annette Watson for providing images from the Harris-Reeves Family Album (HRFA); and Keya Morgan for permission to use his image of Eddy Lincoln. Images marked "JW" are from the author's collection.

I thank Michael Burlingame, Tim Good, Jason Emerson, and John Popolis for reading an early draft of this book and providing valuable feedback. Finally, I thank James Cornelius, Jake Friefeld, Christian McWhirter, and Samuel Wheeler for telling me some of the stories that appear in the pages that follow.

Introduction

Visitors have flocked to the corner of Eighth and Jackson Streets in Springfield, Illinois, for more than a century and a half. It is a magical place where people encounter Abraham Lincoln, the private man. Between 1844 and 1861, people could literally meet "Mr. Lincoln" and his family there. Typically, they got no farther than the parlors to the left of the front doorway or the sitting room to the right. Today, thanks to Robert Todd Lincoln's desire to keep the home open to the public, we are welcome to tour not only the parlors but also the private spaces in which the Lincolns lived—where the future president played with his children, scratched kittens behind the ears, discussed family matters with Mary, read newspapers, and wrote speeches. Walking upstairs with their hands clutched tightly to the railing, tourists are as close to shaking hands with the Great Emancipator as they will ever come. These are, after all, the same stairs that a Wisconsin man saw Lincoln come "tripping down" on July 18, 1860, "as lively as a young man of sixteen years of age—sliding his right hand on the banister."

The Lincolns' home first became a national tourist destination during the 1860 presidential election. At first, the attention must have been exciting. In early June, Mary Lincoln wrote, "We had about twenty of the most prominent Republicans of the State to take supper with us." But soon, the waves of visitors took their toll. In October, Mary complained to a friend, "This summer, we have had immense crowds of strangers visiting us, and have had no time to be occupied, with home affairs."

One of those visitors, a correspondent for a Philadelphia newspaper, described his encounter with the house during a trip to the Illinois capital. "As I was rambling around Springfield, in the vicinity of Mr. Lincoln's home, I accosted a good-natured looking lady, surrounded with a bevy of children, and plucking flowers in a garden close by." When he asked the woman where the Lincolns lived, she turned around and pointed toward the house. Then, with what sounded to the traveler like a blend of naivete and old-fashioned hospitality, she said, "Won't you walk in? you'll be welcome there!" The correspondent later observed that he was "impressed with . . . the true republican simplicity of Mr. Lincoln's character, and of the neighborly cordiality which that character has naturally evoked."

Walking over to the corner of Eighth and Jackson Streets, the Philadelphian remarked that it was "a simple two-storied, double frame house . . . which wears a Quaker tint of light brown, stands upon a plateau elevated three or four feet above the sidewalk." Above the brick foundation wall was "a neat paled fence, with handsome square posts, enclosing the front and side of the property." Behind the house was "a large garden," although the correspondent did not describe what he saw growing in it. "There is no sign of pretension anywhere visible," he observed. "The building is singularly quiet-looking and cozy, just such a home as a sensible man in one of our sensible Pennsylvania towns would care to enjoy."

Many visitors observed the unpretentiousness of the Lincolns' residence. A correspondent for the *New York Herald* opined that the Lincolns' "plain brown" home was "without ornament on it or in the grounds around it. Everything bespeaks a becoming absence of affectation and love of show, and an almost unbecoming absence of taste and refinement." This writer noted that even the interior of the home was "plain but tasteful," which clearly showed "the impress of Mrs. Lincoln's hand, who is really an amiable and accomplished lady." John Locke Scripps, the editor of the *Chicago Tribune*, similarly remarked, "At home he lives like a gentleman of moderate means and simple tastes. A good-sized house of wood, simply but tastefully furnished, surrounded by trees and flowers, is his own." However, the Lincolns may not have planted the flowers. Mary's sister Frances Todd Wallace later recalled that neither Abraham nor Mary "loved the beautiful," so Frances would often go to their house to plant flowers in the front yard "to hide nakedness" and "ugliness."

In truth, Mary Lincoln had her hands full keeping house at Eighth and Jackson Streets, where she prepared meals, corralled children, cared for pets, entertained friends, welcomed strangers, and boarded tenants. When unknown callers came to the door asking for her husband, she might ask them, "Business or politics?" The Lincolns hosted many gatherings, particularly when the state legislature was in session. On Thursday, February 5, 1857, they hosted what Orville Hickman Browning described in his diary as a "large & pleasant party." Another attendee that evening, state legislator Henry G. Little, later remembered that waiters poured coffee while guests served themselves food from a long table that "was stretched nearly the whole length of the room, while above the table was a succession of shelves growing narrower upward. On these shelves the edibles were placed, and the guests . . . were left to help themselves." Little observed Lincoln standing by the table joking, "Do they give you anything to eat here?" Afterward, Mary proudly told her half-sister Emilie Todd Helm, "I may perhaps surprise you, when I mention that I am recovering from a slight fatigue of a very large & I really believe a very handsome & agreable entertainment, at least our friends flatter us by saying so." About 500 guests had been invited, "yet owing to an unlucky rain, 300 only favored us with their presence."

In fact, the Lincoln home was often noisy even when there were not hundreds of guests. The Lincoln children were notoriously rambunctious, in large measure because Lincoln rarely disciplined them (although Mary did). In October 1846, Lincoln described three-year-old Robert as having "a great deal of that sort of mischief, that is the offspring of much animal spirits." As Lincoln was writing this to his best friend, Joshua Speed, a messenger came to tell him that Robert "was lost." Lincoln went straight home, but by the time he "reached the house, his mother had found him, and had him whip[p]ed," Lincoln wrote, "and, by now, very likely he is run away again." Herndon later recollected that Willie and Tad, the Lincolns' two youngest sons, would pile up books into playhouses and tear up papers at the law office. "If they pulled down all the books from the shelves, bent the points of all the pens, overturned inkstands, scattered law-papers over the floor, or threw the pencils in the spittoon, it never disturbed the serenity of their father's good nature," Herndon wrote. "Had they s—t in Lincoln's hat and rubbed it on his boots, he would have laughed and thought it smart."

The boys got away with such hooliganism, Herndon said, because their father was so "frequently absorbed in thought" that "he never observed their mischievous but destructive pranks." By all accounts, the boys could be just as devilish at home. One day, Robert and Tad sent a metal foot tub tumbling down the front staircase. When they told their father that they were trying to imitate the cataracts at Niagara Falls and that the "tub was just the boat bouncing on the rocks going over the falls," Lincoln replied, "Well, boys, you got the right idea, but in the wrong place." He then laughingly added, "Well, that's one way of cleaning the stairs and carpet in short order." On another occasion, when Lincoln was informed that Tad had fallen into the cistern, he did not rush home because Tad "had done this before." In February 1861, when an Ohio politician sent Lincoln a whistle made from a pig's tail, Lincoln "enjoyed the joke hugely," but after practicing on it for nearly an hour, he could not get it to make a sound. His son Tad had more luck, "making the house vocal, if not musical, with the pig-tail whistle, blowing blasts that would have astonished Roderick Dhu."

It was also in this home that the future president let his guard down. More than one visitor later claimed to have seen him in his socks and undershirt. Harriet Chapman, a relative who lived with the Lincolns in the 1840s, remembered one day when several ladies called at the front door.

Abraham was only wearing shirt sleeves when he opened the door and invited them in. According to Chapman, "This made Mrs. L. mad." In 1854, when William Jayne came to urge Lincoln to run for the state legislature, he found Lincoln "the saddest man I Ever Saw—the gloomiest: he walked up and down the floor—almost crying."

Some of the most impactful moments in Lincoln's life took place in the house at Eighth and Jackson Streets, although we do not always know exactly when or in which room they occurred. One case in point involved a vision Lincoln had in 1860 that may have portended his assassination in 1865. In June 1864, when Lincoln received word of his renomination for the presidency, he told the painter Francis B. Carpenter about "a very singular occurrence" that had taken place four years earlier, on May 18, 1860—"the day I was nominated at Chicago." Upon returning home that afternoon, Lincoln went into Mary's sitting room on the first floor and reclined on a couch. As he looked across the room at the mirror, "I saw distinctly *two* images of myself, exactly alike, except that one was a little paler than the other." Lincoln got up and then lay back down and saw the double image again. "It made me quite uncomfortable for a few moments," Lincoln told Carpenter, but soon some friends arrived, and the matter passed out of his mind. The next day, Lincoln retried the experiment and attained the same result, determining "that it was the natural result of some principle of refraction or optics which I did not understand."

Journalist Noah Brooks heard the story from Lincoln shortly after the presidential election in November 1864 (four months after Lincoln told the story to Carpenter). According to Brooks, Lincoln saw this vision on Election Day in 1860, not on the day he was nominated. In Brooks's account, Lincoln was in his bedroom on the second floor, not in the sitting room. As Brooks heard the story, the tips of Lincoln's two noses in the double vision were three inches apart. And according to Brooks, Mary was greatly troubled by the vision, believing it meant that Lincoln would be elected to a second term but "that the paleness of one of the faces was an omen that I should not see life through the last term." According to Brooks, Lincoln would think of the vision every "once in a while," and it "gave me a little pang, as though something uncomfortable had happened." Nevertheless, Brooks concluded in general agreement with Carpenter: "The President, with his usual good sense, saw nothing in all this but an optical illusion; though the flavor of superstition which hangs about every man's composition made him wish that he had never seen it."

Visitors to the Lincoln Home today who walk through the sitting room on the first floor can look in the same mirror Lincoln gazed in more than 160 years ago, although their angles of vision from the carpeted walkway may not enable them to experience the same phenomena Lincoln experienced in 1860. (The mirror above the chest of drawers in Lincoln's bedroom is not his original.)

Of course, working as a lawyer on the Eighth Illinois Judicial Circuit pulled Lincoln away from home for several months each year. With her husband gone so much, Mary often kept a live-in hired girl as a servant. Feeling lonely, she also sometimes had neighborhood children stay with her. The 1860 census listed a 14-year-old boy named Phillip Dinkell residing in the home. According to some accounts, the Lincolns paid 5¢ per night for boys to stay there. James Gourley, a shoemaker who had known Lincoln since the 1830s and who lived one block to the east, later recalled that when Lincoln was away, "the boys & men used to Come to her house in Ls absence and scare her." He remembered one night when Mary was "crying & wailing." She called out, "Mr Gourly—Come—do Come & Stay with me all night—you Can Sleep in the bed with Bob and I. I don't want boys: they'd go to Sleep to[o] Soon & won't & can't watch—Come do—Sleep with Robt. & myself." Another acquaintance similarly testified that the Lincolns took in boarders because "Mrs. Lincoln was afraid to be alone."

On occasion, Abraham remained at home while Mary took a trip. Journalist Henry Villard reported that when Mary went to New York City in January 1861, "the President elect has been keeping house alone." Whatever Lincoln's qualifications were for political leadership, Villard joked that he was "sadly destitute of both talent and experience" in his "management of the kitchen and other domestic concerns." In fact, Lincoln anxiously awaited Mary's return from New York City. One newspaper reported, "Mr. Lincoln is a model husband. For three successive nights, each stormy with snow, he waited at the Springfield railroad depot for the return of his wife." Witnesses saw him walking with an umbrella to shield himself from the snow, and some worried that "his conjugal fidelity" might bring about "bronchitis, neuralgia, and diphtheria." When Mary finally returned home, Henry Villard wondered "whether she got a good scolding from Abraham for unexpectedly prolonging her absence."

The home that visitors walk through today is not the same structure that the Lincolns moved into in 1844. Originally constructed as a one-and-a-half-story cottage in 1839, the Lincolns made several improvements to the property over the years, most notably raising it to a full two stories in 1856. When the Lincolns departed Springfield in February 1861, the home became a rental property. In 1883, when Lincolniana collector Osborn Oldroyd moved in, he turned the downstairs parlors into a private museum. In 1887, Robert Lincoln transferred the title of the home to the State of Illinois for $1, insisting that the state keep the property in good repair and free and open to the public. Finally, in 1972, the house became a component of the National Park Service, still upholding Robert's desire to remain open to the public free of charge.

This book traces the history of this national landmark as well as the stories of many of the people who have walked through its doors, including the Lincolns' family and friends, politicians, foreign dignitaries, and generations of tourists. What draws so many people to walk through the door with the "A. Lincoln" nameplate? Perhaps Mary captured this in a letter she wrote to Francis B. Carpenter in November 1865, seven months after her husband's assassination. Mary noted that Lincoln seemed happier in the last three weeks of his life, as the war was coming to a close. During this time, she observed that he was spending "most of the time *away* from" Washington, "where he had endured such conflicts of mind." He had become "almost boyish in his mirth & reminded me, of his original nature, what I had always remembered of him, in our own home—free from care, surrounded by those he loved so well & by whom, he was so idolized."

One

There I Grew Up

Lincoln's Early Homes

Abraham Lincoln rose from abject poverty to a place of highest regard in American history. His transformation from a poor farm boy to a respectable attorney and politician can be traced in the places he lived. For his first 22 years, he resided with his family in log cabins in Kentucky, Indiana, and Illinois. As a young man, he boarded in strangers' homes, in stores, and in taverns. It was not until 1844 that he finally purchased a home of his own.

Perhaps no one understood the significance of Lincoln's rise from poverty more than Frederick Douglass. In his famous 1876 speech dedicating the statue of Lincoln at Lincoln Park in Washington, DC, Douglass pointed out that Lincoln had been "born and reared among the lowly, a stranger to wealth and luxury, compelled to grapple single-handed with the flintiest hardships of life." But from "tender youth to sturdy manhood," Lincoln "grew strong in the manly and heroic qualities demanded by the great mission to which he was called by the votes of his countrymen." Overcoming the "hard condition of his early life," Douglass said, had given Lincoln "the heroic spirit" he needed to accomplish the great tasks set before him as a wartime president.

Douglass believed that rising from humble origins gave Lincoln a sense of authenticity when he interacted with those around him. "In all my interviews with Mr. Lincoln I was impressed with his entire freedom from popular prejudice against the colored race," Douglass wrote in 1886. "He was the first great man that I talked with in the United States freely, who in no single instance reminded me of the difference between himself and myself, of the difference of color." Douglass believed this was, in part at least, "because of the similarity with which I had fought my way up, we both starting at the lowest round of the ladder." Lincoln, in short, had learned both politics and basic human decency as a boy and young man splitting rails on the frontiers of Kentucky, Indiana, and Illinois.

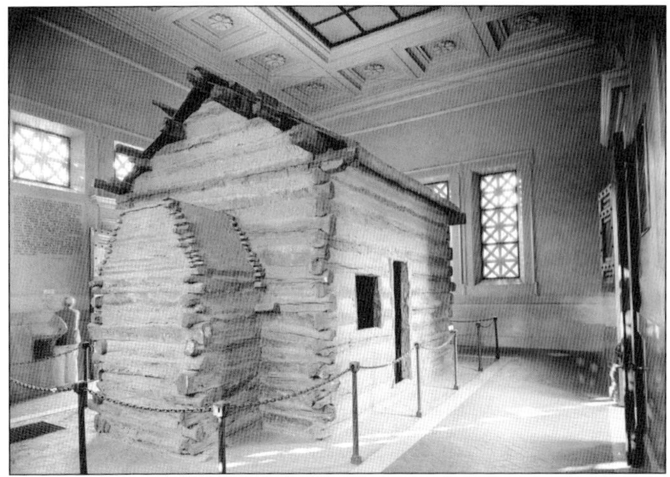

Abraham Lincoln was born in a one-room log cabin in Hodgenville, Kentucky, on February 12, 1809, to Thomas and Nancy Lincoln. The cabin was 16 by 18 feet with a dirt floor and no door or glass in the windows. In 1894, New York restaurant owner Alfred Dennett tried to turn the farm into a resort, but tourists did not flock to Kentucky, so he put the cabin on display at several places, including Coney Island. (LOC.)

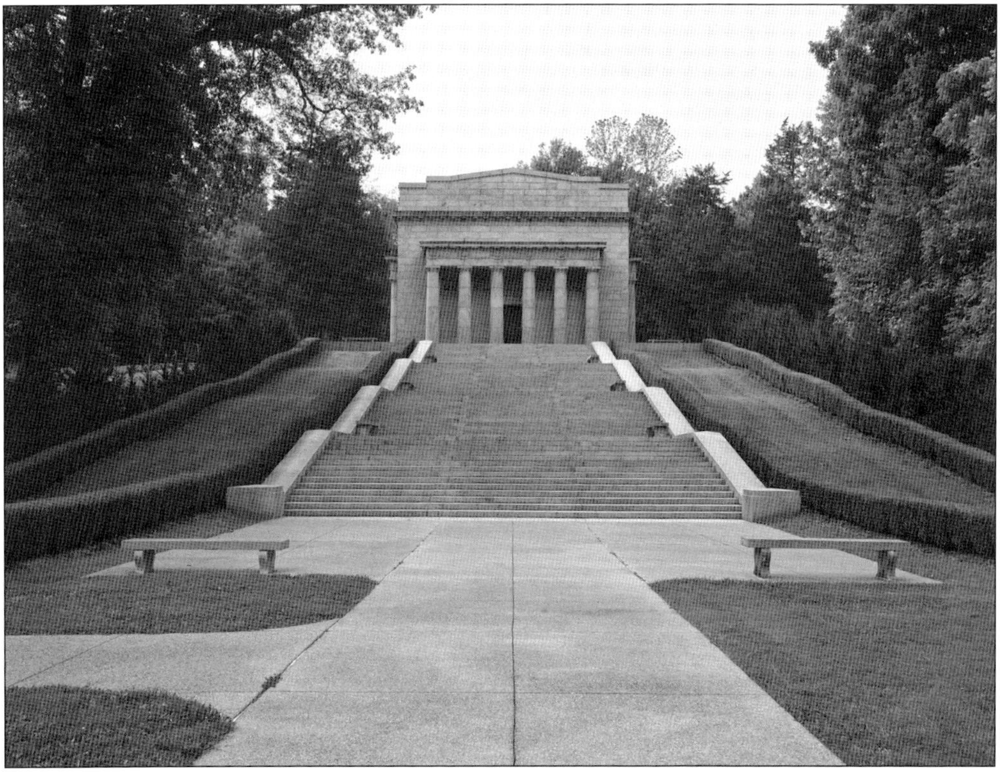

Lincoln lovers like Mark Twain, Theodore Roosevelt, and William Howard Taft formed the Lincoln Farm Association in 1905 to raise money to bring the cabin back to Kentucky. Architect John Russell Pope designed a temple to house it with 56 steps leading up to the entrance, one for each year of Lincoln's life. In 2004, tree ring sampling determined that the cabin is actually from the 1850s, so it is now called the "symbolic" birth cabin. (LOC.)

When Lincoln was two, his family moved a few miles north to the Knob Creek Valley. One day, he almost drowned when he and his friend Austin Gollaher were chasing birds near the creek. Fortunately, Austin saved young Abe by reaching a stick into the water and pulling him out. Pictured here is the cabin "as it now stands" in the late 19th century. (JW.)

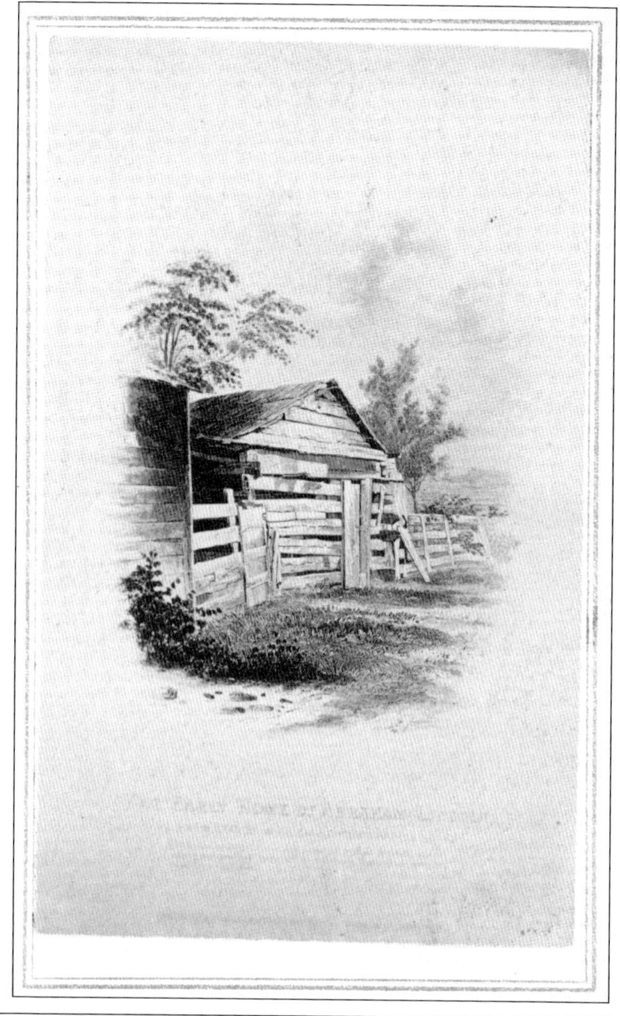

Thomas Lincoln moved his family to the new free state of Indiana in 1816, as Abraham later explained, "partly on account of slavery, but chiefly on account of the difficulty of land titles in Kentucky." Thomas purchased 160 acres and built a cabin near Little Pigeon Creek. For several months, the family lived in a half-faced camp, like this one, while they cleared the land and built a home. (LOC.)

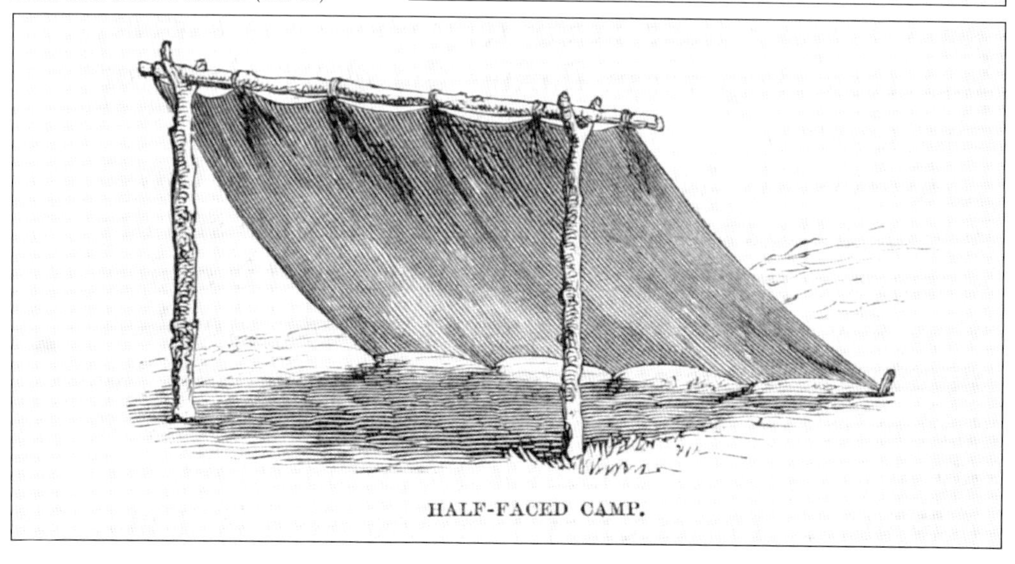

HALF-FACED CAMP.

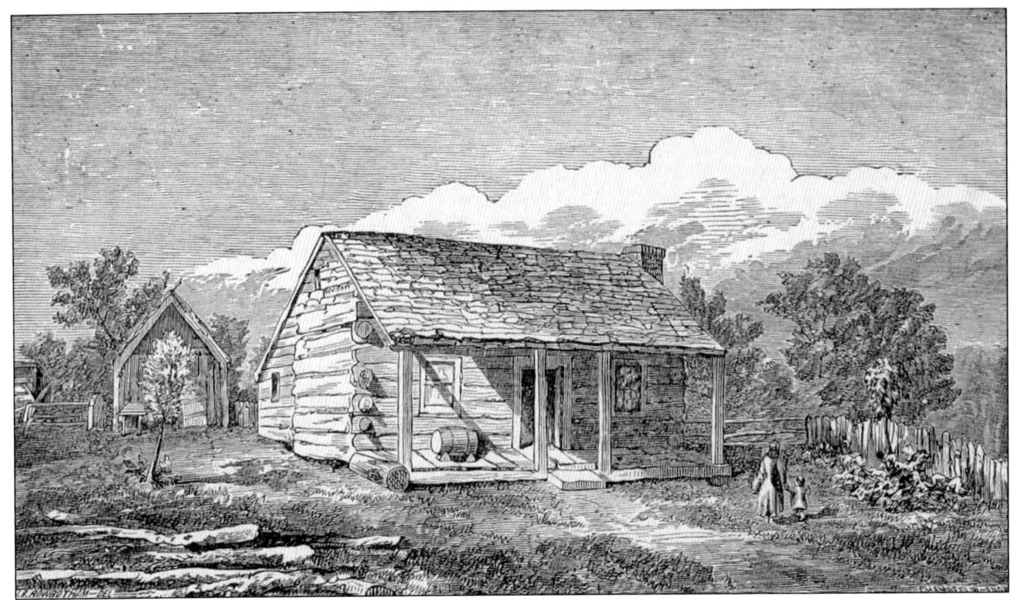

In 1859, Lincoln described Spencer County, Indiana, as "a wild region, with many bears and other wild animals still in the woods. There I grew up." Lincoln worked diligently to educate himself in this region, reading any book he could get his hands on. He later remarked, "If a straggler supposed to understand latin, happened to so-journ in the neighborhood, he was looked upon as a wizzard." (University of Illinois.)

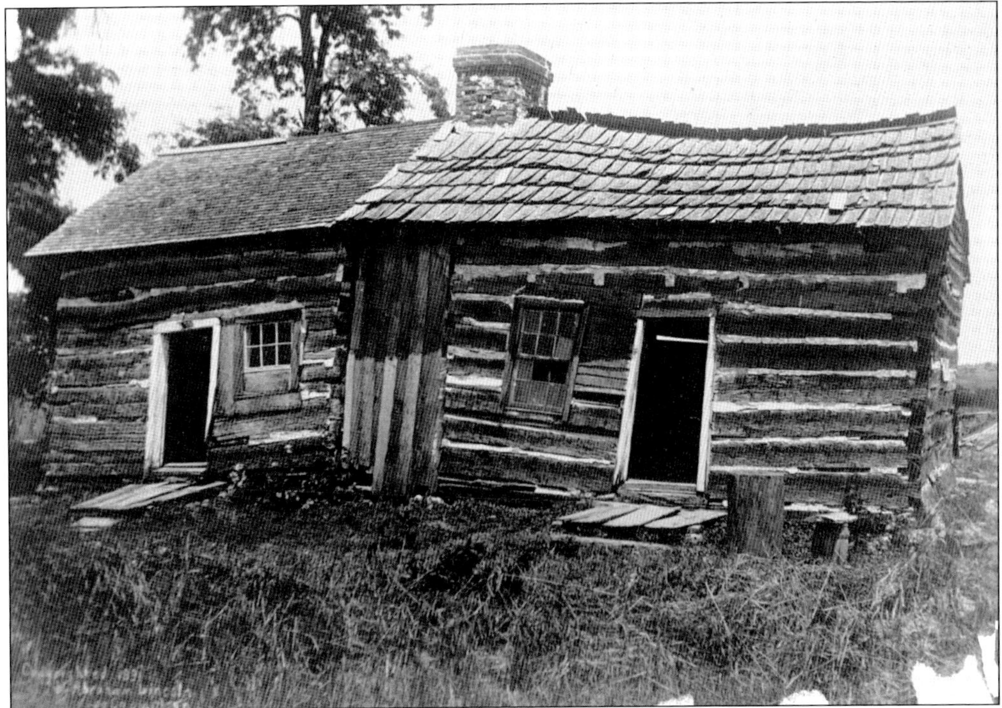

Thomas Lincoln moved his family to Illinois in 1830. Now 21 years old, Abe was old enough to go off on his own, but he agreed to help his family set up a new farm. The first winter in Illinois was brutally cold, with blizzards. When spring came, Lincoln left his family and farming forever. (LOC.)

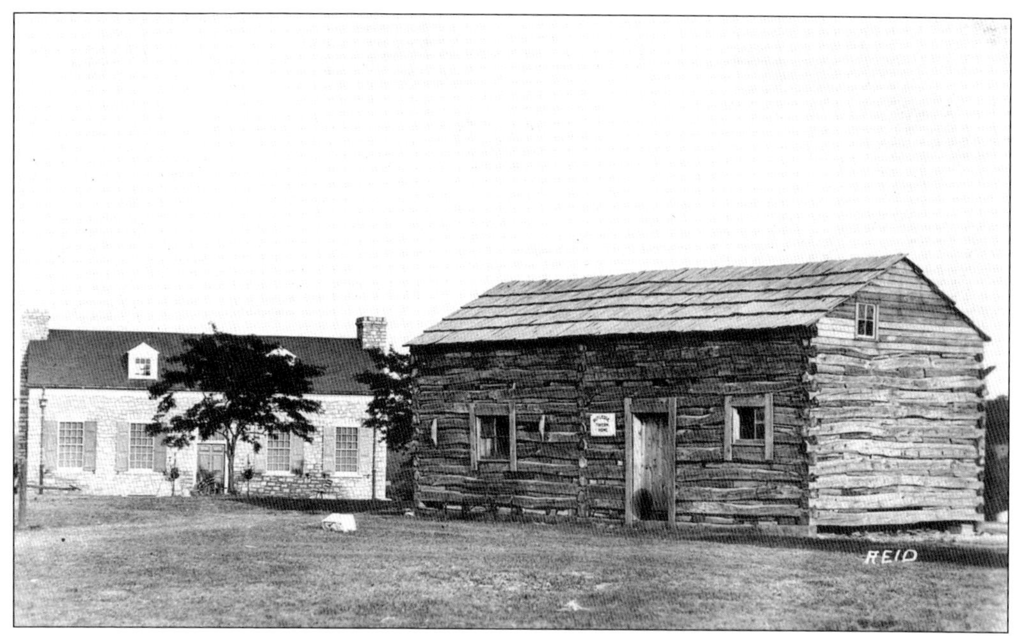

In 1831, Lincoln settled in New Salem, Illinois, a small village where he came of age working as a surveyor, postmaster, shopkeeper, militia captain, politician, and lawyer. For a time, he boarded in the tavern of millwright James Rutledge, where he came to know (and reportedly fall in love with) Ann Rutledge. Sadly, Ann died of typhoid fever in 1835 at the age of 22. This recreated Rutledge Tavern was built around 1918. (LFFC.)

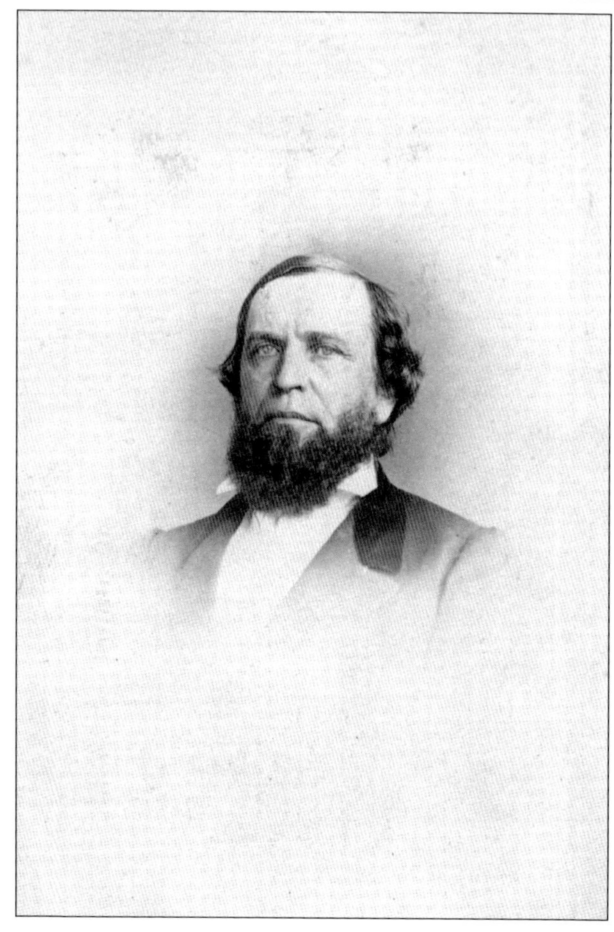

Joshua Speed later recalled how Lincoln rode into Springfield in 1837 "with no earthly goods but a pair of saddle-bags, two or three law books, and some clothing." Seeing Lincoln's destitution, Speed offered to let him share his double bed in the room above the store. Lincoln went upstairs, dropped off his belongings, and came back down "with a face beaming with pleasure." He said, "Well, Speed, I'm moved." (LMU.)

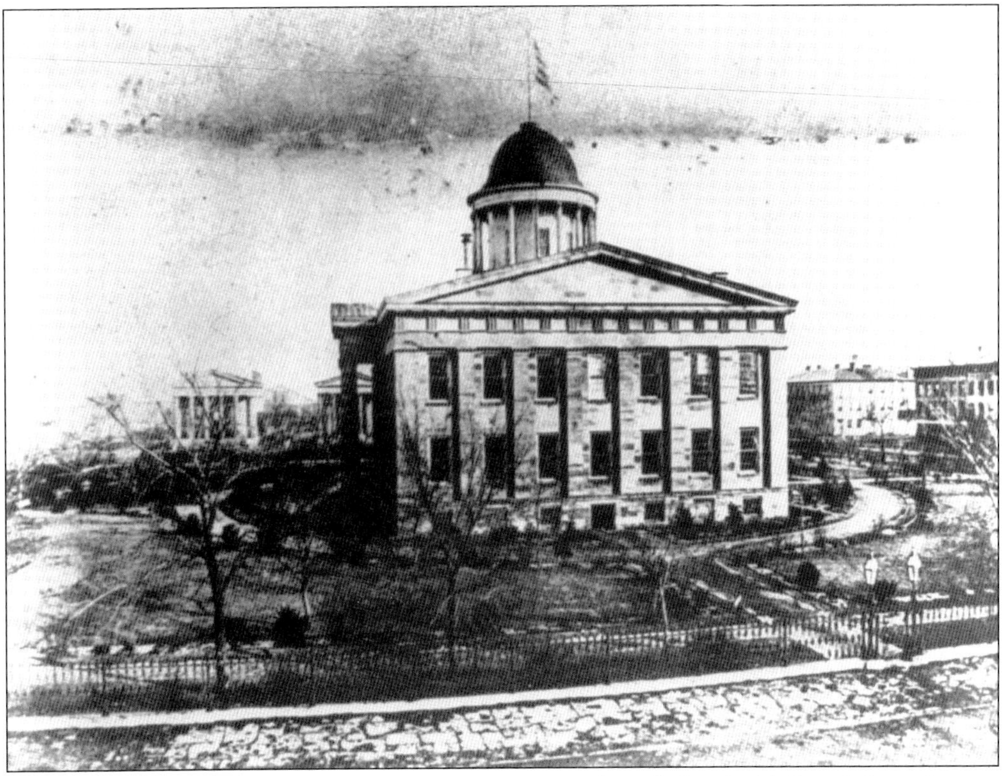

Lincoln lived with Speed above the store until 1841, and the two men became best friends. The building, which was destroyed by fire in 1855, stood on the southwest corner of Washington and Fifth Streets, facing the state capitol building (which was constructed between 1837 and 1840). Looking out of his front window, Lincoln would have seen a view like this. (LOC.)

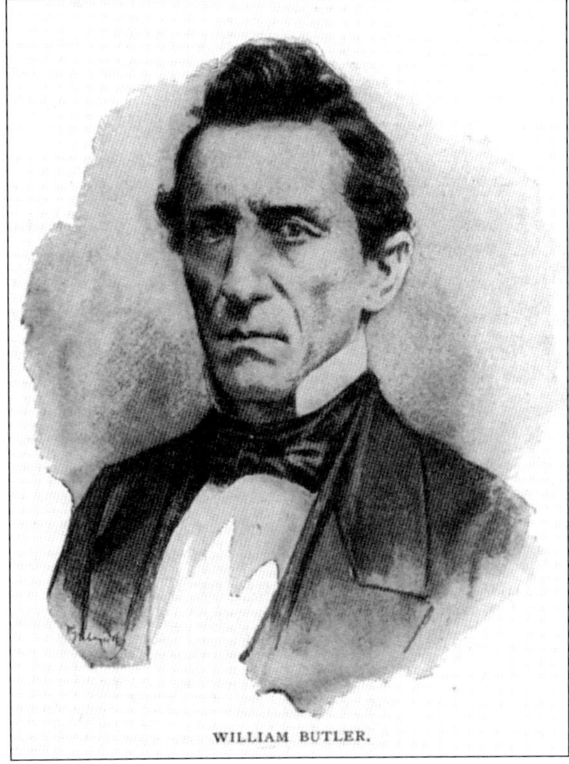

WILLIAM BUTLER.

When Speed returned to Kentucky in the spring of 1841, Lincoln moved into the boardinghouse of his friend William Butler (pictured here) on the southwest corner of Madison and Third Streets. During this time, Lincoln's courtship with Mary Todd went through a rough patch. According to William H. Herndon, Butler "did not charge Lincoln one cent for the board" because he saw Lincoln's gloom and sadness and "deeply Sympathized with him" and "wanted to help him." (ALPLM.)

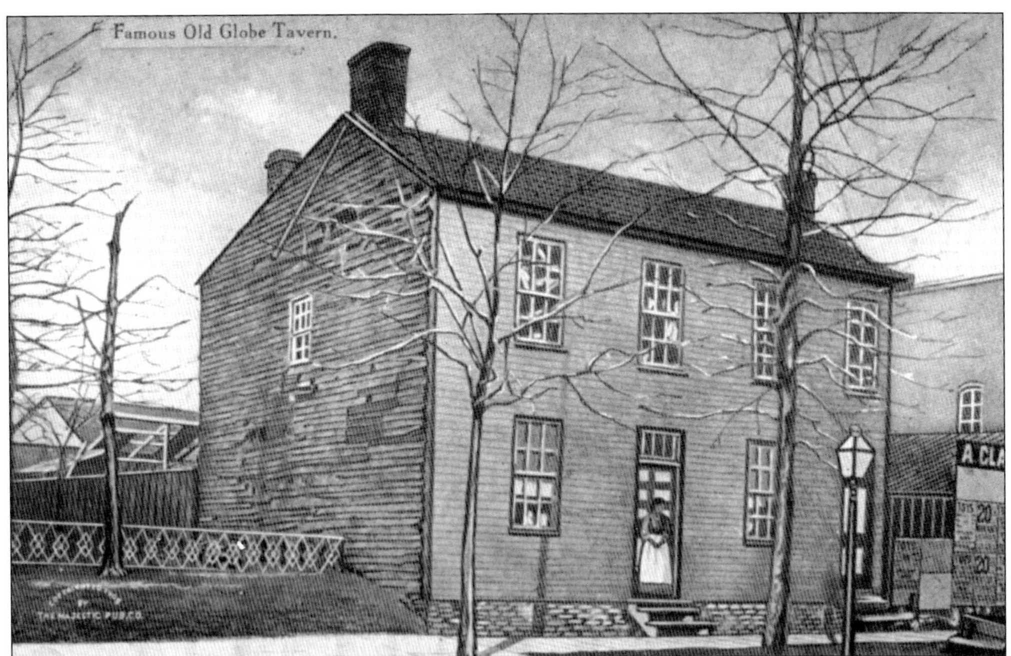

Following their wedding on November 4, 1842, Abraham and Mary Lincoln moved into the Globe Tavern on Adams Street between Third and Fourth Streets. They lived in the same rooms that Mary's sister Frances Jane Todd and her husband, Dr. William S. Wallace, had lived when they were first married. (LOC.)

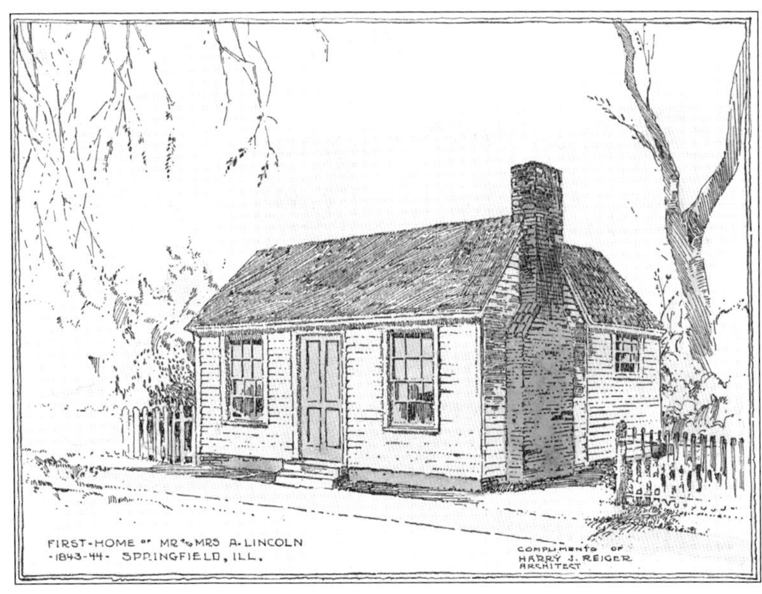

After Robert Lincoln was born on August 1, 1843, the quarters at the Globe Tavern became too cramped for the growing family. According to some accounts, other boarders complained about Robert's crying at night. For a brief period, the Lincolns rented this small one-story house at 214 South Fourth Street. (ALPLM.)

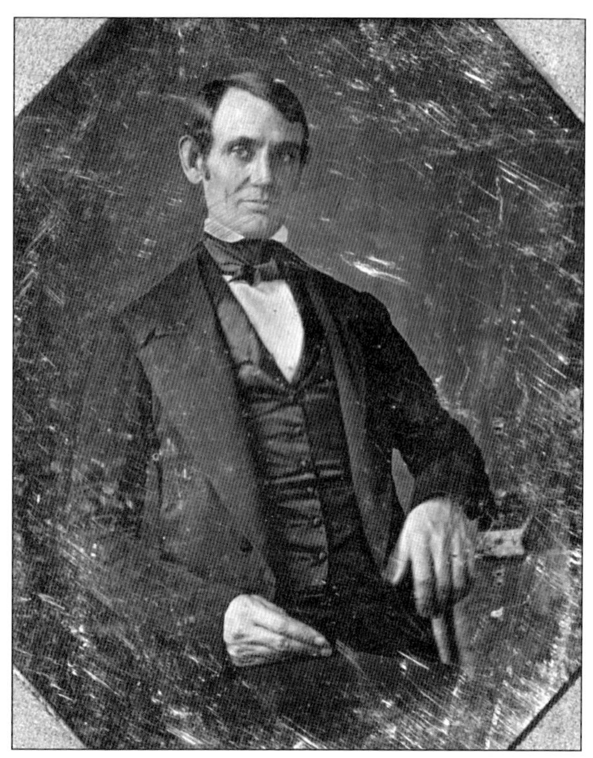

Accounts of the Lincoln marriage vary wildly. One neighbor later claimed that Mary "was quite disposed to make a servant girl" of her husband, forcing him "to get up and get the breakfast and then dress the children, after which she would join the family at the table, or lie abed an hour or two longer as she might choose." William H. Herndon later claimed that Mary drove him "from home, by a club, knife, or tongue." By contrast, another old friend recollected that "Lincoln & his wife got along tolerably well, unless Mrs. L got the devil in her." According to this acquaintance, Mary had often said that she "could love him better" if he were not traveling on the judicial circuit so much. These are the earliest known photographs of Abraham and Mary Lincoln, taken by N.H. Shepard of Springfield around 1846, when Lincoln was elected to Congress. (Both, LOC.)

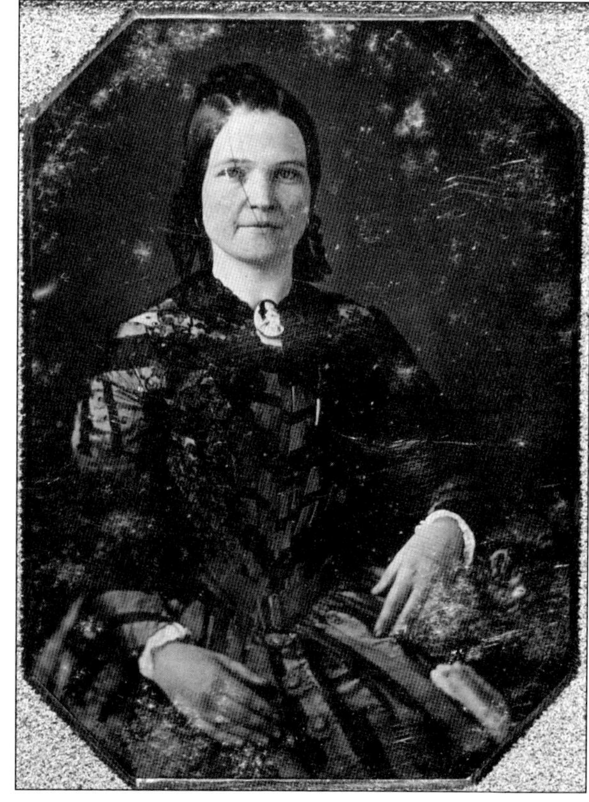

Two

WHERE MR. LINCOLN LIVES

THE HOUSE AT EIGHTH AND JACKSON STREETS

The house on the northeast corner of Eighth and Jackson Streets was the only home that Abraham Lincoln ever owned. It was here that three of his four boys were born and, sadly, one would die. Within these walls, he and Mary played with their children, entertained guests, interacted with neighbors, and went through the daily routines of life. Writing in 1870, Mary stated that "a nice home—loving husband & precious child are the happiest stages of life."

In the years after Lincoln's death, old neighbors remembered what it was like to live so close to the great man. James Gourley recalled that "Lincoln was a poor landscape gardener and his yard was graced by very little shrubbery." Once, according to Gourley, Lincoln planted some rosebushes, "but in a short time he had forgotten all about them." Gourley claimed that Lincoln "never planted any vines or trees of any kind; in fact, seemed to take little, if any, interest in things of that kind." Another friend recalled, "It was notorious that his fences were always in need of repair, his gate wanted a hinge, the grass in his yard needed cutting, and the scene about his home betrayed a reckless indifference to appearances."

One day, when William A. Richardson and Lincoln drove up to the home after eight weeks on the circuit, they found "a great and surprising change." The grass was mowed, the gate fixed, and the fence painted. "Everything was spick and span; it didn't look like the same place." Mary had fixed up the place while Lincoln was gone and now was waiting at the door so that she could "enjoy the excitement her improvements would create." Lincoln pulled up his horse next to the house but did not get out of the buggy. "You will excuse me, my good woman, but can you tell me where Mr. Lincoln lives?" he asked her. Richardson recalled that this "nettled Mrs. L." and she replied, "You get out and come in here. I'll show you personally where Mr. Lincoln lives."

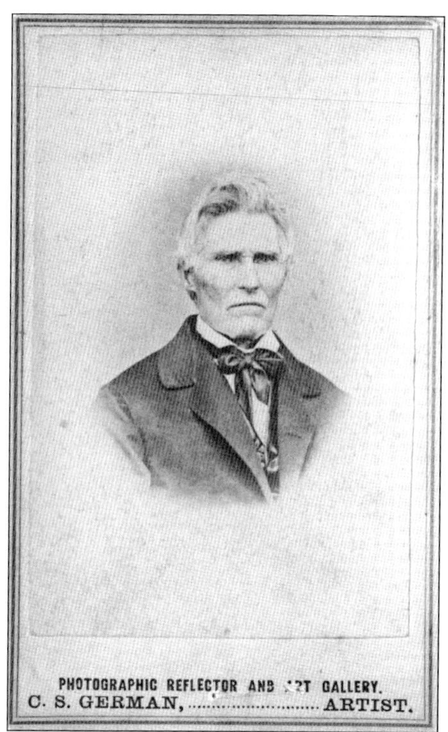

The first white owner of the property that Lincoln would eventually own was Pascal P. Enos, who acquired title to it in 1824. In 1825, Enos sold the land to Elijah Iles (pictured here), who in turn had it surveyed and platted in 1836. Known as Elijah Iles's "Addition to Springfield," Iles sold a parcel to Dr. Gersham Jayne, who in turn sold Lot 8 in Block 10 to Rev. Charles Dresser for $300 on April 23, 1839. (LFA.)

Construction of Dresser's cottage took place from May through December 1839. In August, Dresser had to purchase part of the adjoining lot to the north from neighbor Francis Webster because the contractor made an error when siting the foundation. The finished home was a modest one-and-a-half-story cottage. In July 1841, Dresser attempted to sell or rent his home, but, unable to find either a buyer or a tenant, his family remained in the house. Pictured here are Rev. Charles and Louisa Dresser in the 1850s. (ALPLM.)

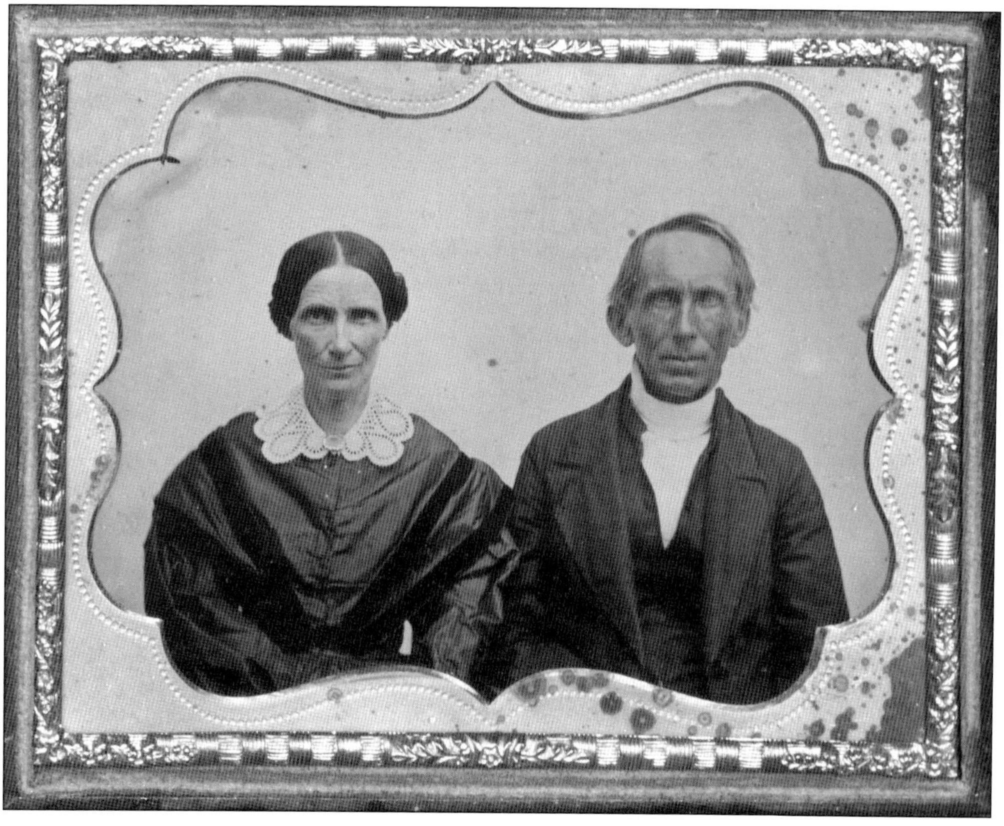

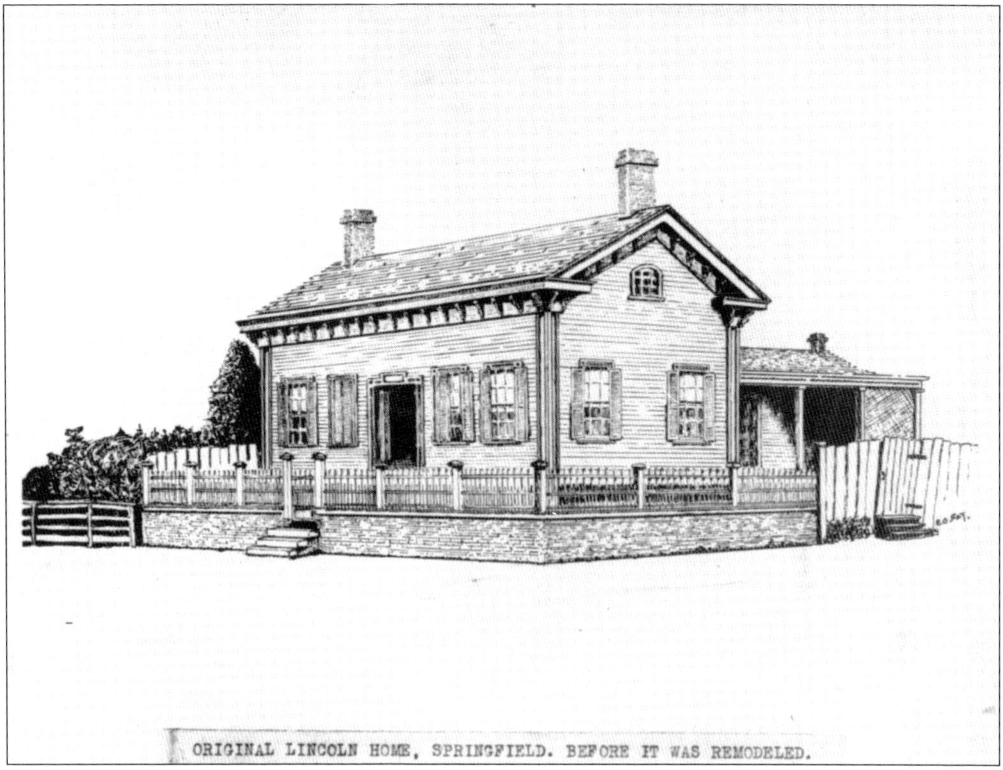

ORIGINAL LINCOLN HOME, SPRINGFIELD. BEFORE IT WAS REMODELED.

Lincoln may have first visited his future home on his wedding day when he asked Reverend Dresser to officiate the ceremony. Lincoln reportedly told the Episcopalian, "I want to get hitched tonight." He and Mary had planned to wed in the Dresser cottage, but when Ninian Edwards, Mary's brother-in-law, heard this, he said, "That will never do. Mary Todd is my ward. If the marriage is going to take place, it must be at my house." (SVC.)

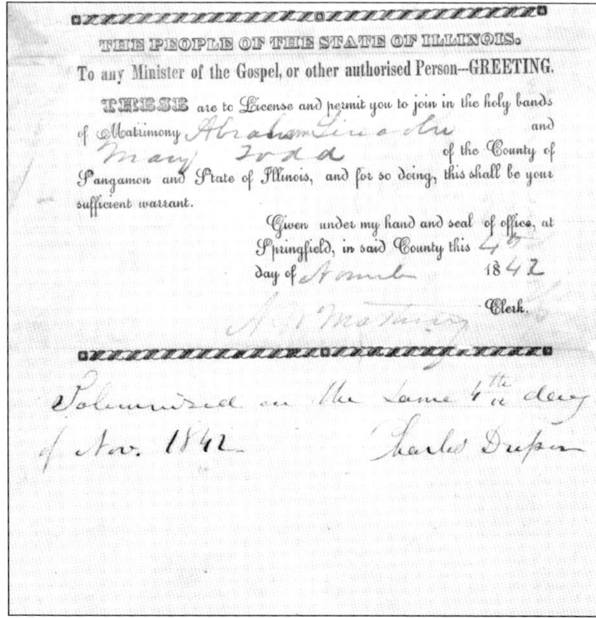

THE PEOPLE OF THE STATE OF ILLINOIS.

To any Minister of the Gospel, or other authorised Person—GREETING.

THESE are to License and permit you to join in the holy bands of Matrimony Abraham Lincoln and Mary Todd of the County of Sangamon and State of Illinois, and for so doing, this shall be your sufficient warrant.

Given under my hand and seal of office, at Springfield, in said County this 4th day of Novr 1842

N. W. Matheny Clerk.

Solemnized on the same 4th day of Nov. 1842

Charles Dresser

Abraham Lincoln and Mary Todd were married in Ninian and Elizabeth Edwards' home on the evening of November 4, 1842. Lincoln gave her a wedding ring engraved with the words, "A.L. to Mary, Nov. 4, 1842. Love is Eternal." Pictured here is the Lincolns' marriage license, signed by Reverend Dresser. (ALPLM.)

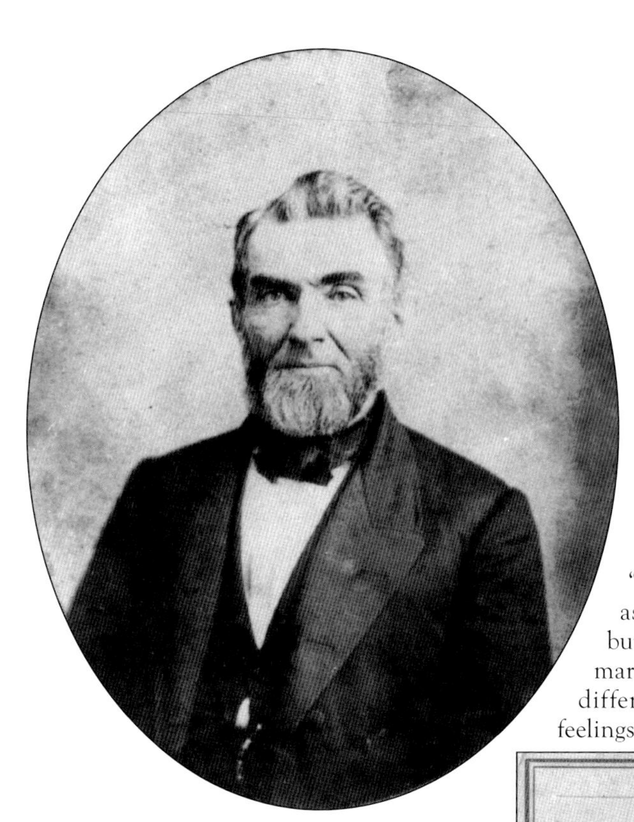

Ninian and Elizabeth Edwards (Mary's older sister) had not supported Abraham and Mary's courtship. Elizabeth later recalled that Lincoln "would listen and gaze on her [Mary] as if drawn by some superior power," but she and Ninian advised Mary not to marry Lincoln because "they were raised differently and had no congeniality, no feelings alike, etc." (Left, LFFC; below, LFA.)

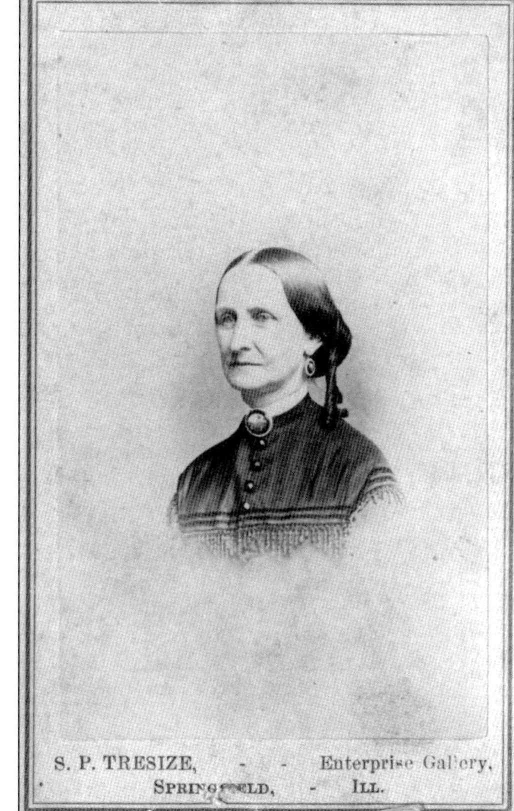

A little more than a year after the Lincolns' wedding, on January 16, 1844, Lincoln contracted with Dresser to purchase the cottage for $1,200 plus a downtown lot worth $300. They moved into their new home on May 2, 1844, when Robert was about one year old. It may have taken the young couple some time to fully furnish their new residence. "I went to housekeeping myself once—with a husband—I loved better than all the world beside & a baby," wrote Mary in 1869, "and with not a great deal in my house so I know by experience—what it is to wait patiently." Pictured here are the contract Lincoln signed with Dresser to purchase the home as well as Lincoln's city tax receipt from 1844. (Both, ALPLM.)

This memorandum witnesseth that Charles Dresser and Abraham Lincoln of Springfield Illinois, have contracted with each other as follows. The said Dresser is to convey to or procure to be conveyed to, said Lincoln, by a clear title in fee simple, the entire premises (ground and improvements) in Springfield, on which said Dresser now resides, ~~on or before~~ and give him possession of said premises, on or before the first day of April next— for which said Lincoln, at or before the same day, is to pay to said Dresser twelve hundred dollars, or what said Dresser shall then at his own option accept as equivalent thereto. and also to procure to be conveyed to said Dresser, by a clear title in fee simple, the entire premises (ground and building) in Springfield, on the block immediately West of the Public square, the building on which is now occupied by H A Hough as a shop. being the same premises some time since conveyed by N. W. Edwards & wife to said Lincoln & Stephen T. Logan— Said Dresser takes upon himself to arrange with said Hough for the possession of said shop and premises—

Jany 16th 1844 (signed duplicates)

Charles Dresser
A Lincoln

CITY OF SPRINGFIELD, Sep 1844.

Received **of** A Lincoln Six 56/100 **Dollars, in full for his City Tax, for the year 1844, on the following described property, to-wit: Lot** 12.13 **Block** 7 E Iles **Ad. Valuation, $** 1600
Lot 8 & 10 ft 7. Blk 10 E Iles **Personal Property,** 150

A A Garland **City Collector.**

Prior to departing for Washington to take his seat in Congress in 1847, Lincoln wrote and signed an agreement between himself and Cornelius Ludlum to rent the Lincolns' home. Ludlum agreed to pay "the sum of ninety dollars in quarter yearly payments, to be especially careful to prevent any destruction by fire, [and] to allow said Lincoln, the use of the North-up-stairs room, during the term, in which to store his furniture." (ALPLM.)

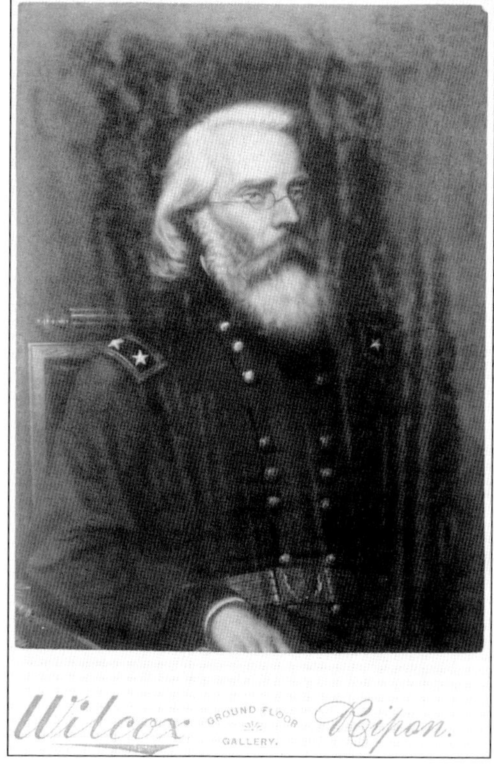

When Ludlum moved out of the Lincoln home, Mason Brayman, a local printer, took over. On June 8, 1848, Brayman told his sister Sarah, "We have an excellent house and garden–with plenty of cherries and currants, and peaches growing–with vegetables of my own raising." The Braymans' lease was not yet up when the Lincolns returned to Springfield, so the Lincolns moved back into the Globe Tavern for a short time. (HRFA.)

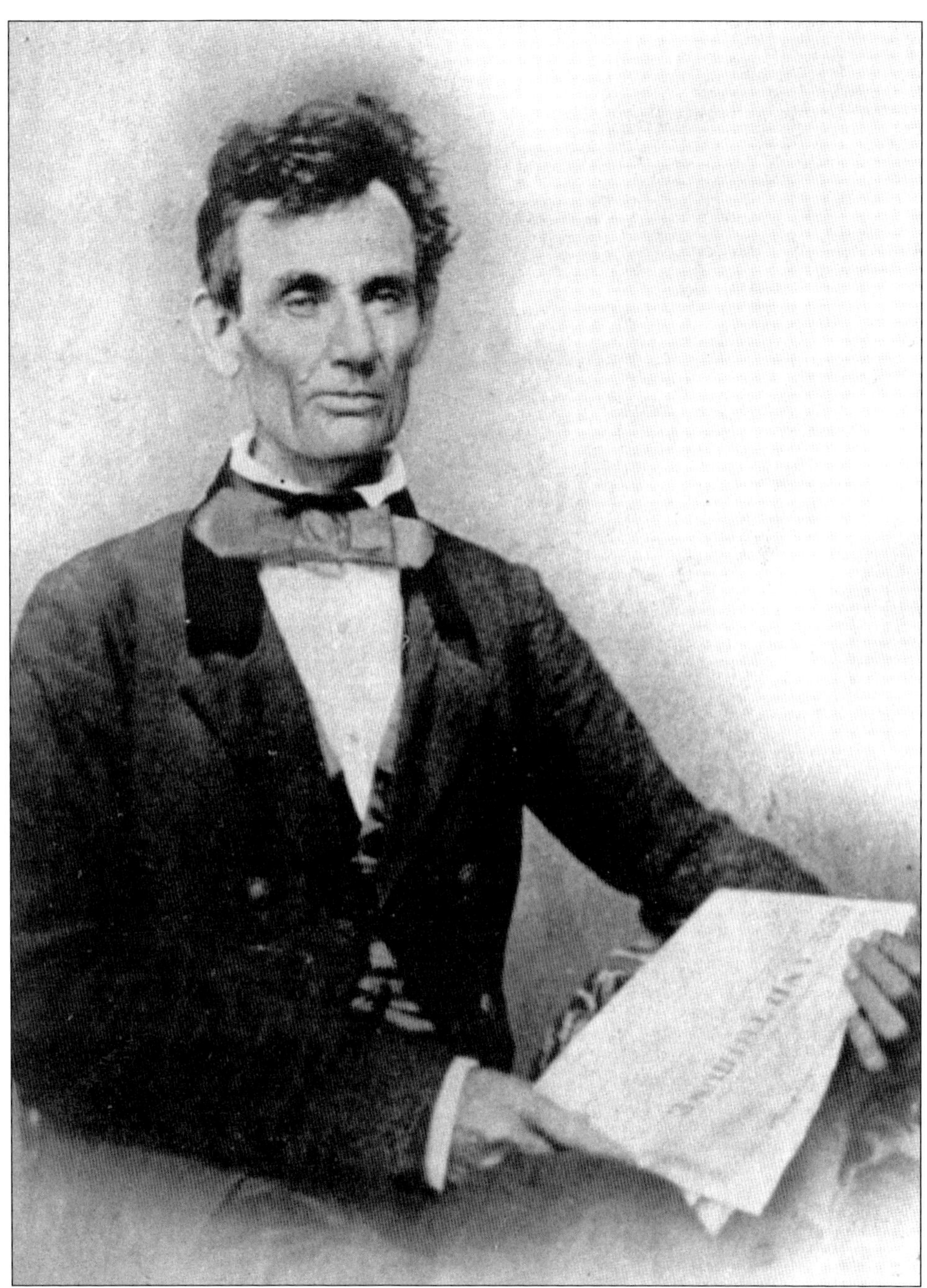

Fire nearly destroyed the home in early 1855. Mary Lincoln's half-sister Emilie Todd recalled that the Lincolns had gone to a party at the Ridgely home, but Mary grew restless and said, "Mr. Lincoln, we must go home." Although Abraham did not wish to leave the party, Mary insisted, "We must go home, Mr. Lincoln." Lincoln replied, "I will take you home. We will find everything all right and then we can come back and enjoy the rest of the evening." But when they got home, they found the house on fire, the maid fast asleep, and the children's lives in danger. According to Emilie, Lincoln said he was glad he had a wife who could "sniff fire a quarter of a mile away." This photograph was taken on October 27, 1854. (LOC.)

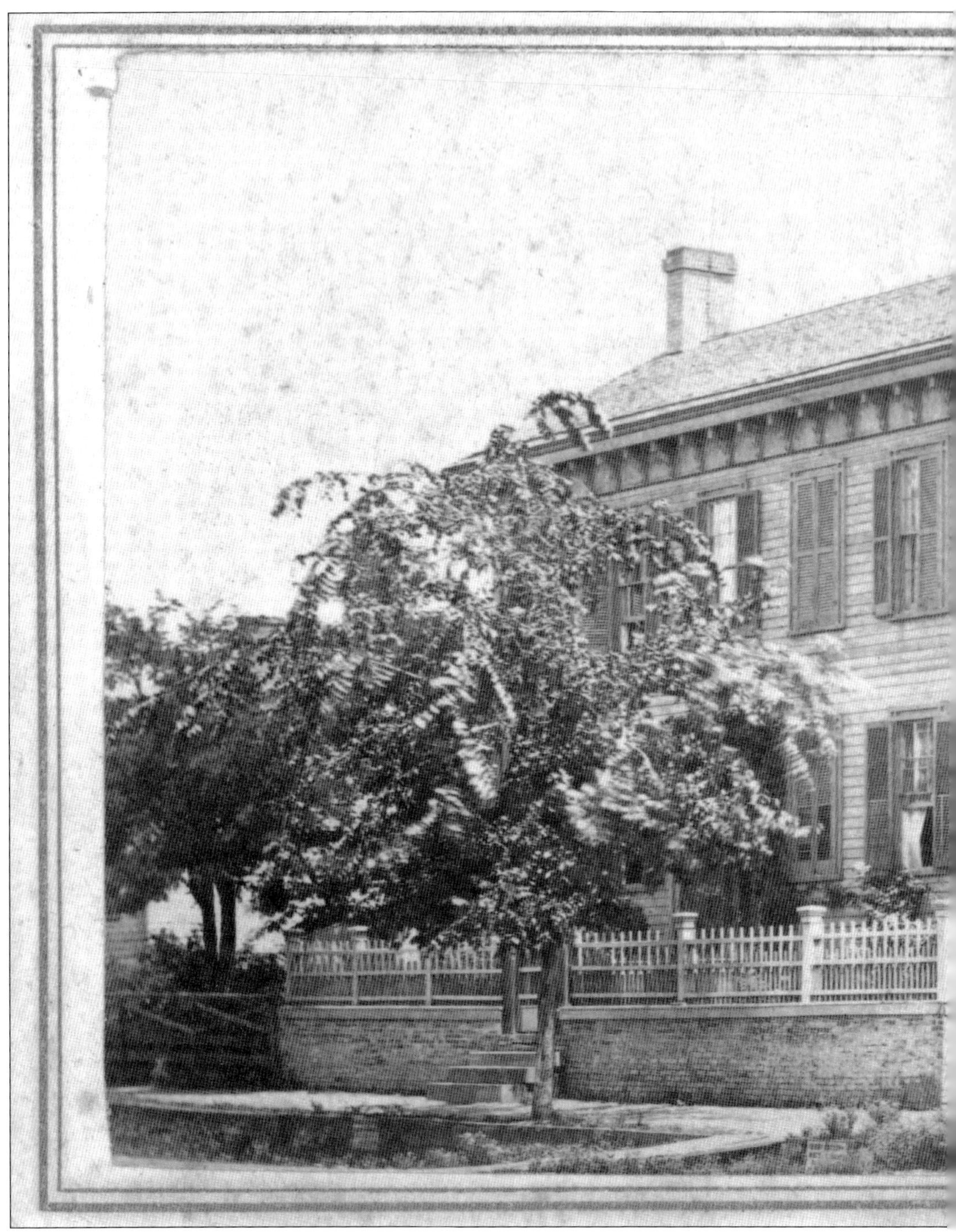

The Lincolns did several remodeling projects at their home between 1846 and 1855, including adding the brick retaining wall so that they could install a fence. In 1856, they enlarged their home, likely because of Lincoln's rising status in Illinois politics, Mary's desire for a "more pretentious" house, and because of their growing family. In addition to raising the home to two full stories, they added four bedrooms on the second floor. This is also likely when they created the two parlors on

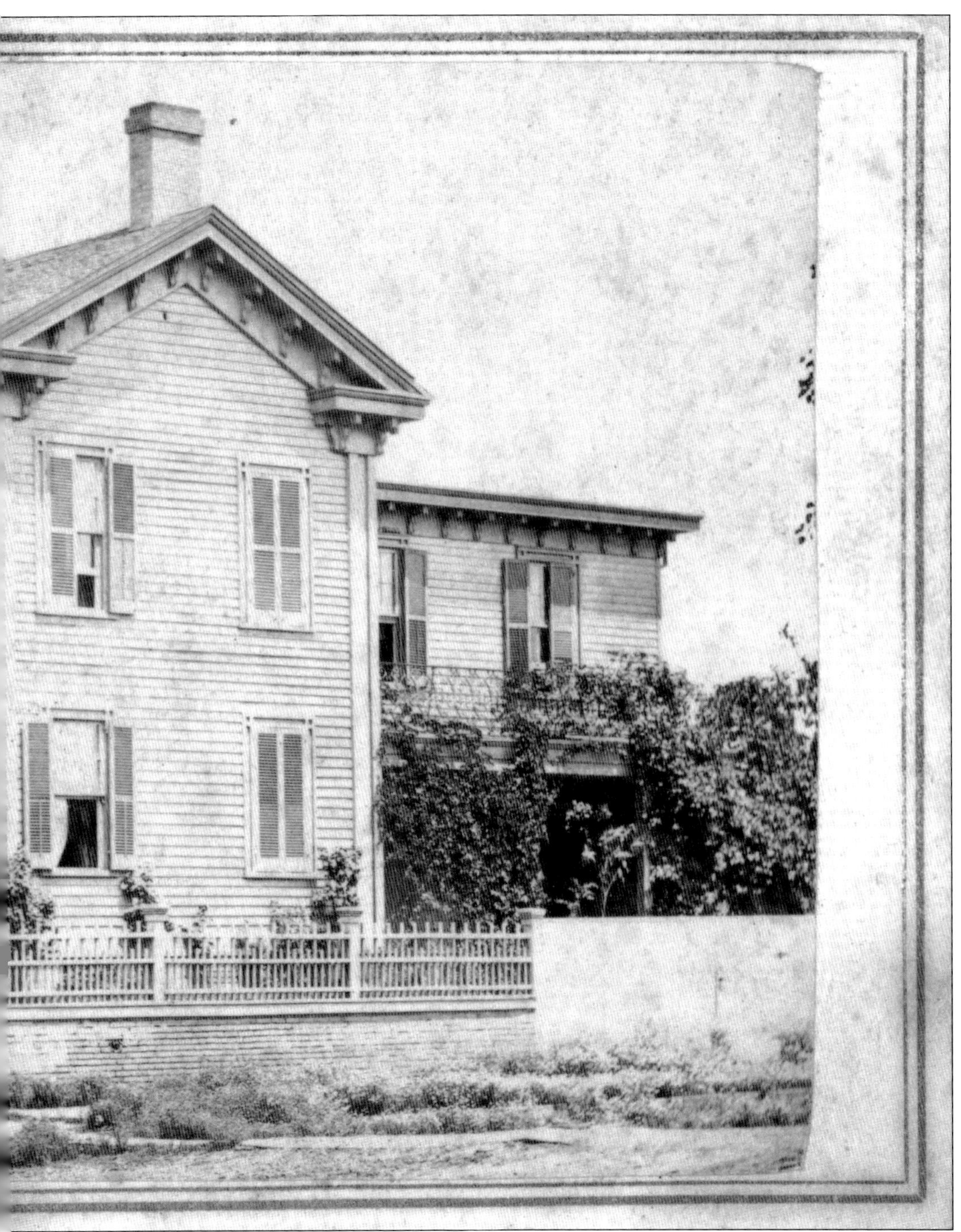

the north side of the first floor (prior to this time, Abraham and Mary slept in the area that is now the back parlor). The renovation cost $1,300. Mary wrote her half-sister Emilie Helm on February 16, 1857, "You will think we have enlarged our borders, since you were here." Mary T. Stuart, the wife of Mary's cousin John Todd Stuart, observed snidely: "I think they will have room enough before they are done, particularly as Mary seldom ever uses what she has." (LOC.)

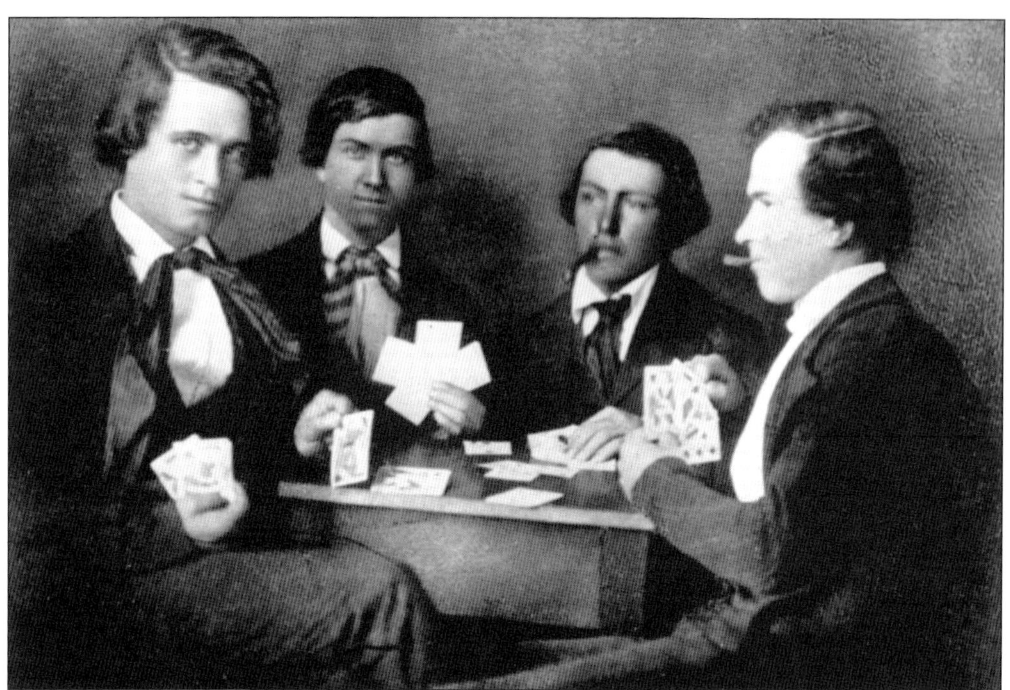

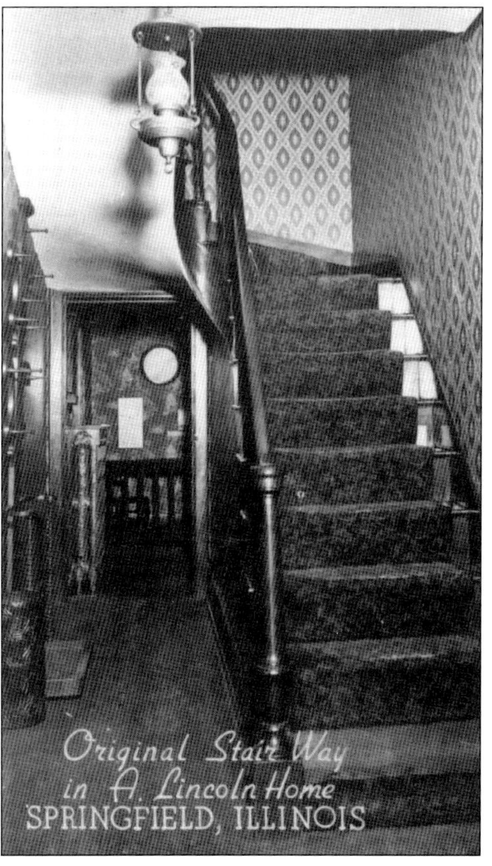

One frequent visitor to the Lincoln home, law student Gibson William Harris, remembered an evening around 1850 when Lincoln came into the office after dinner "smiling beyond even his wont." Lincoln told Harris that he had been resting when "he heard a tremendous clatter on the stairs." Lincoln rushed to the staircase and found Robert "getting up on all fours from the floor of the hallway below, unhurt but sadly bewildered." Robert had put on Lincoln's boots and tried to walk around in them when he fell down the stairs. "You ought to have seen him, Gibson," Lincoln laughed, "he looked so comical with the bootlegs reaching clear up to his little body." Pictured here in the early 1840s are, from left to right, Lincoln's best man, James H. Matheny; Samuel Baker; Gibson W. Harris; and Zimri A. Enos. (Above, SVC; left, JW.)

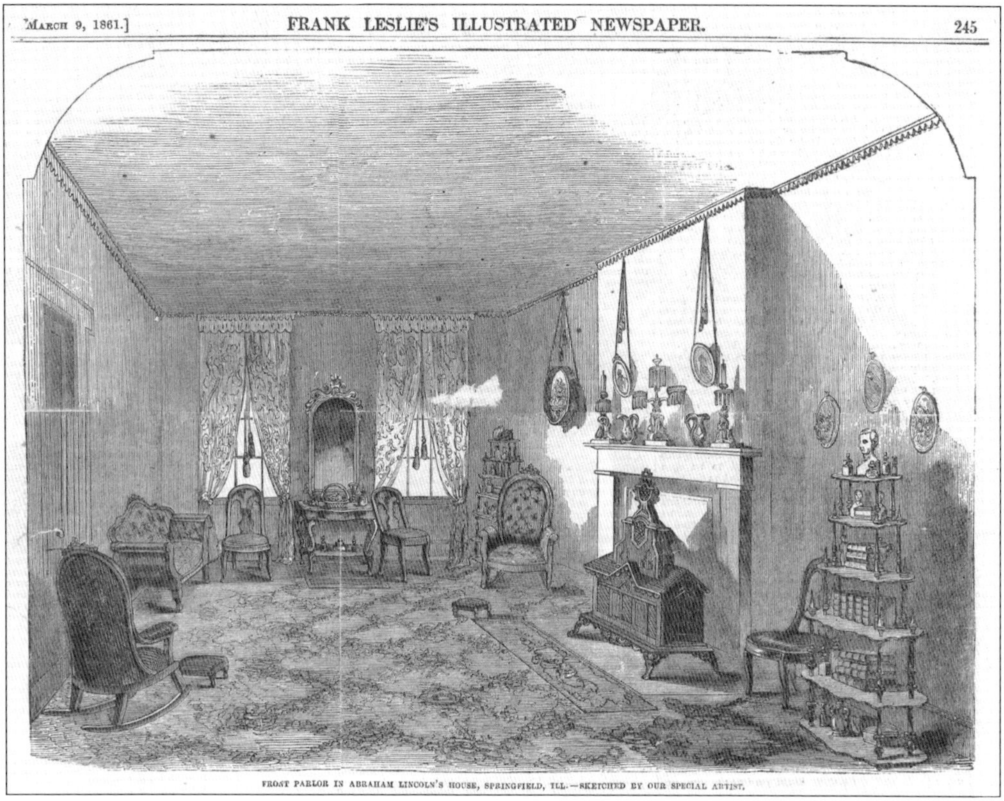

March 9, 1861.] FRANK LESLIE'S ILLUSTRATED NEWSPAPER. 245

FRONT PARLOR IN ABRAHAM LINCOLN'S HOUSE, SPRINGFIELD, ILL.—SKETCHED BY OUR SPECIAL ARTIST.

In 1860, Republican politician George Ashmun of Massachusetts noted that the furniture in the two parlors on the first floor was "without pretension to show, was neat, and in admirable keeping with what is understood to be his moderate pecuniary ability." Everything Ashmun saw in the home tended to reflect "a man who has battled hard with the fortunes of life, and whose hard experience has taught him to enjoy whatever of success belongs to him, rather in solid substance than in showy display." Another visitor said that the home was "furnished in the style usual in well-to-do educated families," with "strong, well-made furniture" designed "for use and not for show." The front parlor (above) and sitting room (seen on the following page) appeared in *Frank Leslie's Illustrated Newspaper* on March 9, 1861. The back parlor (below) appeared in *Frank Leslie's* on December 10, 1864. (Both, LIHO.)

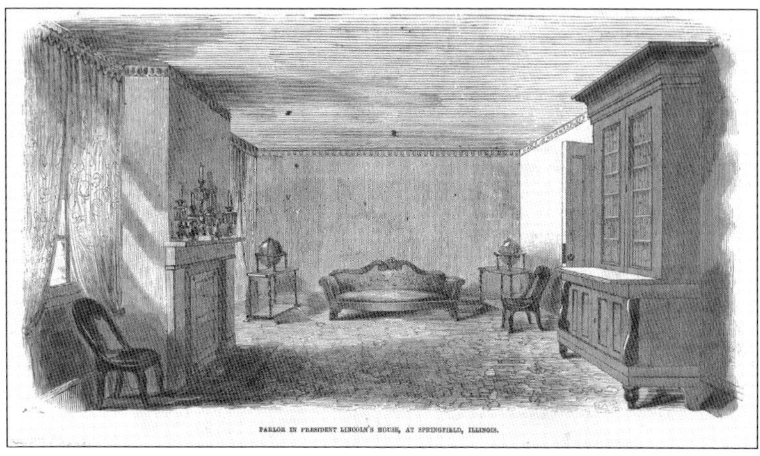

PARLOR IN PRESIDENT LINCOLN'S HOUSE, AT SPRINGFIELD, ILLINOIS.

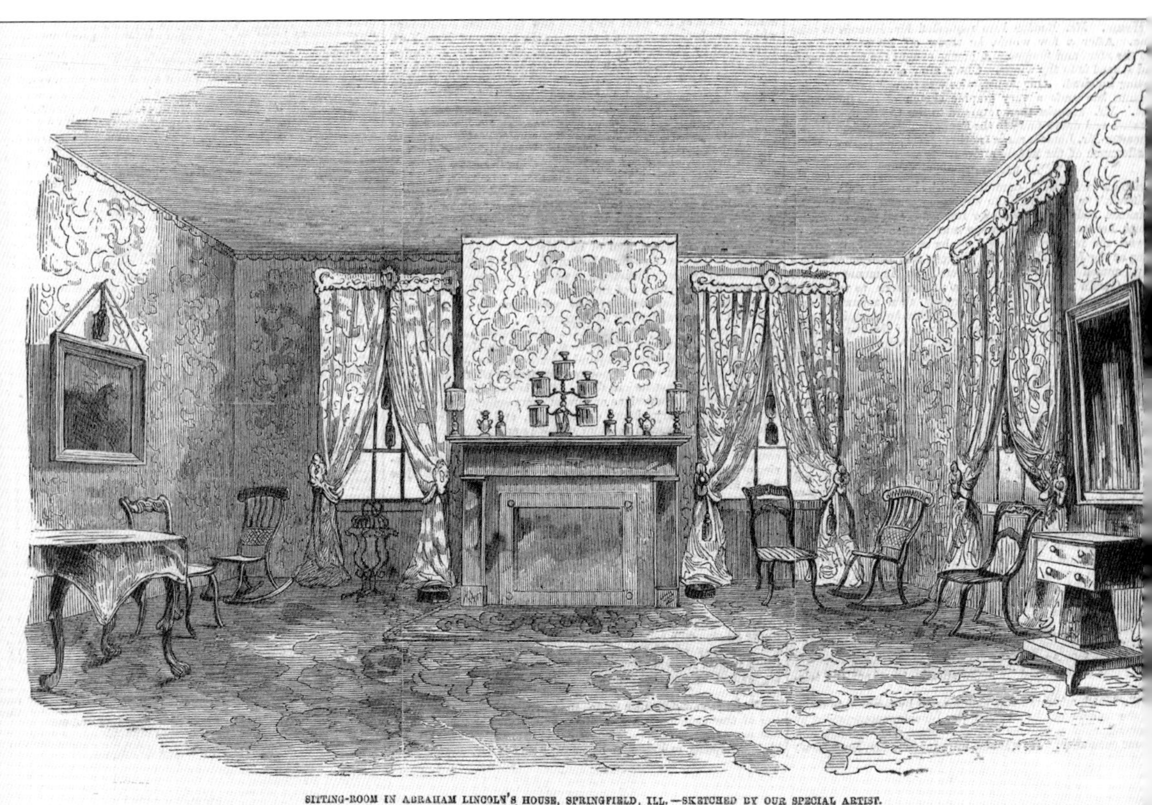

SITTING-ROOM IN ABRAHAM LINCOLN'S HOUSE, SPRINGFIELD, ILL.—SKETCHED BY OUR SPECIAL ARTIST.

In the sitting room, the family played games, looked at three-dimensional images in their stereoscope (the original is still in the room today), read books, and sewed. Lincoln would often read aloud, typically to the annoyance of those around him. Emilie Helm recalled playing checkers with Robert one night as Lincoln looked "thoughtfully into the fire and apparently did not hear what Mary was saying." Finally, Mary put down her embroidery and said, "Your silence is remarkably soothing, Mr. Lincoln, but we are not quite ready for sleep just yet." When Lincoln again did not respond, Mary got up and took his hand. "I fear my husband has become stone deaf since he left home at noon," she said. Lincoln replied, "I believe I have been both deaf and dumb for the last half hour, but now you shall not complain." He then told a funny story about one of his law clients, "which broke up the game of checkers and left us all speechless with laughter." The mirror hanging on the wall today (pictured in this image at far right) is likely the one in which Lincoln saw his double image in 1860. (LIHO.)

William H. Herndon joked that in the law office, Lincoln would sit on a sofa with "one foot on one chair and one foot on the table. He spilt himself out easily over of the room." At home, Lincoln liked to read on the floor. To make himself comfortable, he would turn a chair upside down and put a pillow on it, while most of his body would be on the carpet. (JW.)

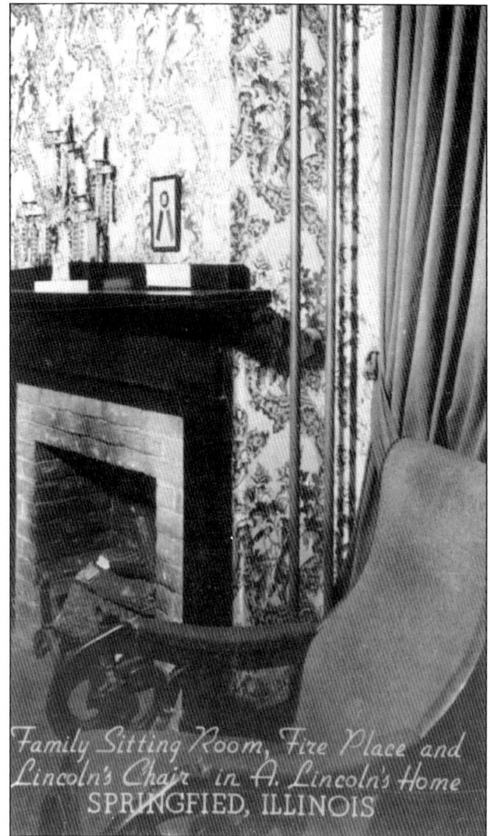

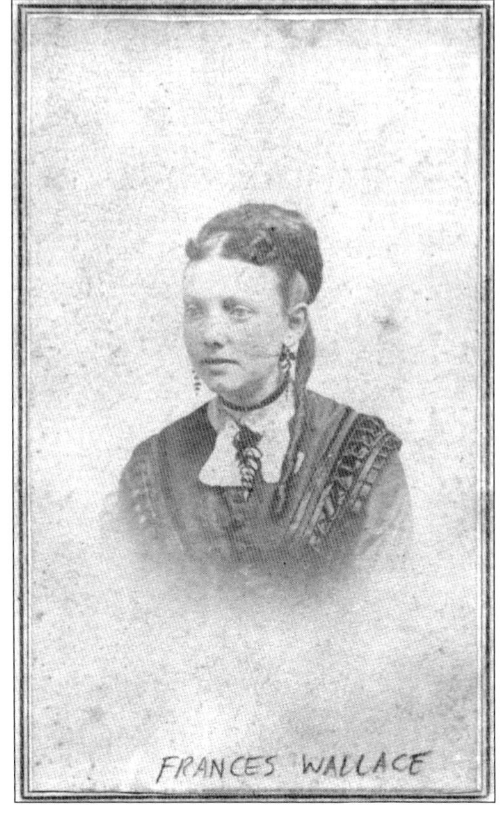

Mary Lincoln's sister Frances Todd Wallace spent many days and evenings at the Lincolns' home in pleasant conversation. She recalled, "Lincoln would lean back—his head against the top of a rocking Chair—sit abstracted that way for moments—20-30 minutes—and all at once burst out in a joke—though his thoughts were not on a joke." (LFA.)

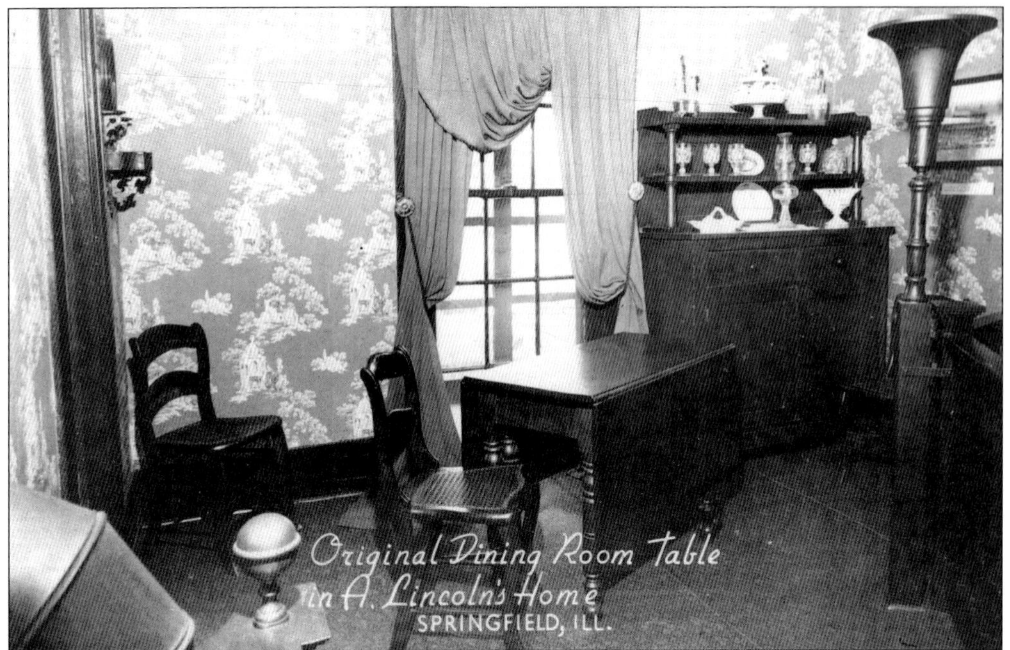

Frank Fuller, a friend of Robert's, recalled having supper at the Lincolns' during a visit in July 1860. When Lincoln asked Fuller if he said grace before meals, Fuller replied that his custom was to recite a few lines of poetry by Albert Laighton. After everyone was seated at the table, Lincoln asked Fuller to recite the lines, which he did. The conversation then turned to the Bible, and Lincoln recited Psalm 23. (JW.)

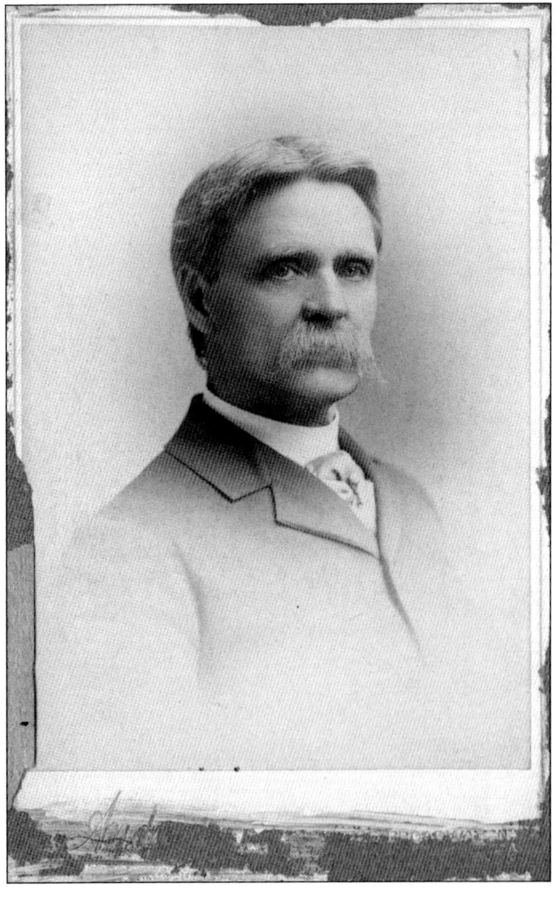

After supper, Frank Fuller (pictured here later in life) spread posters for an Independence Day festival around on the floor. "The boys climbed all over me and I interested them in my repeating watch, which also attracted the attention of Mr. Lincoln, who had never before seen a repeater." The time spent with the Lincolns "constituted the red letter day of my whole life," Fuller later wrote. "I was taken to the hearts and home of a charming family." (LDS.)

Emilie Todd Helm recalled one evening when Lincoln was two hours late for supper. When he finally sauntered in, completely unaware that the others had been waiting, Mary said, "I am afraid the chickens are burned to a crisp." Lincoln smiled and made a wisecrack about being two minutes late. "Two minutes!" cried Robert and Emilie in unison, "two hours you mean." Lincoln joked, "Just bring on the cinders and see how quickly they will disappear." (LFA.)

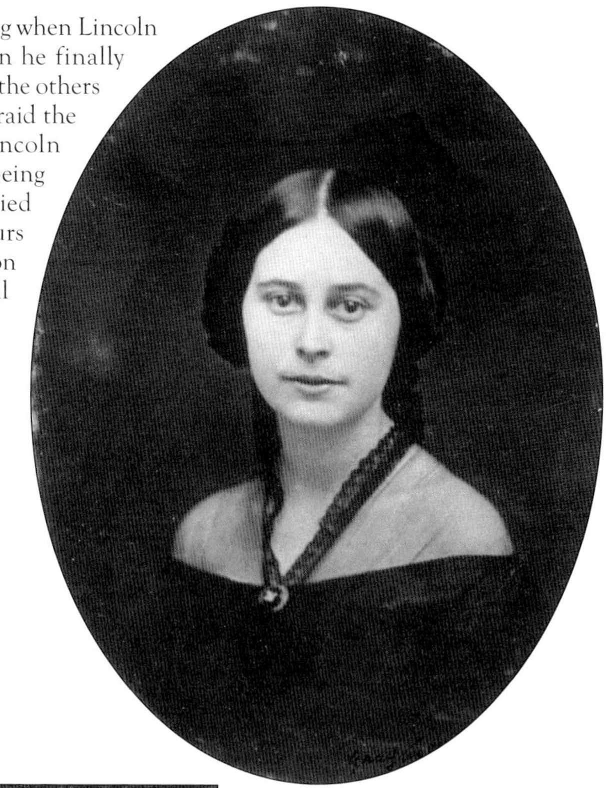

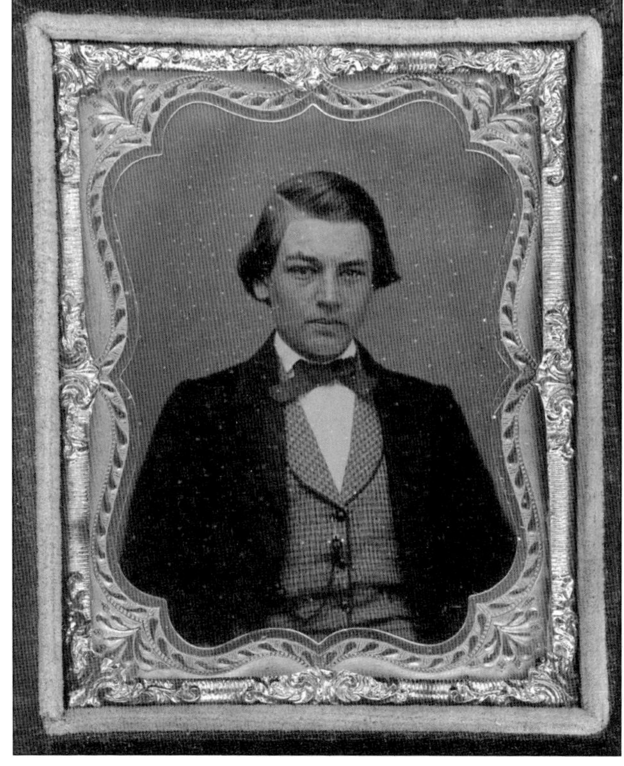

In the spring of 1855, Mary Lincoln read the novels of Sir Walter Scott to Robert (pictured here around 1859). One day, "hearing sounds of strife," Emilie and Mary ran to the window and saw Robert and a playmate "having a battle royal" with Robert wielding "a fence paling in lieu of a lance" and shouting, "This rock shall fly from its firm base as soon as I." Mary, bursting with laughter, called out, "Gramercy, brave knights. Pray be more merciful than you are brawny." (LFA.)

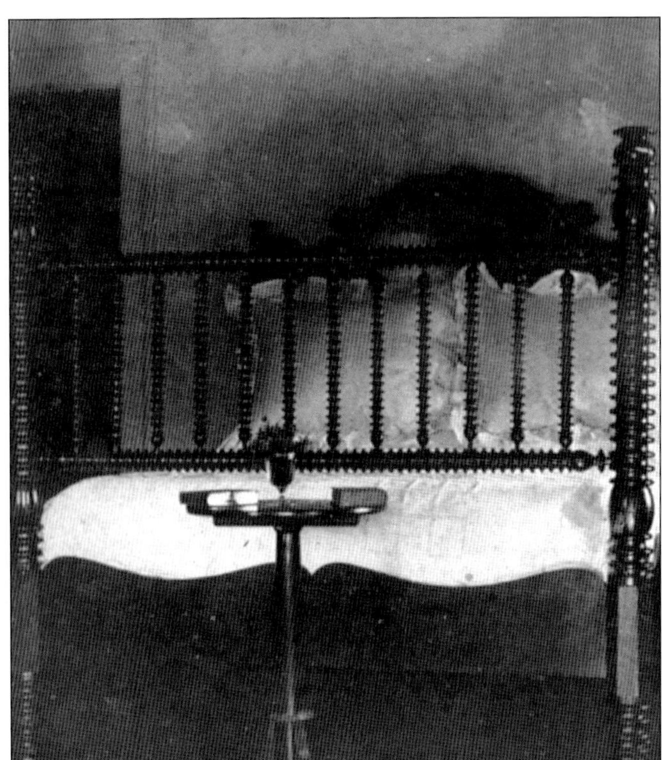

William H. Herndon later claimed that "Lincoln was a good Sleeper" who went to bed about 11:00 p.m. and rarely awoke before 7:00 or 8:00 a.m., "unless *Mrs* Lincoln chucked beat him out with a stick of stove wood in order to make him go to market for some beef for breakfast." Pictured here is Lincoln's bed in 1865. It was destroyed in the Chicago fire in 1871. (LIHO.)

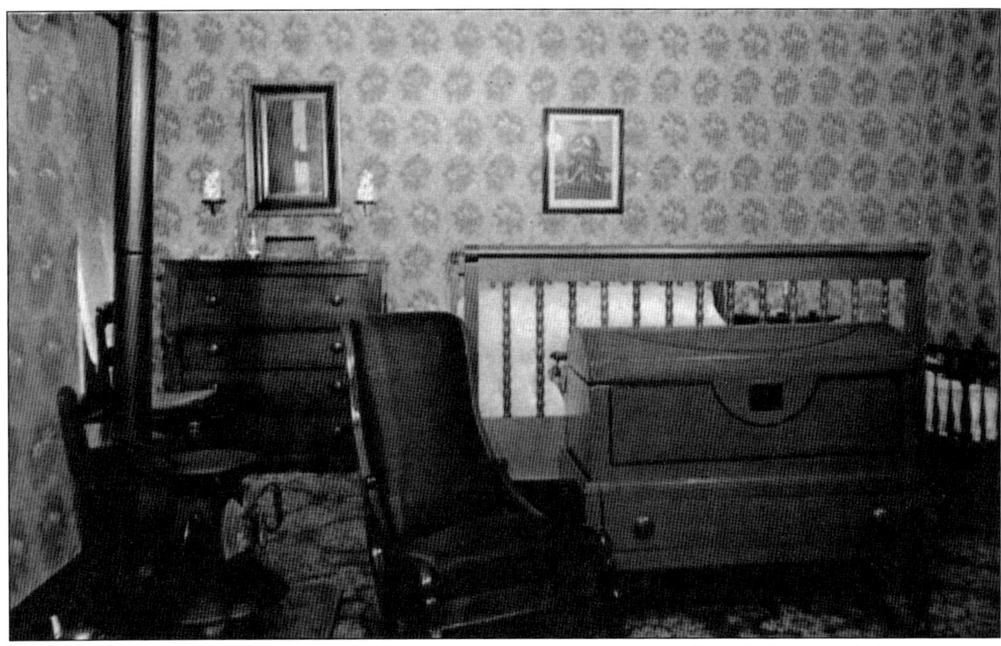

Two weeks before the presidential election of 1860, Mary wrote a friend, "I scarcely know how I would bear up under defeat. I trust we will not have the trial." When the night finally came, Lincoln went home about 1:30 a.m. and found Mary fast asleep (her bedroom is pictured here). He gently touched her shoulder and whispered, "Mary," to which she "gave no answer." Lincoln then "spoke again, a little louder," saying, "'Mary, Mary! we are elected!'" (LFFC.)

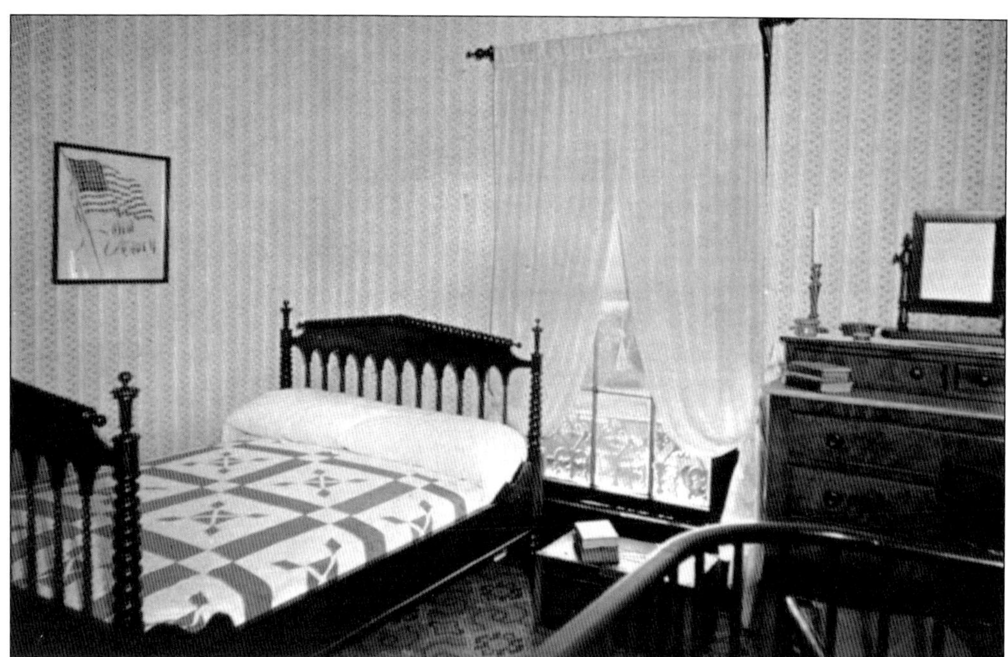

The last time Robert Lincoln visited his childhood home was on February 12, 1909—the 100th anniversary of his father's birth. He went inside and greeted his relatives Albert and Josephine Edwards, who were custodians of the home. He then went upstairs to his old bedroom. "In the sacred presence of memory he was left alone in the room and remained there some time," reported a newspaper, "friends keeping intruders from venturing inside to disturb whatever thought the visit recalled to his mind." Robert is pictured here around 1910, and his room appears as it was displayed in the 1950s. (Above LFFC; right, LFA.)

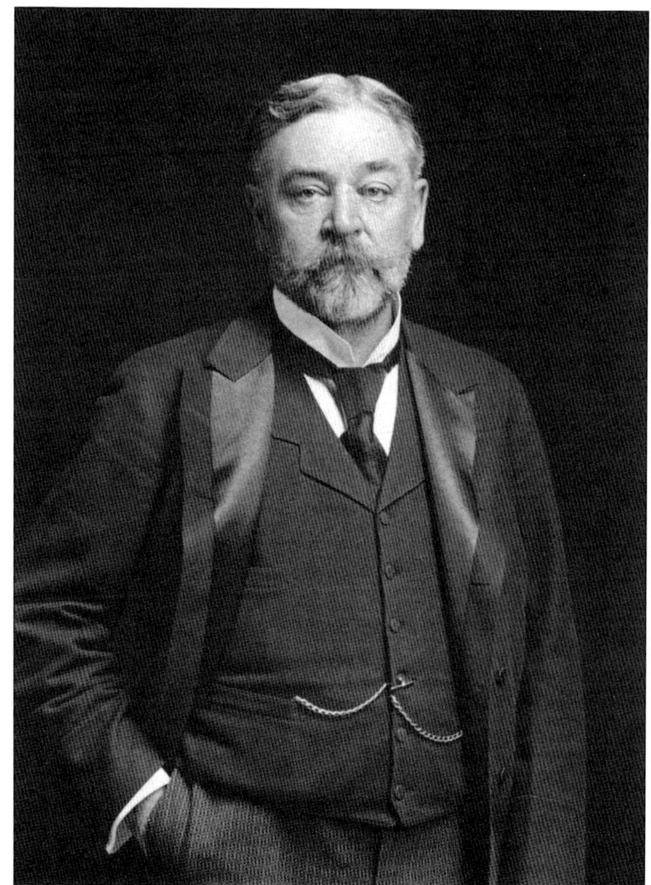

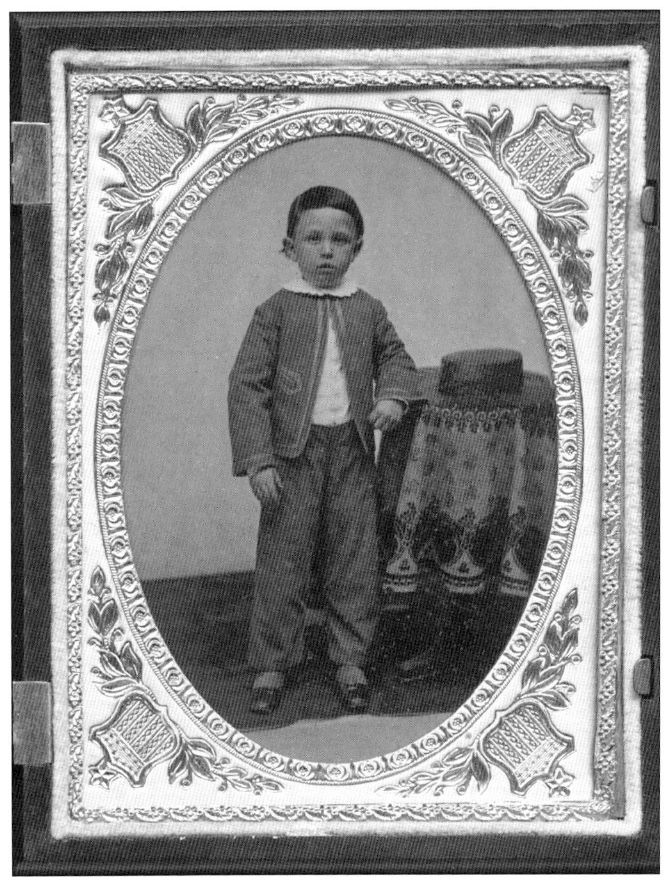

On February 28, 1859, Mary wrote a worried letter to family friend (and Illinois secretary of state) Ozias M. Hatch asking him to let Lincoln know "that our dear little Taddie, is quite sick." The doctor thought it might be "a slight attack of lung fever," a 19th-century phrase for pneumonia. "I am feeling troubled & it would be a comfort to have him, at home," she wrote. "He passed a bad night, I do not like his symptoms, and will be glad, if he hurries home." Pictured here are Tad in 1859 and the Lincolns' family cradle. (Left, LFA; below, ALPLM.)

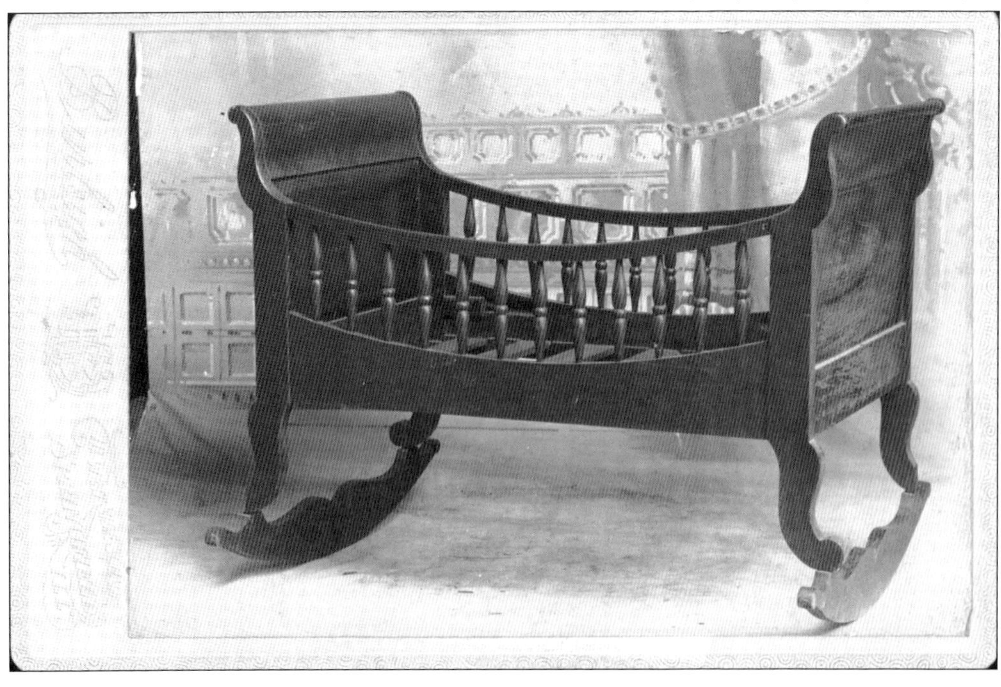

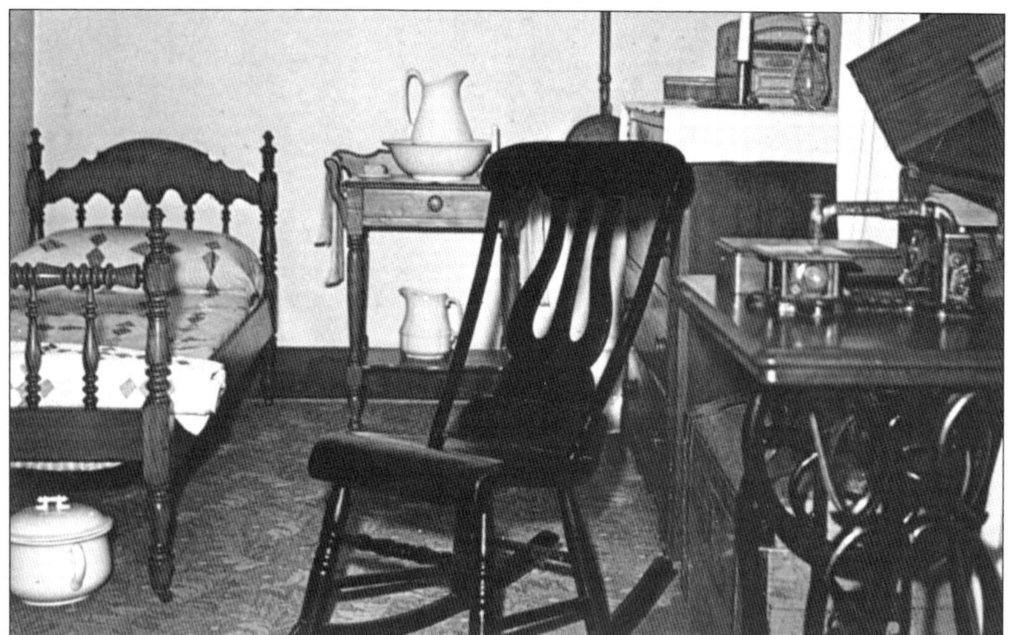

Early in their marriage, Mary did most of the housework. On December 31, 1846, the Lincolns purchased a copy of Eliza Leslie's *Directions for Cookery* from a local shop for 87¢. They also purchased *The House Book: Or, a Manual of Domestic Economy for Town and Country* by the same author. After the expansion of the home in 1856, this room became the maid's quarters. Mary described some of her servants as "wild Irish." (LFFC.)

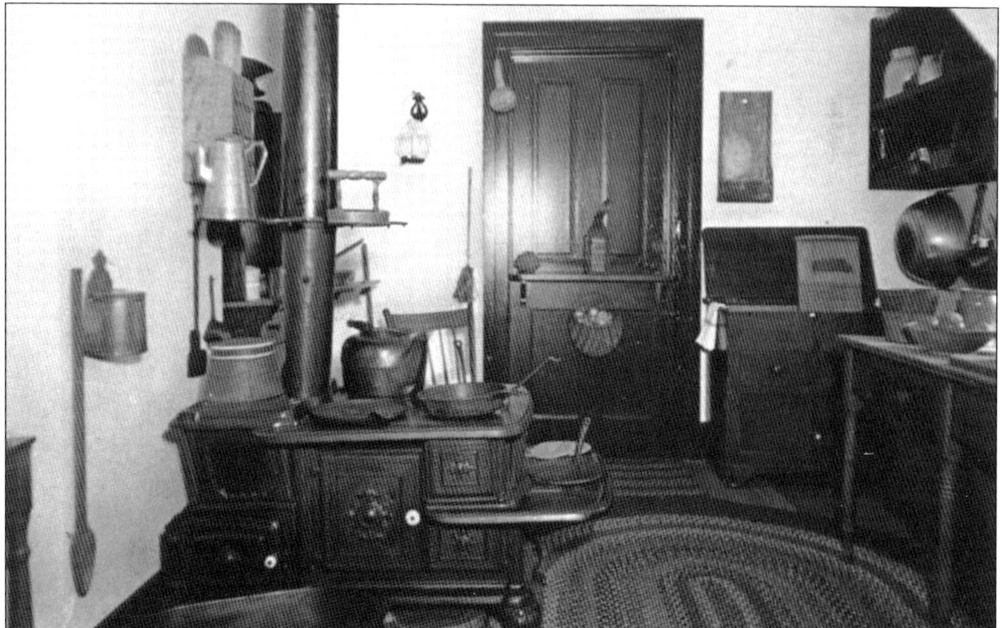

Margaret Ryan, a servant who had lived in the Lincoln home, later claimed that Lincoln would sneak into the house through the kitchen when he got home at night to see if Mary "was all right before going in front of house." Ryan also claimed that she once saw Mary "strike L. on [the] head with [a] piece of wood while reading paper in South Parlor" and "cut his nose." (LFFC.)

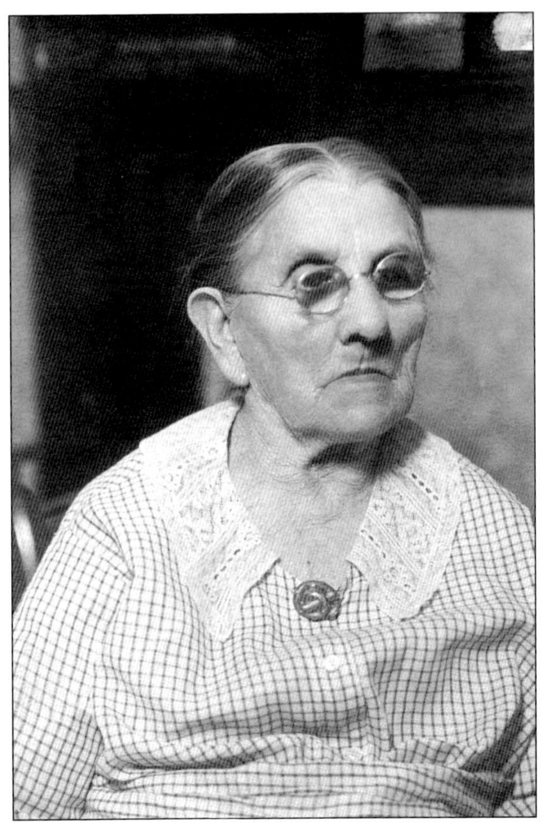

Charlotte Rodrigues De Souza was six years old when she emigrated from Portugal to Springfield in 1849 as part of a wave of exiles escaping religious persecution. Working as a seamstress for Mary Lincoln during the summer of 1860, she had many encounters with Lincoln in the lead-up to the presidential election. When she was about 90 years old, she recalled, "I believe our people [Portuguese immigrants] thought him a saint sent from heaven." (SVC.)

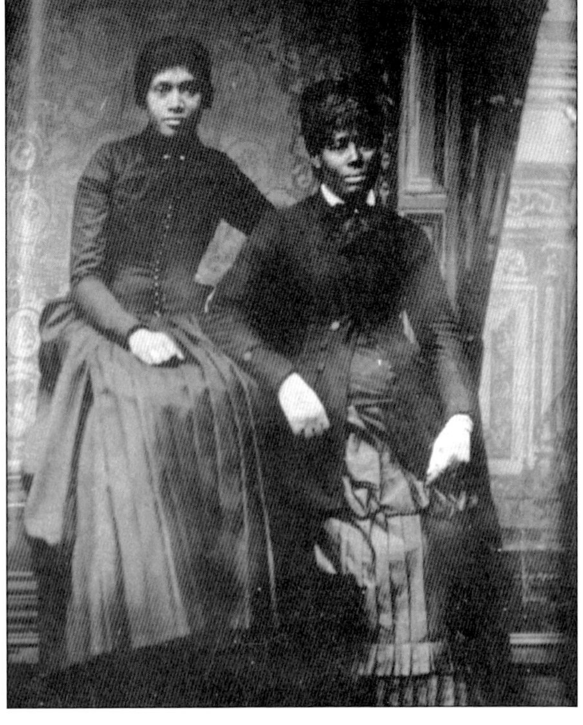

Mariah Vance, a free woman of color, worked for the Lincolns throughout the 1850s, doing laundry and cooking for the family. According to her obituary in 1904, "She packed his belongings when he was elected president, and did not see him again until he was taken home dead." Vance is pictured here at right with one of her daughters. (SVC.)

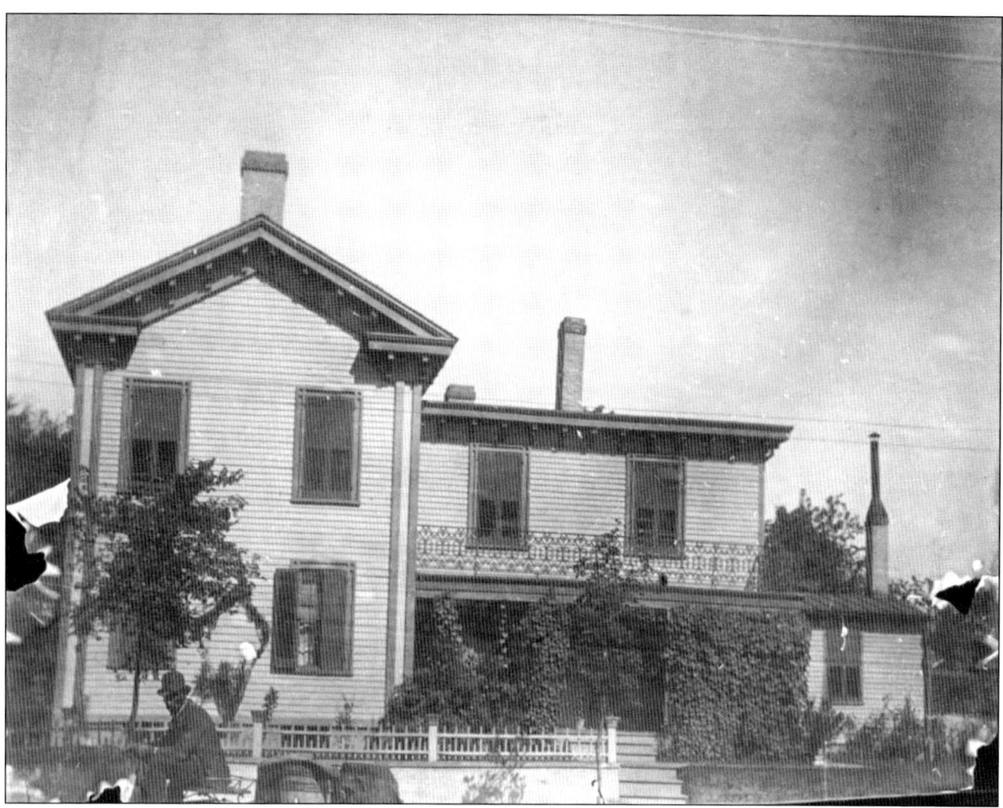

Not all was domestic tranquility in the Lincoln home. Several stories survive of Mary Lincoln lashing out at her husband. Neighbor Stephen Whitehurst later claimed that in 1856 or 1857, he saw Mary chasing Abraham "with a table knife or butcher knife in her hand." They ran through the garden, heading east toward Whitehurst's house. Whitehurst watched the scene from his backyard, while others on the street saw the commotion, some thinking it "was sport or fun." After some time, Lincoln turned and caught his wife by the shoulder and hip and "hustled her to the back door of his house," saying, "There d—n it, now Stay in the house and don't disgrace us before the Eyes of the world." (ALPLM.)

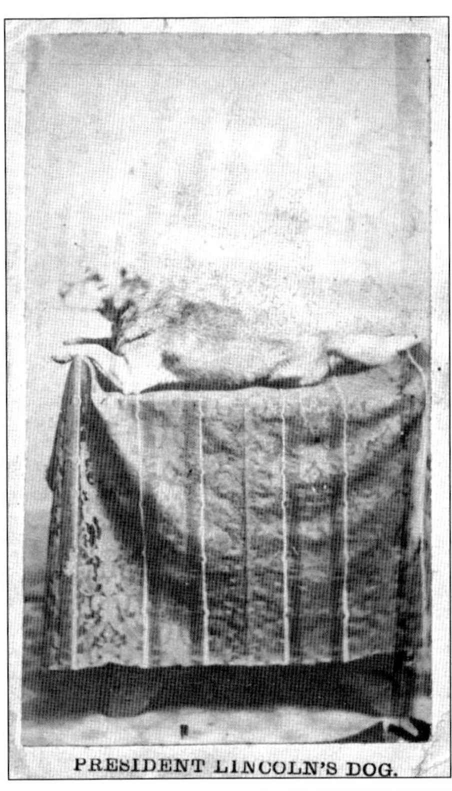
PRESIDENT LINCOLN'S DOG.

Bringing stray cats home was apparently a "hobby" of Lincoln's, although William H. Herndon claimed that Lincoln was not fond of animals. Nevertheless, Herndon said, "If L's children wanted a dog—cat—rat or the Devil it was alright and well treated—housed—petted—fed—fondled &c." On another occasion, Herndon described the "dogs & kittens[,] pups & chicks running around Lincolns house." Pictured here is the Lincolns' dog Fido. (LFA.)

Lincoln may have pondered the nation's problems while sitting in the privy. Once, as a small boy, Robert got into the lime box by the outhouse and got some of the poisonous powder into his mouth. Mary ran into the yard shouting, "Bobbie will die! Bobbie will die!" but a neighbor came and washed out his mouth. (LOC.)

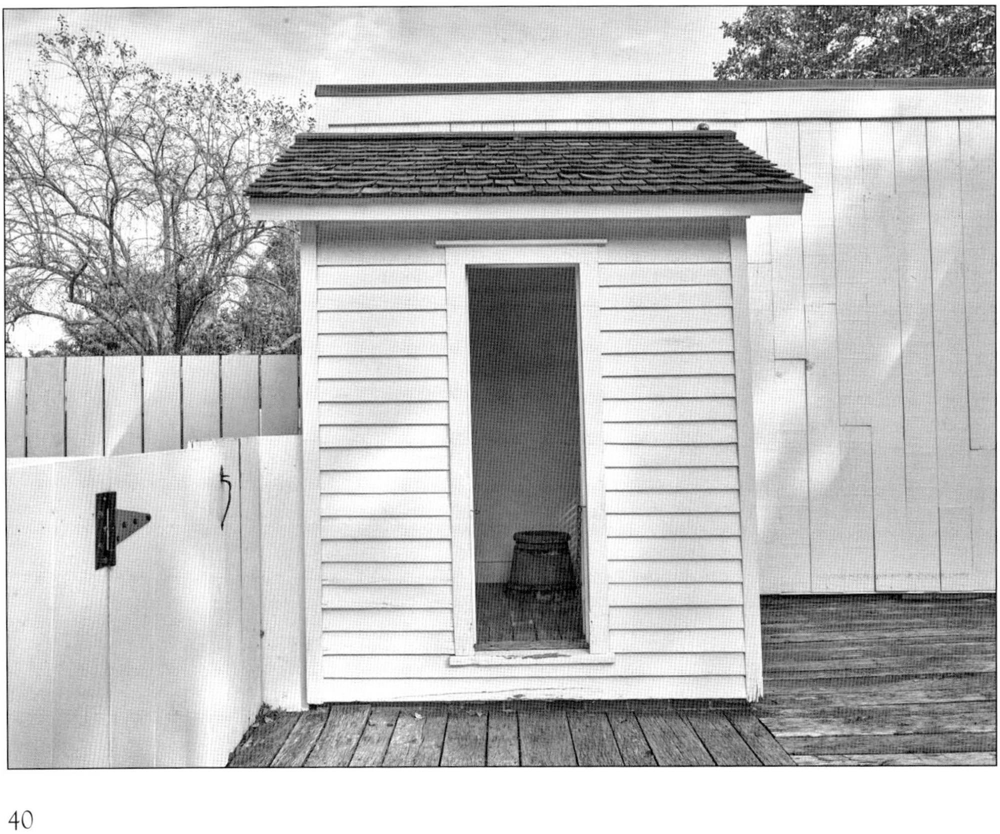

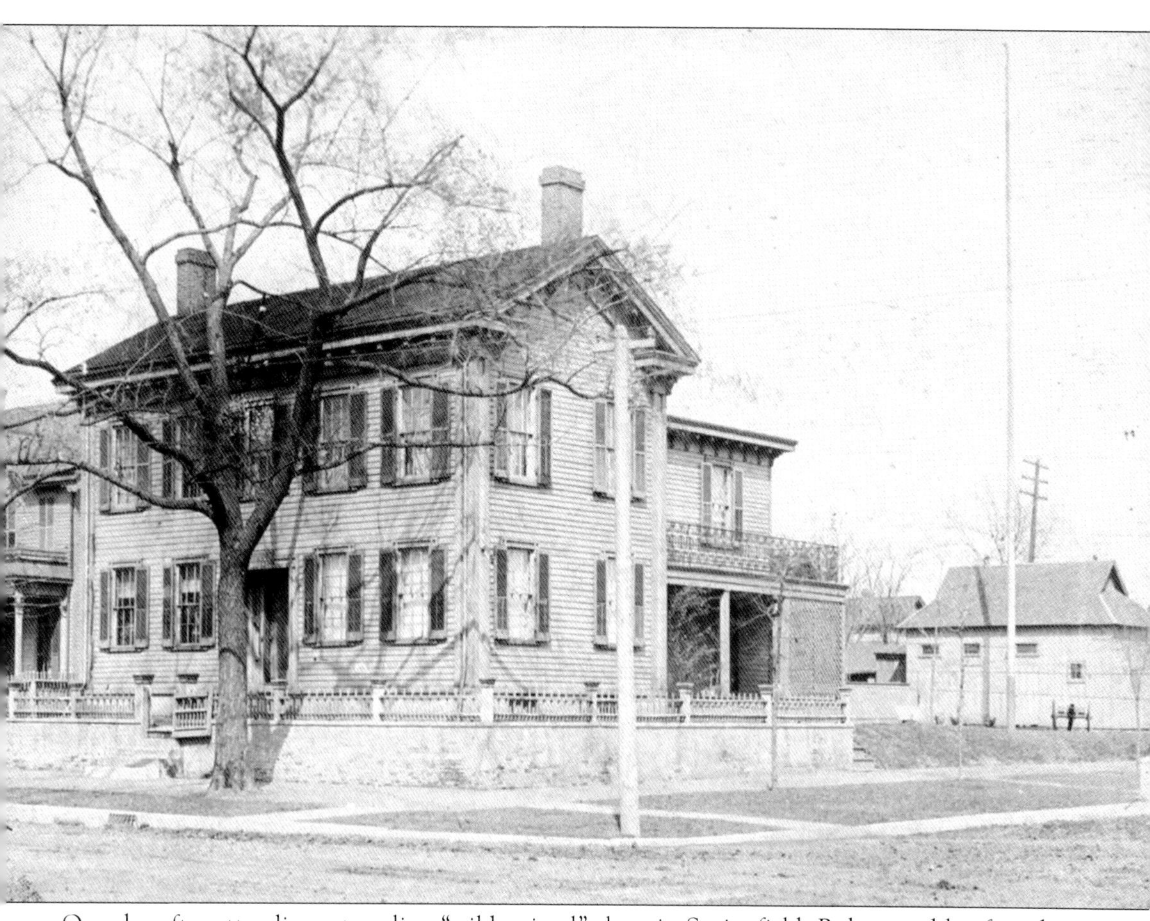

One day after attending a traveling "wild animal" show in Springfield, Robert and his friends attempted to put on a show of their own in the barn behind the Lincolns' house. The boys put ropes around the dogs' necks and slung them over the roof beams, hoping to yank the poor creatures up onto their hind legs like the lions they had seen at the circus. A neighbor heard the dogs yelping and ran to Lincoln's law office to tell him that "the dogs were being hung in his barn." Lincoln hurried home, rescued the animals, and swatted the boys. To his dying day in 1934, one of the boys "delighted in telling of a spanking he received as a boy of 7 years at the hands of Abraham Lincoln." Lincoln also split wood and cared for animals in the backyard. Mary Lincoln's sister Frances Todd Wallace recalled that he used the backyard as a woodpile and would "Saw wood for Exercise" there because "he really loved to do it." (ALPLM.)

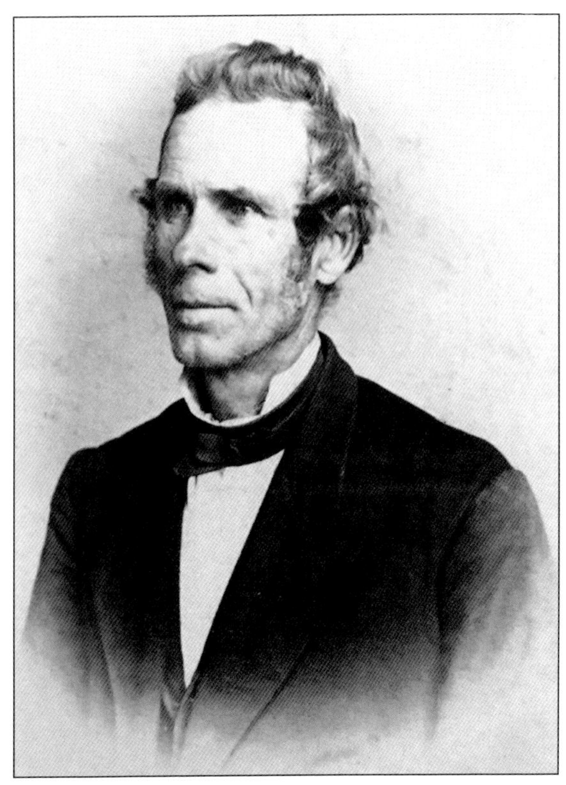

John B. Weber remembered one day when Mary Lincoln called for him to "Keep this little dog from biting me." Weber recalled, "The dog was a little thing & was doing nothing." On another occasion, Weber heard Mary screaming "Murder!" as she leaned over the fence, waving her hands in the air. Weber looked and saw an "umbrella man" walking from her house, muttering, "Should be sorry to have such a wife." (Find-a-Grave.)

Once, a workman determined that he could not finish his job "without Cutting down a pretty & valuable Shade tree in front of the house." He told Mary Lincoln that either the tree would need to come down or the plan would have to be altered. "Cut the tree down," she replied. Feeling uncertain, the workman asked Lincoln what to do. "Have you seen Mrs. Lincoln?" he asked. "Yes." "Then in God's name cut it down clean to the roots." (LOC.)

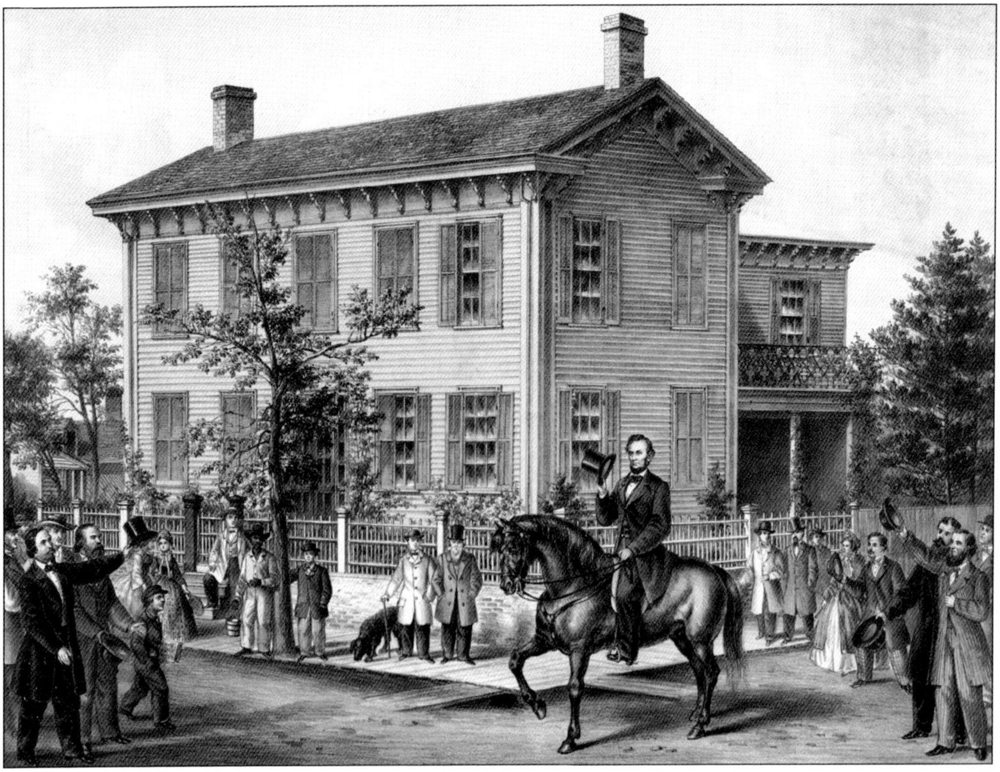

Three

Going to Housekeeping

Hospitality and Entertainment

The Lincolns welcomed many friends and neighbors into their home. Harriet Chapman, a relative who lived with them in the 1840s, recalled that Mary liked "to put on style." In 1881, Isaac N. Arnold recollected "the old-fashioned, generous hospitality of Springfield" in Lincoln's day. With "sad pleasure," he remembered attending "the dinners and evening parties given by Mrs. Lincoln. In her modest and simple home, everything orderly and refined, there was always, on the part of both host and hostess, a cordial and hearty Western welcome, which put every guest perfectly at ease." According to Arnold, Mary Lincoln's table was famous for "the excellence of many rare Kentucky dishes, and in season, it was loaded with venison, wild turkeys, prairie chickens, quail and other game, which was then abundant."

Strangers also found hospitality there. In 1860, a Pennsylvania Democrat named Jackson came to Springfield to see the Republican nominee. Unfortunately, one of the Lincoln boys was too sick for Lincoln to leave the house, so he invited Jackson to come see him at home. Jackson knocked at the door, was welcomed in, and sat down in the parlor. As he waited for the tall Illinoisan, he "look'd at every thing"—the carpet, chairs, and bookcase—and wondered whether this man "will ever be presdt of these U.S." Soon, Lincoln came downstairs in his socks and shirt sleeves. The two men shook hands and talked for an hour and a half. Jackson went away thinking, "He's a man of great good sense—familiar and honest. He's not an ugly man—but is a good looking man." And perhaps most surprisingly, the Democrat concluded, "I intend to vote for that man."

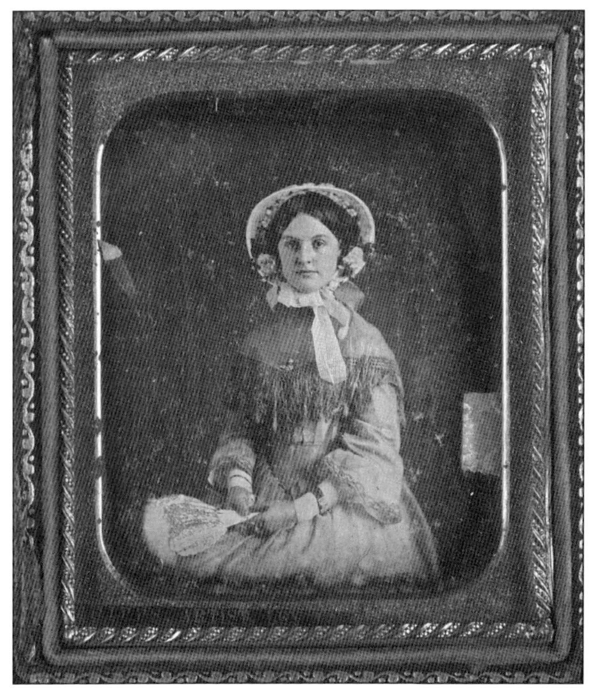

Mary's younger half-sister Emilie Todd was so beautiful as a little girl that a childless couple in Lexington, Kentucky, tried to kidnap her. An occasional long-term visitor to the Lincoln home, Emilie observed that Mary "mothered her husband as she did her children, and he seemed very dependent on her." For his part, Lincoln joked that Emilie "has a tongue like the rest of the Todds." This photograph was made while Emilie lived with the Lincolns around 1855. (MTL.)

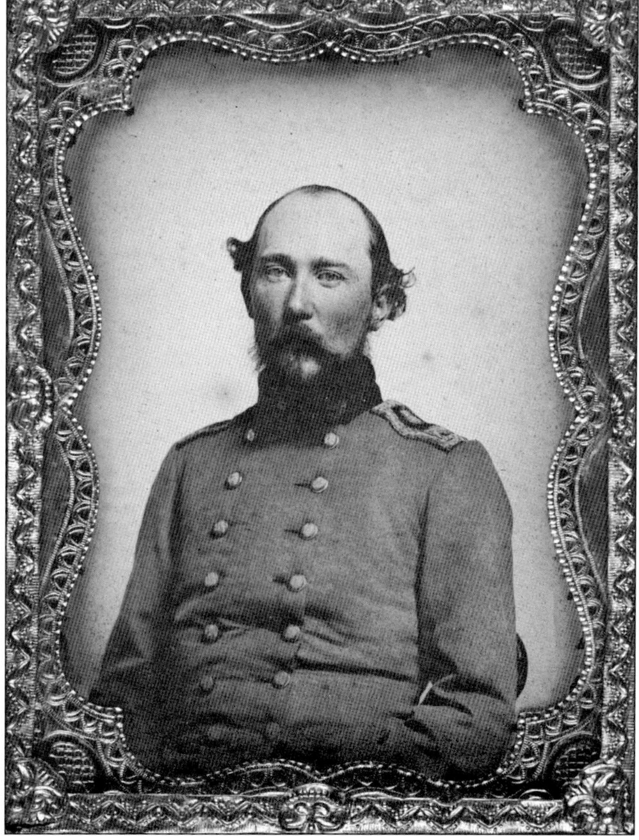

In 1857, Benjamin Hardin Helm (Emilie's new husband) visited Springfield to argue a law case. When he called at the Lincolns' home, Mary greeted him with, "So this tall young Kentuckian is Little Sister's husband; he shall have a double welcome as a Kentuckian and as a brother." Lincoln insisted that Helm stay with them for the week. Sadly, Helm would join the Confederate army and be killed at Chickamauga in September 1863 at the age of 32. (MTL.)

The Lincolns' second child, Edward Baker Lincoln, was born in the home on March 10, 1846. When Lincoln went to Congress in 1848, the little boy, who could not pronounce the word "Capitol," said that his father had "gone tapila." Sadly, Eddy died in the home of tuberculosis on February 1, 1850, after 52 days of sickness. Lincoln wrote privately, "We miss him very much." This is a daguerreotype by N.H. Shepard from around 1849. (Keya Morgan Collection, LincolnImages.com.)

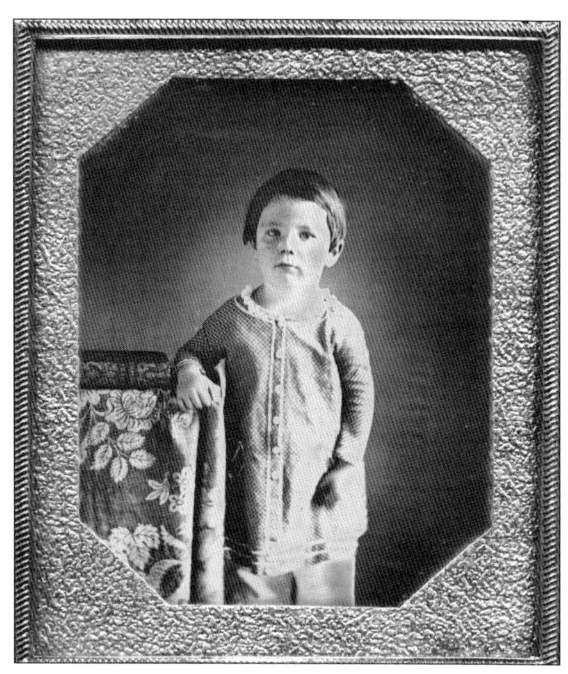

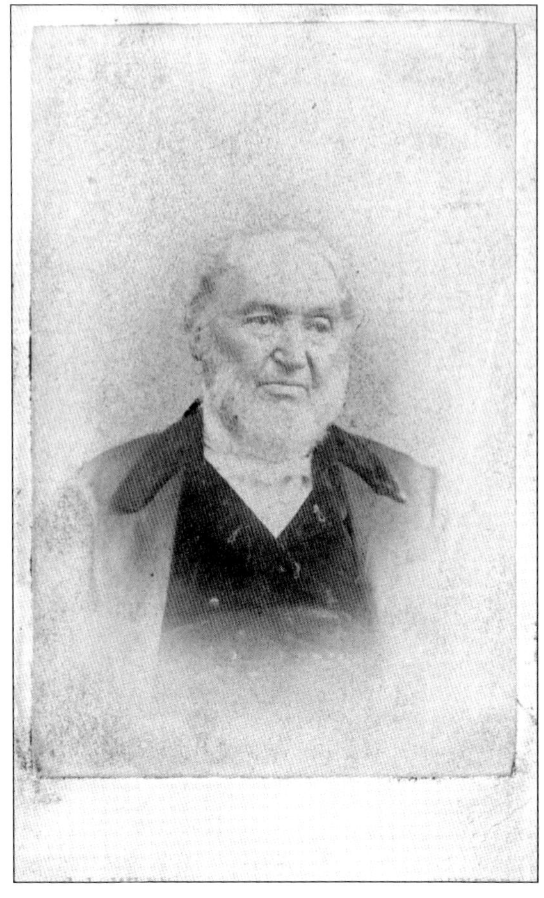

Rev. James Smith conducted Eddy's funeral in what is now the back parlor of the home. From 1850 to 1861, Smith "was a welcome caller at the house on Eighth Street, engaging Abraham Lincoln in probing philosophical discussions and providing Mary Lincoln with the strength to look ahead." Mary told Emilie Helm in 1856 that "Dr. Smith is talented & beloved." (ALPLM.)

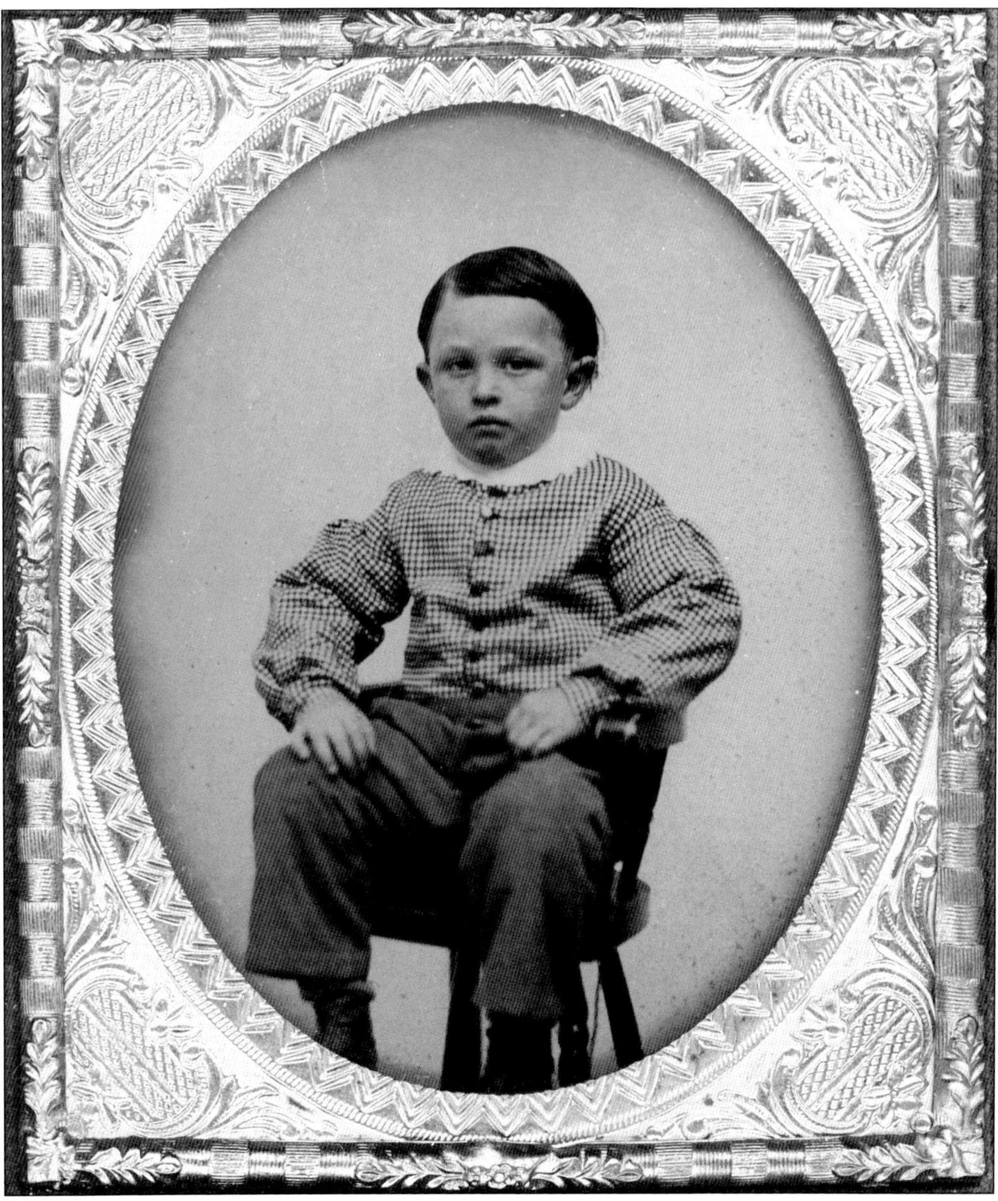

As an elderly woman, next-door neighbor Anna Eastman recalled a summer afternoon when she heard commotion coming from the Lincoln home. When she opened her kitchen window so that she could see and hear, she saw Mary Lincoln loudly accusing Tad (born April 4, 1853, and pictured here in 1858) of having taken a dime that was meant for groceries. "Tad," she declared, "You are a bad boy, I am afraid you are a thief." Tad interjected that he had lost the money, not stolen it. As Mary Lincoln rapt a switch across Tad's legs, Abraham walked in. "What does this mean?" he asked. Mary told him what Tad had done, but he replied, "But, are you sure? Perhaps." Lincoln turned out Tad's pockets and out popped the missing dime. Lincoln turned to his wife and said in a soft, gentle voice, "Mary! Mary!" (LFA.)

When Robert Lincoln (pictured here in 1860) left for Harvard in August 1859, Mary wrote a friend, "I am feeling quite lonely, as Bob, left for College, in Boston, . . . and it almost appears, as if light & mirth, had departed with him." Four weeks later, she added, "I miss Bob, so much, that I do not feel settled down." After "a long year" of his absence, she wrote in 1860, "at times I feel wild to see him." (LFA.)

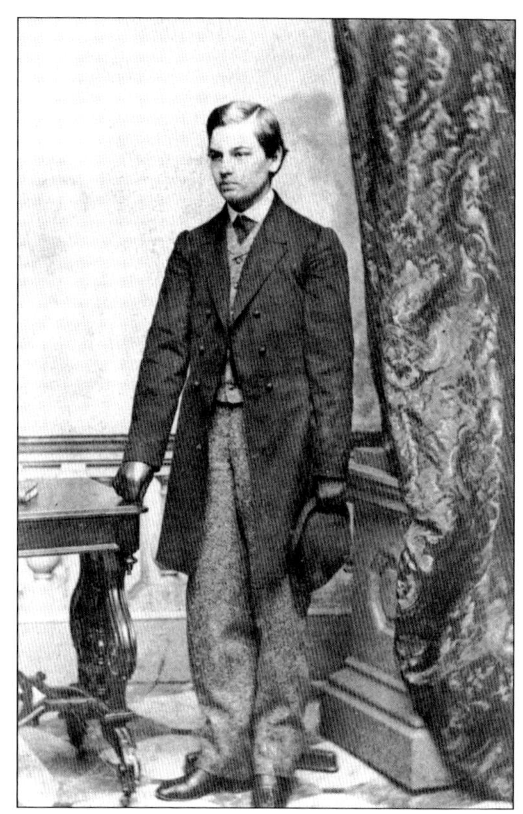

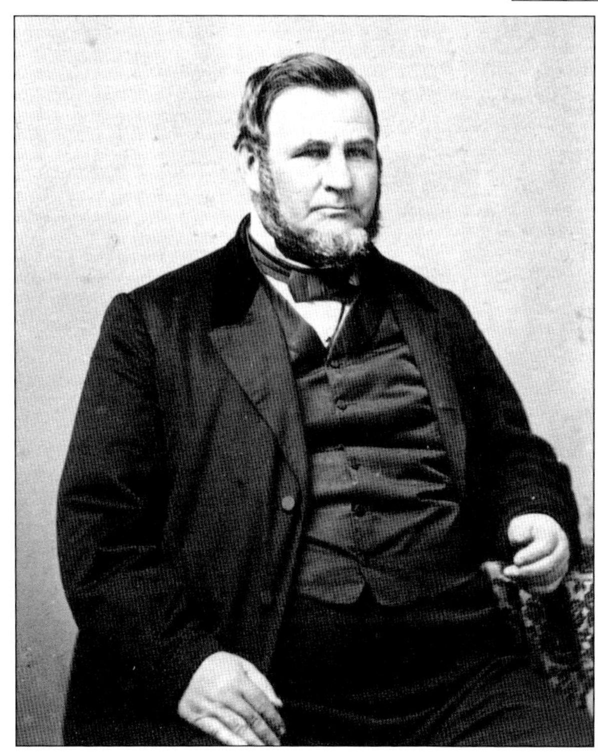

In August 1847, Lincoln invited about 20 delegates from the state constitutional convention to his home. David Davis, a delegate from Bloomington, wrote to his wife, "No ladies present—not even Mrs. Lincoln. . . . The Bill of fare the same as is usual in this town." As for Lincoln, Davis wrote, "You cant make a gentleman in his outward appearance, out of Lincoln to save your life." (LFA.)

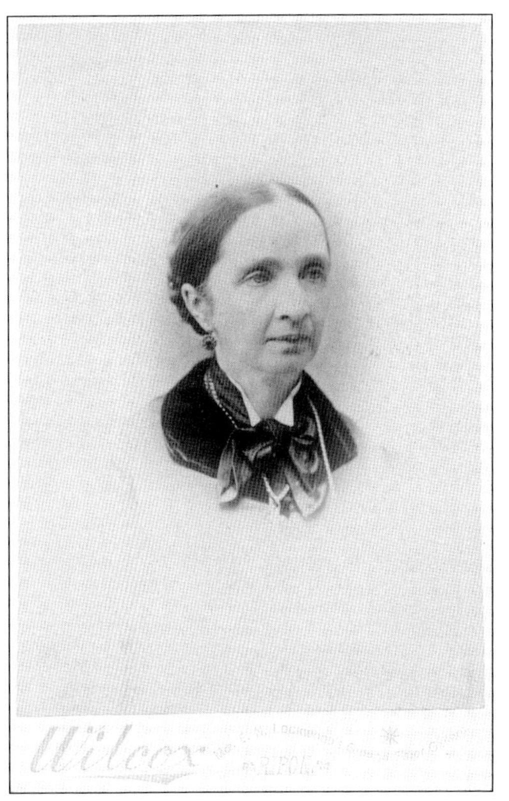

One Saturday evening in the late 1850s, Mary Lincoln wrote to her friend Mary Brayman (pictured here later in life), "If your health will admit of venturing out, in such damp weather, we would be much pleased to have you, Mr. B—and the young ladies come round, this eve about seven and pass a social evening also any friend you may have with you." (HRFA.)

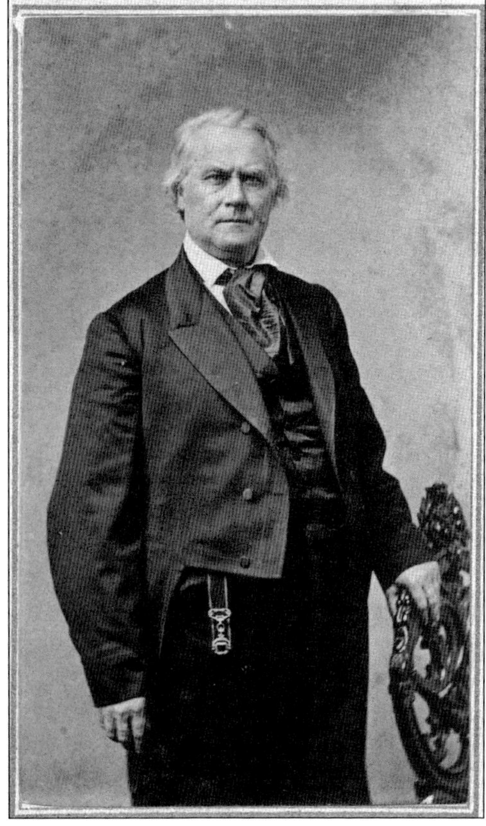

Lincoln had served with Jesse K. Dubois (pictured here) in the state legislature since the 1830s, and in the 1840s, they became neighbors (the Dubois home still stands in the Lincoln Home National Historic Site). In April 1859, Mary wrote that "Mr. Dubois' family and Mr. [Ozias M.] Hatch took tea with us a few evenings since." (LFA.)

Lincoln's friend and political associate Orville Hickman Browning (pictured here) wrote in his diary about several suppers and parties he enjoyed at the Lincoln home in the 1850s. Although Lincoln's law partner William H. Herndon does not appear to have ever attended any of these gatherings, he complained that the Lincolns never served wine, beer, or liquor. It may have been because, as Lincoln told a friend, alcohol "always makes me feel flabby and undone." (LOC.)

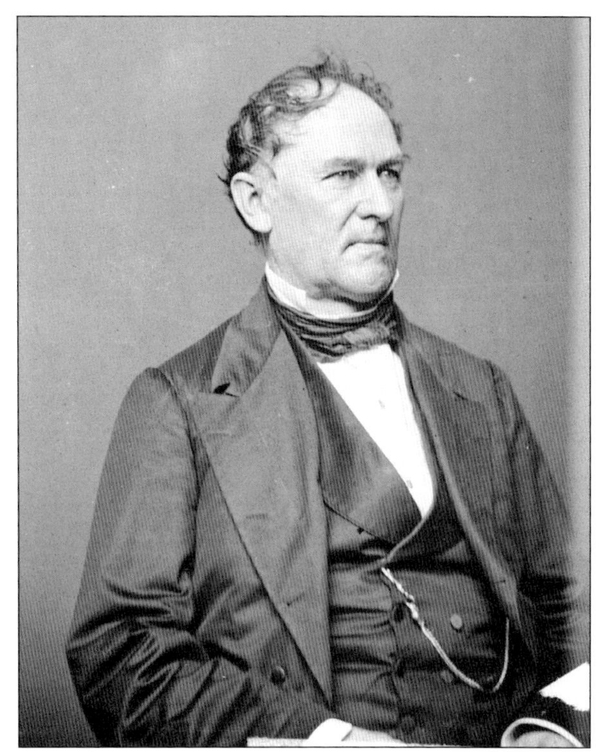

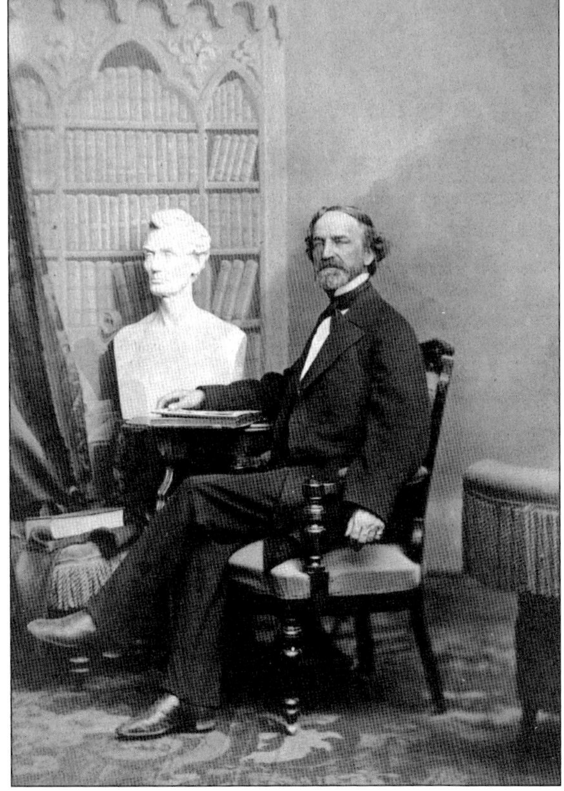

Some of Lincoln's associates claimed that Mary never permitted Lincoln to invite his friends to dinner. However, Isaac N. Arnold, a former Democrat-turned-Republican, remembered Mary Lincoln's "genial manners and ever-kind welcome" at parties, adding that "Mr. Lincoln's wit and humor, anecdote and unrivalled conversation, . . . formed the chief attraction." (LFFC.)

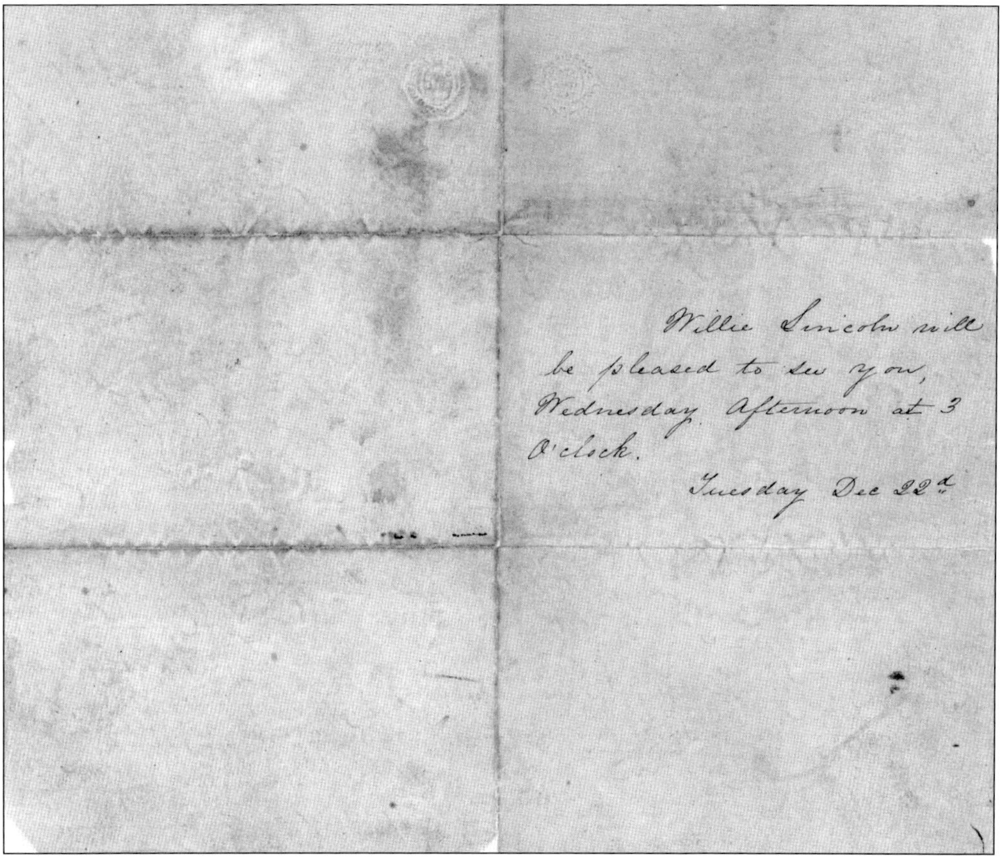

Willie Lincoln will be pleased to see you, Wednesday Afternoon at 3 O'clock.

Tuesday Dec 22d

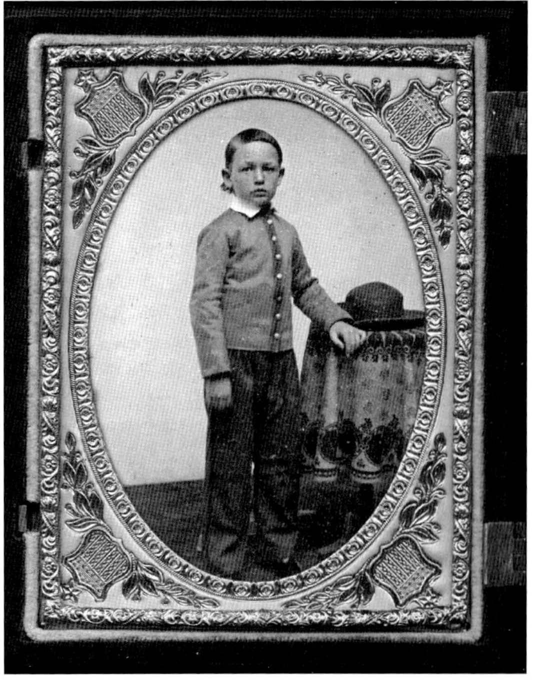

On December 23, 1859, the Lincolns hosted a ninth birthday party for Willie (born December 21, 1850, and pictured here around 1859). Invitations, such as this one to Isaac Diller, said that "Willie Lincoln will be pleased to see you." Mary later told a friend that "as I had long promised him a celebration, it duly came off. Some 50 or 60 boys & girls attended the gala, you may believe I have come to the conclusion, that they are nonsensical affairs." In 1938, Diller, now about 84 years old, wrote, "I treasure the invitation written by Mrs. Lincoln to attend Willie's party." (Above, ALPLM; left, LFA.)

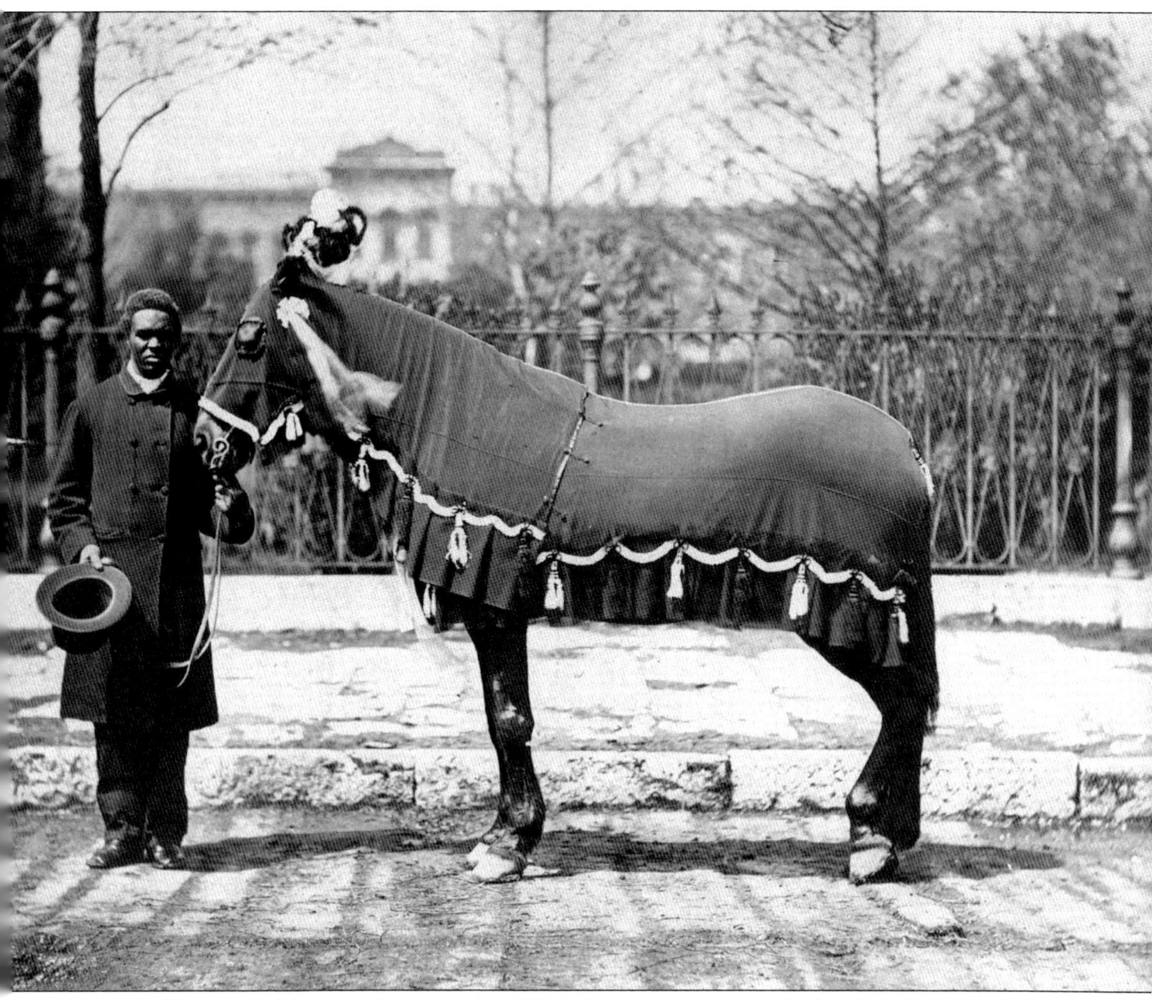

Joseph P. Kent, who lived on the east side of Eighth Street, occasionally lived with the Lincolns and cared for their horse when Lincoln and Robert were away from home. One Sunday in the summer of 1859, several other neighborhood boys persuaded Kent to ask if he could borrow the horse. Kent approached the house from the side entrance on Jackson Street. When Lincoln opened the door, Kent recalled, "I promptly stated my business. Mr. Lincoln told me to go and get the horse. Prompted by Mr. Lincoln's ever generous favors in the past, I presumed too far that time." Kent then asked if he could borrow the carriage as well. With a broad smile on his face, Lincoln replied, "No, Joseph, there are two things I will not loan, my wife and my carriage." Pictured here is Lincoln's horse (sometimes identified as "Old Bob" and sometimes as "Old Robin") with Rev. Henry Brown in May 1865, at the time of Lincoln's funeral. (LFA.)

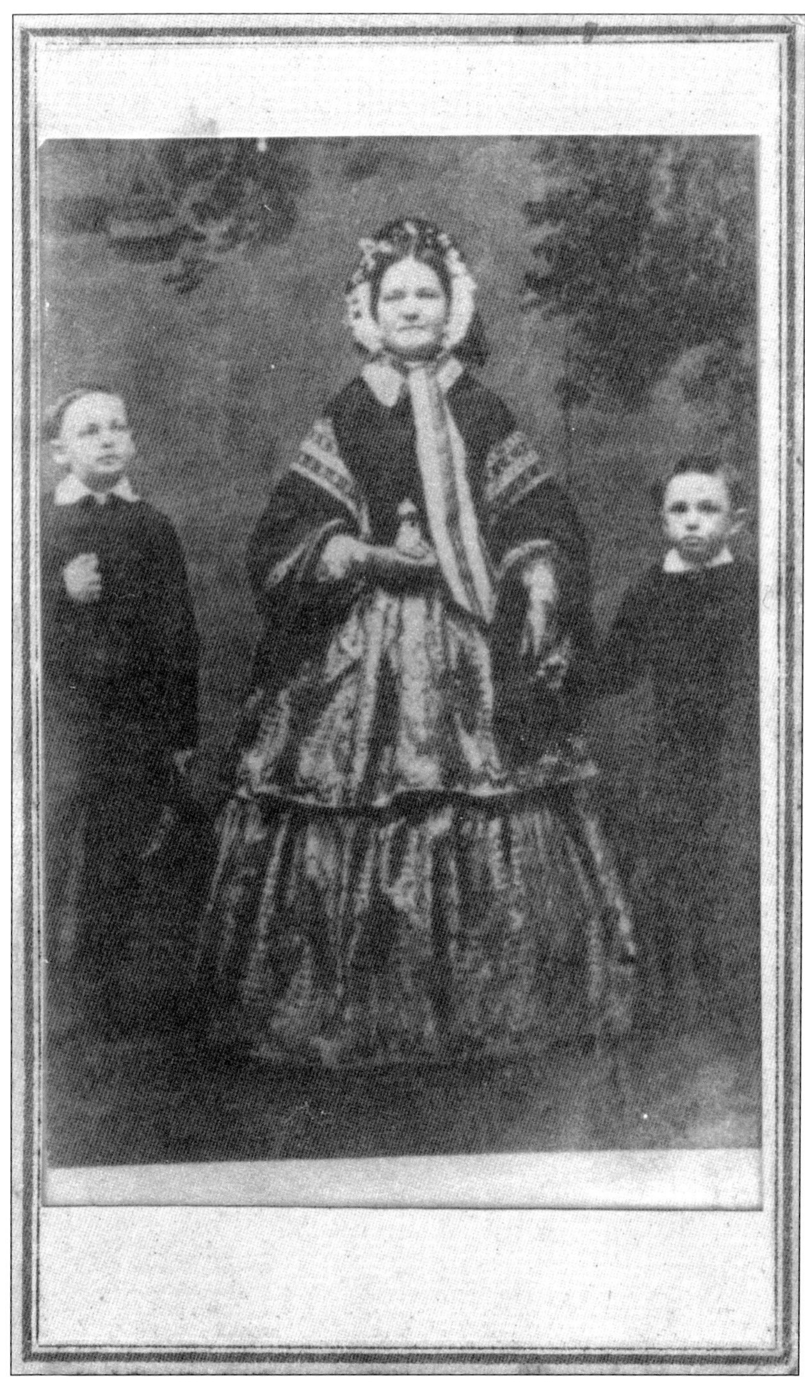

One evening, Abraham and Mary were invited to a party at the home of Jesse K. Dubois, just down the street. As Mary was getting dressed, Willie and Tad "came home from a candy pull . . . smeared with molasses candy from head to foot." When they asked to go, Mary firmly said no, at which point "the two boys set up a cry . . . kicking and screaming." Lincoln came in and overruled his wife, and the five Lincolns walked to the party—Abraham with the two younger boys, and Mary following shortly after with Robert. Mary is pictured here with Willie and Tad in November 1860. (LFFC.)

After Lincoln lost the 1858 US Senate race, Norman Judd, chairman of the state Republican Party, asked Lincoln for a financial contribution to pay down the party's debt. Lincoln, who had forgone the practice of law to campaign, replied, "I am willing to pay according to my ability; but I am the poorest hand living to get others to pay. I have been on expences so long without earning any thing that I am absolutely without money now for even household purposes." (LOC.)

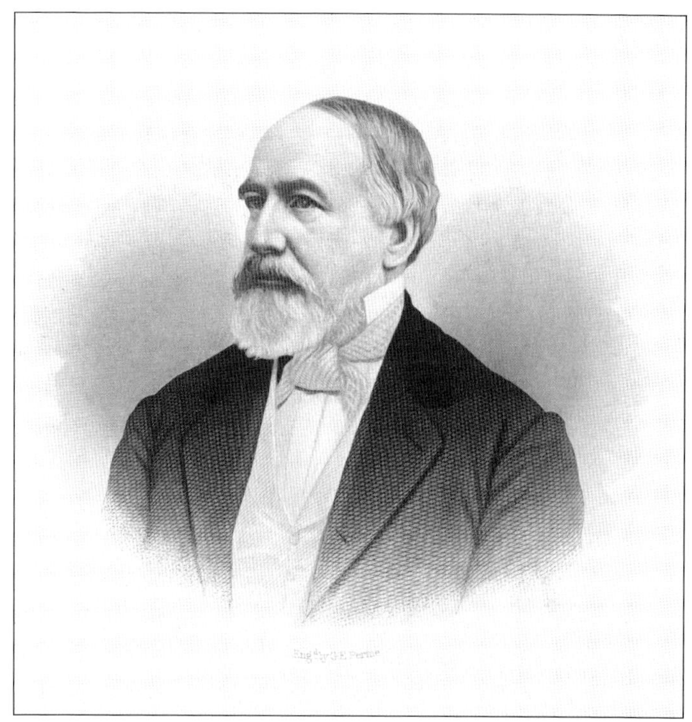

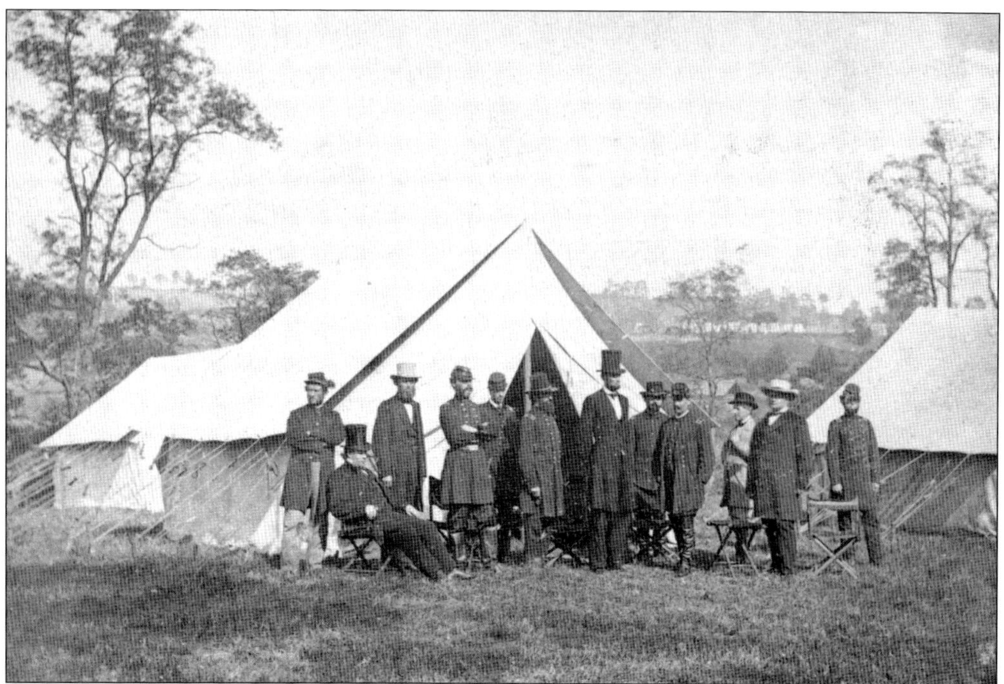

Illinois secretary of state Ozias M. Hatch was a close friend and important political ally of Lincoln's. On October 1, 1859, he made, in Mary's words, "one of his social, agreeable calls." Mary later wrote him that she "would be pleased to have you wander up our way, to see us this evening" because "I should like to see you." Hatch is pictured here (third from left) visiting Antietam with Lincoln in October 1862. (LOC.)

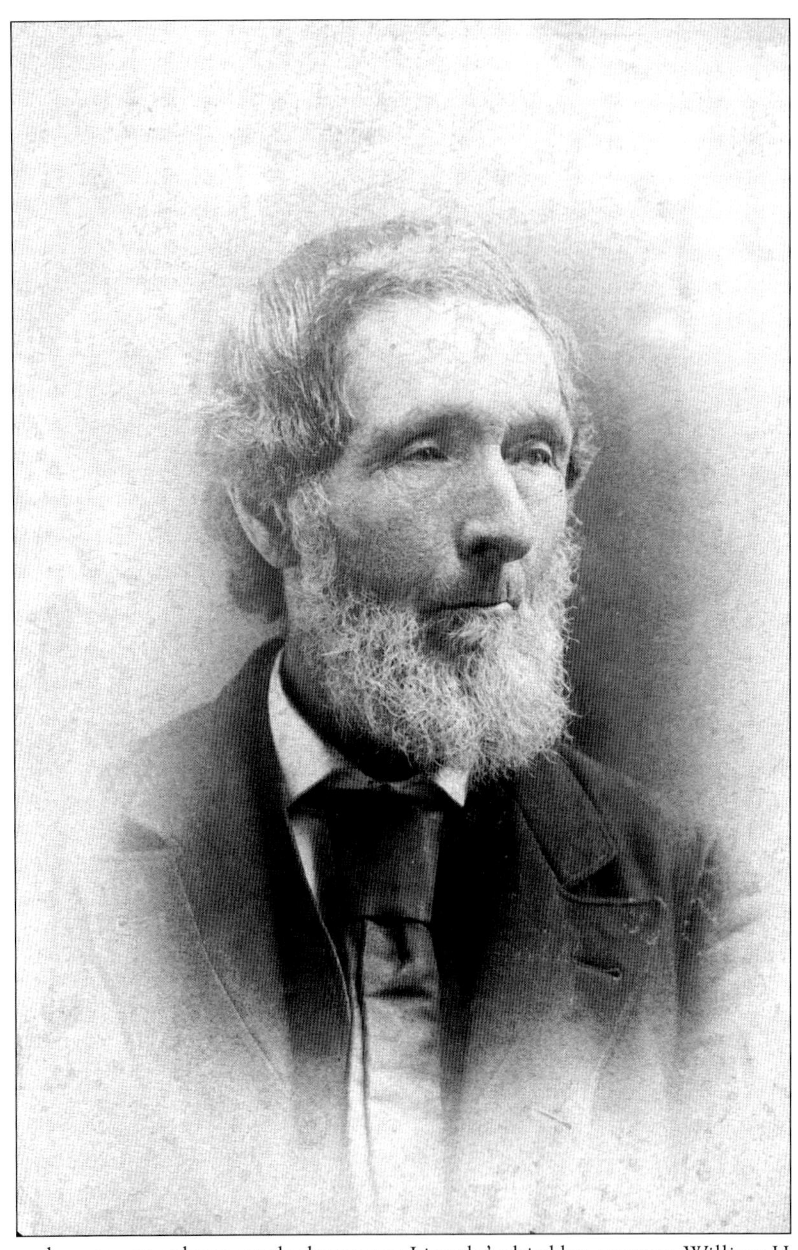

One person who was not welcome at the home was Lincoln's third law partner, William H. Herndon. Mary did not care for Herndon, whom she considered "a drunkard, an outrageous story-teller," a "thief," and "a dirty dog." Herndon, for his part, groused that Mary was "cold & repulsive to visitors that did not suit her cold aristocratic blood." Herndon later claimed that "I never put my foot in his house but once and that on business which I could not avoid after he was elected President." Mary affirmed this in a private letter to David Davis: "Mr Herndon, had always been an utter stranger to me, he was not considered an habitué, at our house. The office was more, in his line." Herndon claimed that the Lincolns' "house was cold—exclusive and aristocratic, with no soul—fire—cheer or fun in it," like an "ice cave in mid summer." He also claimed that Lincoln did so much work on the circuit because "his home was Hell and he did not wish to burn long nor often." In response, Mary lamented "that wretched Herndon & all his falsehoods, and villanies." (LFFC.)

Four

Make Yourself at Home

Visitors during the 1860 Campaign

A correspondent for the *Utica Morning Herald* visited Springfield on June 21, 1860. After "vainly searching for a hack," he determined to walk to Lincoln's home, "in the truly democratic way of going afoot, and unattended by any guide save my own wits." With "little difficulty" he located the house at the corner of Eighth and Jackson Streets. "A modest-looking two story brown frame house, with the name 'A. Lincoln' on the door plate, told me that my pilgrimage was ended." A servant met him at the door, ushered him into the parlor, and took his note upstairs to Lincoln. "The house was neatly without being extravagantly furnished. An air of quiet refinement pervaded the place." He saw flowers on the table and pictures hanging on the wall. "The adornments were few, but chastely appropriate; everything was in its place and ministered to the general effect. The hand of the domestic artist was everywhere visible." Without thinking, the visitor involuntarily blurted, "What a pleasant home Abe Lincoln has."

At that moment, the visitor heard footsteps coming down the staircase. He looked and saw "a tall, arrowy, angular gentleman, with a profusion of wiry hair, 'lying around loose' about his head, and a pair of eyes that seemed to say 'make yourself at home.' " Lincoln shook his visitor's hand, and the two men sat down in the parlor to talk politics. After a bit of conversation, the visitor asked Lincoln if he "was not very much bored with calls and correspondence." Lincoln replied that he "liked to see his friends" and that he "took care not to answer" many of his letters. Although the visitor had not intended to stay more than 10 minutes, the conversation lasted nearly two hours. "More than once I rose to leave, but he was kind enough to assure me that he did not regard my call as a bore. I found him one of the most companionable men I have ever met. Frank, hearty and unassuming, one feels irresistibly drawn toward him. . . . One feels, in talking with him, that his utterances come from the heart."

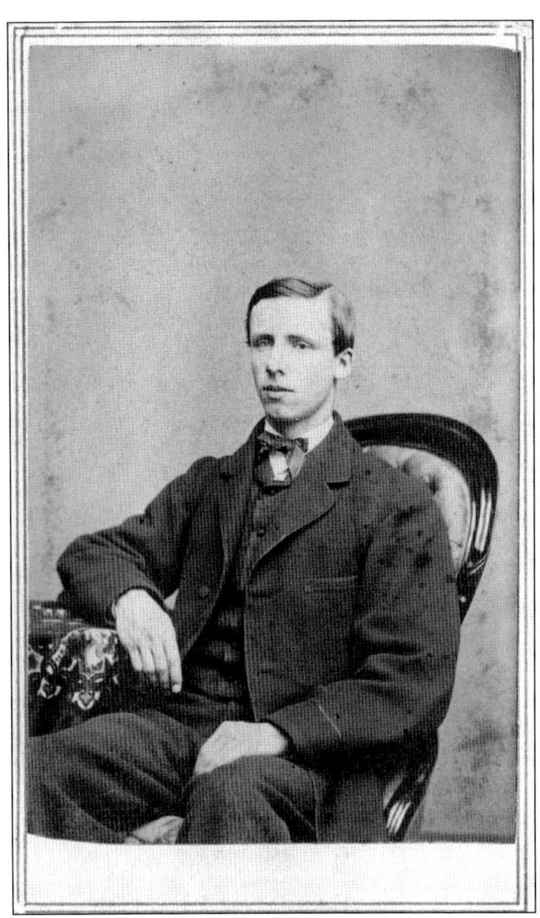

Robert Lincoln's childhood friend Clinton L. Conkling (pictured at left) vividly remembered the day Lincoln received the Republican nomination for president on May 18, 1860. In 1920, he recalled that Lincoln had been visiting his father, James C. Conkling, when he said, "Well, Conkling, I believe I will go back to my office and practice law." A moment after Lincoln departed, word came in across the telegraph that he had received the nomination. The younger Conkling ran outside and shouted, "Mr. Lincoln! You're nominated!" Lincoln turned, smiled, and shook the 12-year-old's hand. "Well, Clinton, then we've got it!" (Left, LFA; below, LOC.)

[FORM 2.]

CATON LINES.

Illinois and Mississippi Telegraph Company.

IN CONNECTION WITH ALL OTHER LINES IN THE UNITED STATES AND CANADAS.

TERMS AND CONDITIONS ON WHICH MESSAGES ARE RECEIVED BY THIS COMPANY FOR TRANSMISSION.

The public are notified, that, in order to guard against mistakes in the transmission of messages, every message of importance ought to be repeated, by being sent back from the station at which it is to be received to the station from which it is originally sent. Half the usual price for transmission will be charged for repeating the message. This Company will not be responsible for mistakes or delays in the transmission or delivery of unrepeated messages, from whatever cause they may arise; nor will it be responsible for damages arising from mistakes or delays in the transmission or delivery of a repeated message, beyond an amount exceeding two hundred times the amount paid for sending the message; nor will it be responsible for delays arising from interruptions in the working of its Telegraphs, nor for any mistake or omission of any other Company over whose lines a message is to be sent to reach the place of destination. All messages will hereafter be received by this Company for transmission, subject to the above conditions.

J. D. CATON, Pres't, Ottawa, Ill.

1860

By Telegraph from Chicago 18 [May] 1860

To Hon A Lincoln

Dear Sir: A Committee of the convention will wait upon you by Special train Saturday Eve to inform you officially of your nomination for Prest of the United States —

2696 28 wd ch 1.45 PM George Ashmun President

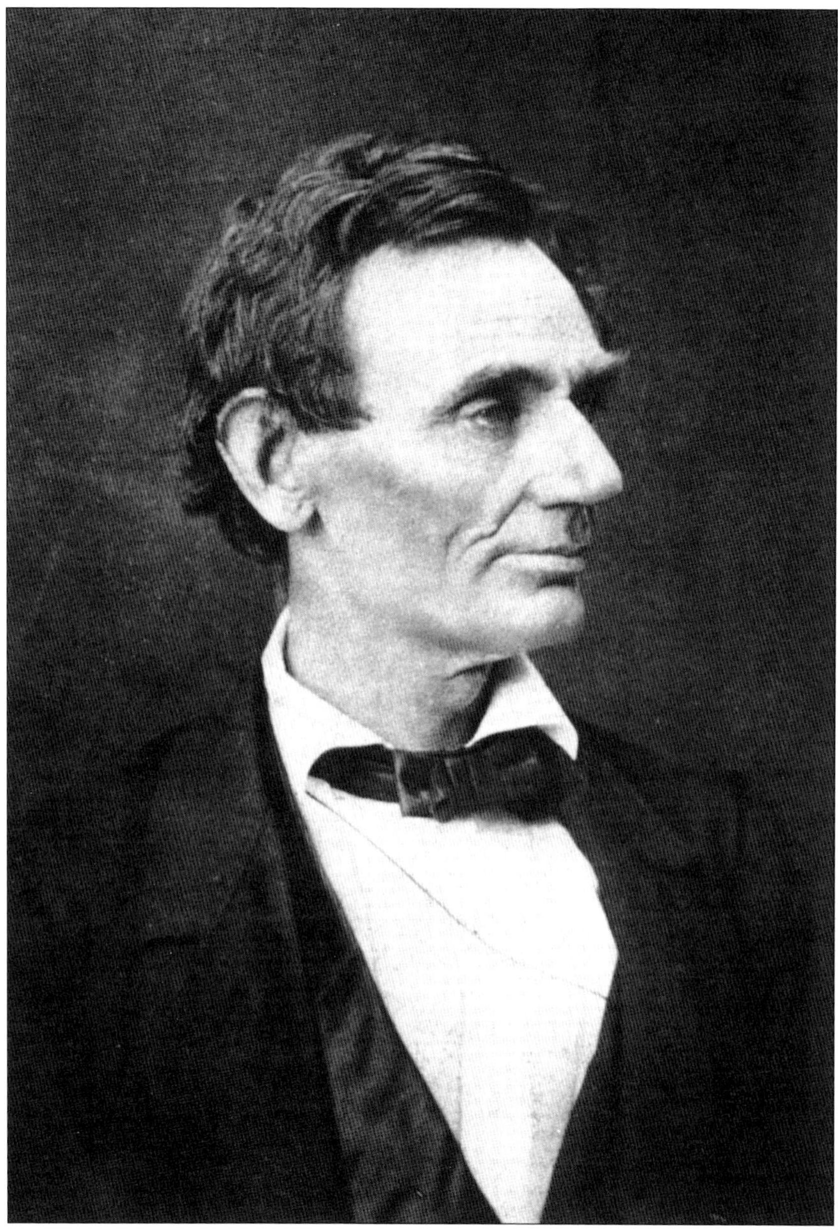

The people of Springfield were "considerably excited" when Lincoln received the Republican nomination for president, firing cannons and ringing church bells for the rest of the day. In the evening, when a crowd showed up at his home, Lincoln came out and made a few remarks, then said "he would invite the whole crowd into his house if it was large enough to hold them, but as it could not contain more than a fraction of those who were in front of it, he would merely invite as many as could find room." One of the revelers shouted joyously, "We'll give you a larger house on the fourth of next March!" As one local reporter stated, "Deafening cheers greeted the invitation, and in less than a minute Mr. Lincoln's house was invaded by as many as could 'squeeze in.' The invaders were warmly received and many of them had the pleasure of shaking the right hand of their hospitable host." Likely to Lincoln's chagrin, many stayed past midnight. This photograph was taken at Springfield by Alexander Hesler on June 3, 1860. (LOC.)

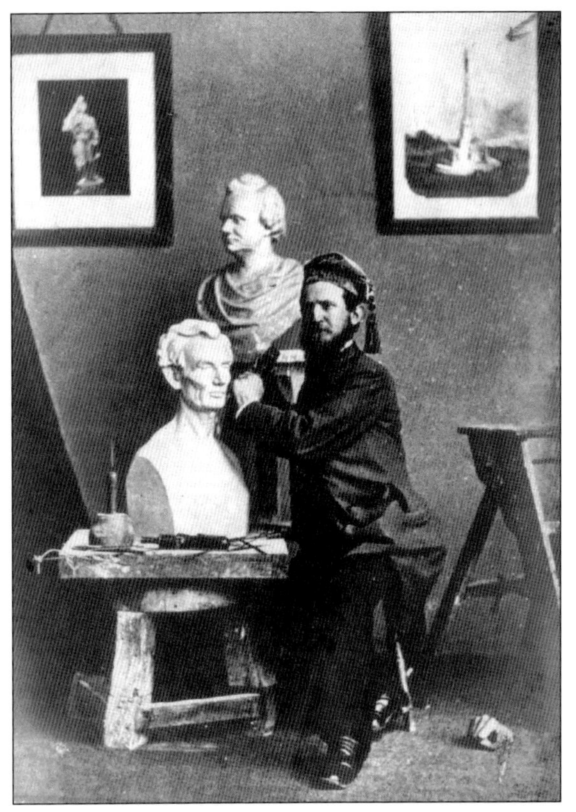

On the same day Lincoln received the Republican nomination, Chicago sculptor Leonard Volk (pictured here in 1868) visited Springfield to make a statue of Lincoln. Looking out his window, Lincoln saw the sculptor approaching and went out to greet him. "I am the first man from Chicago, I believe, who has the honor of congratulating you on your nomination for President," Volk said. After the two men shook hands, Volk told the nominee that he wished to make a statue of Lincoln and that he would "do my best to do you justice." Lincoln replied, "I don't doubt it, for I have come to the conclusion that you are an honest man." Lincoln invited Volk into the parlor so that they could talk. Soon, Mary entered the room carrying a bouquet of roses. Volk gave her a cabinet-size bust of Lincoln (pictured here at ALPLM), a replica of which can still be seen on the "whatnot" shelf in the Lincolns' parlor. (Left, GBC; below, JW.)

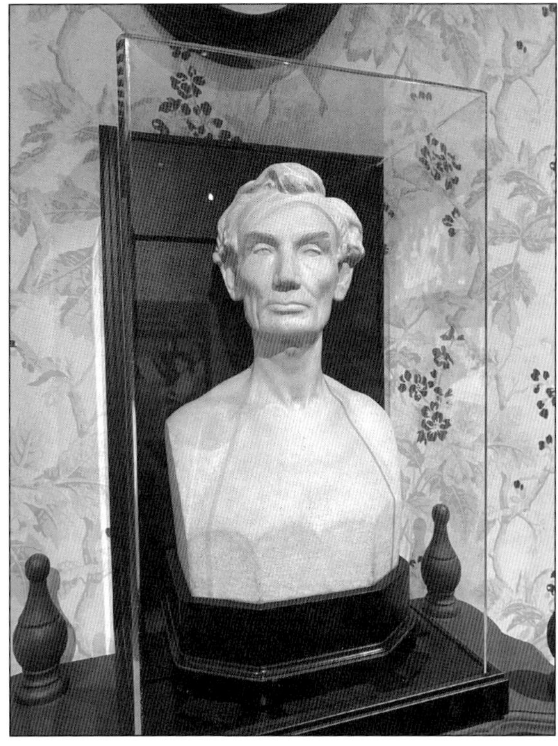

Gustave Koerner (right) and Ebenezer Peck (below) arrived at the Lincoln home a few hours before the Republican committee. In the sitting room, Koerner saw a "long table set on one side, on which stood many glasses, a decanter or two of brandy, and under the table a champagne basket. Cakes and sandwiches were just being placed on the table by a colored man." They went in and asked the servant what it was for. He replied, "O, this is for the Chicago folks, that come down to congratulate master." When Mary Lincoln came in, Koerner and Peck encouraged her to remove the alcohol since several members of the committee "were strictly temperance people." Mary argued with them, but Lincoln walked over from the parlor and said, "Perhaps, Mary, these gentlemen are right. After all is over, we may see about it, and some may stay and have a good time." (Right, Supreme Court of Illinois; below, ALPLM.)

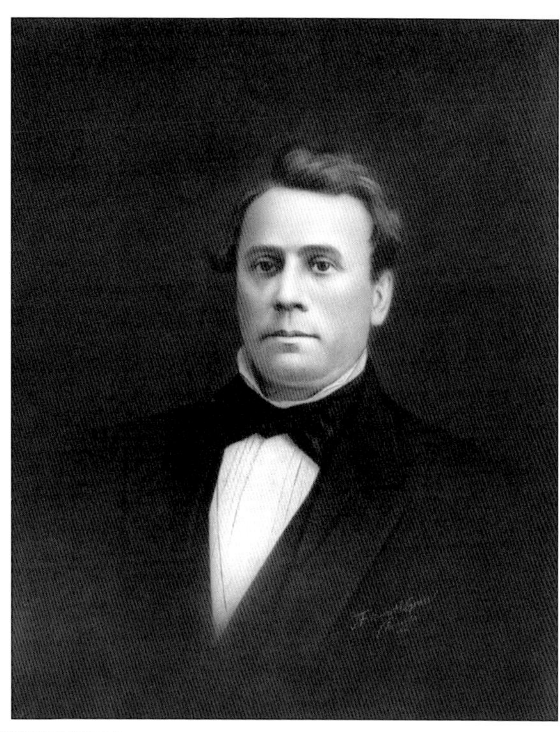

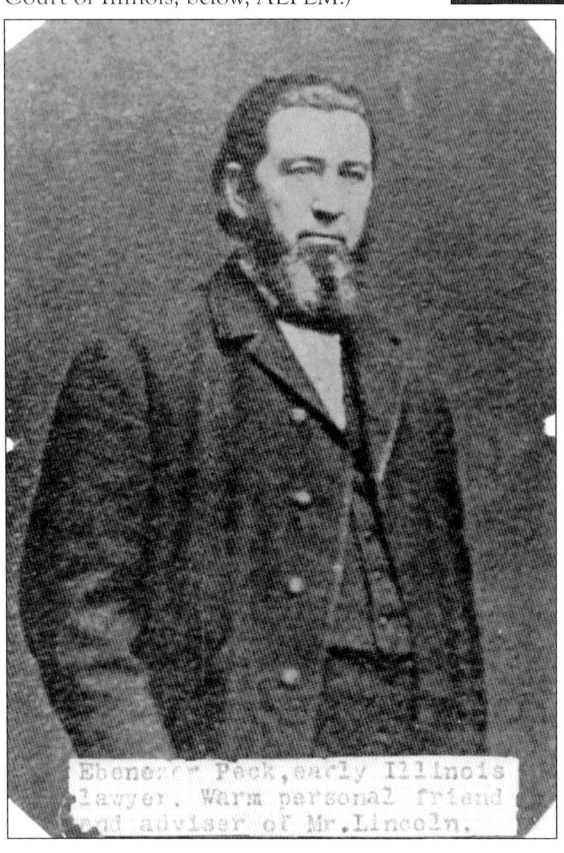

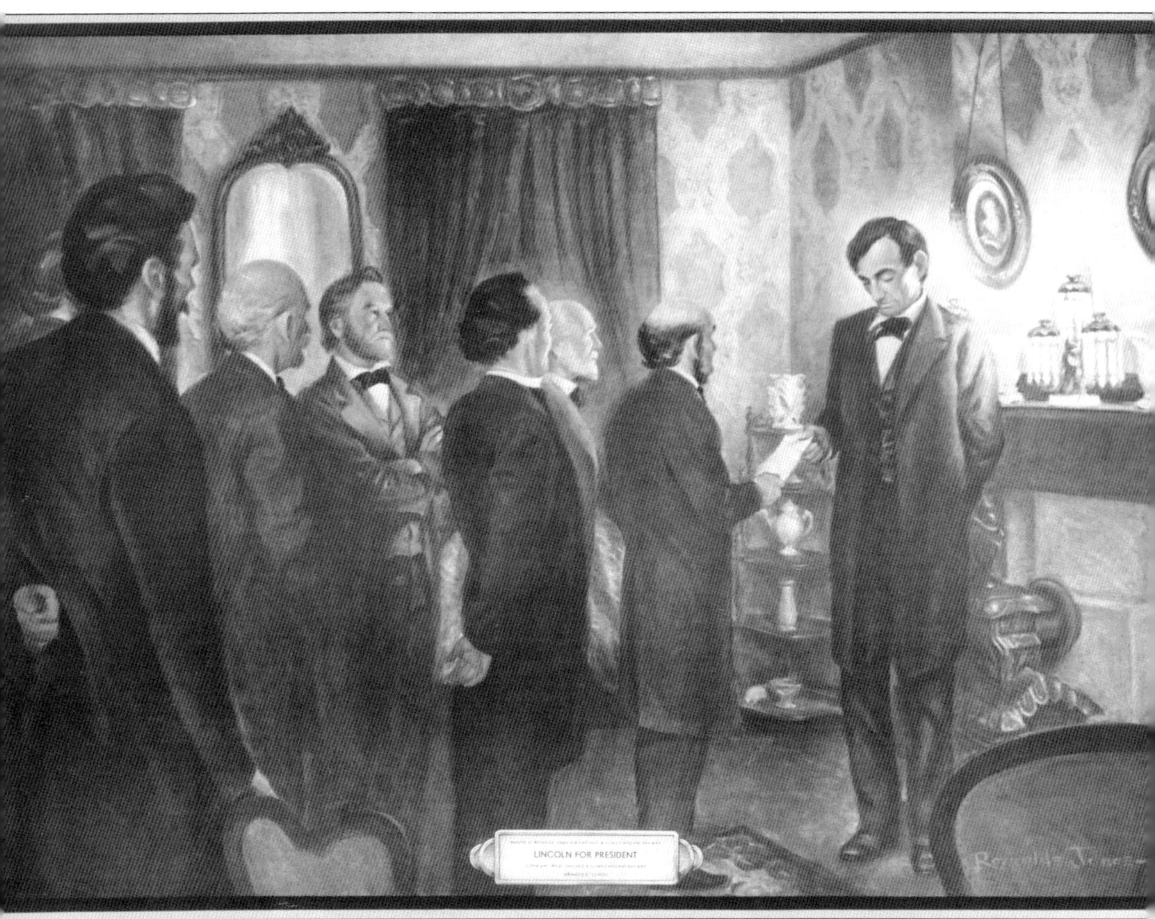

As the committee approached the Lincoln home about 6:00 p.m., they encountered Willie and Tad perched on the gateposts. Upon entering the house, they found Lincoln standing at the rear of the double parlor. Lincoln greeted them, according to Koerner, "standing on the threshold of the back parlor and leaning somewhat on an arm-chair." While Carl Schurz later recalled many years later that Lincoln appeared "tall and ungainly in his black suit of apparently new but ill-fitting clothes, his long tawny neck emerging gauntly from his turn-down collar, his melancholy eyes sunken deep in his haggard face," a journalist writing at the time stated that Lincoln "was dressed with perfect neatness" and "stood erect, displaying to excellent advantage his tall and manly figure." Schurz recalled, "Most of the members of the committee . . . gazed at him with surprised curiosity. He certainly did not present the appearance of a statesman as people usually picture it in their imagination." Later, Congressman William D. Kelley told his colleagues, "Well, we might have done a more brilliant thing, but we could hardly have done a better thing." (LFFC.)

George Ashmun, a former congressman from Massachusetts and the head of the committee, made a few remarks, to which Lincoln replied by offering "my profoundest thanks for the high honor done me, which you now formally announce." After a few other words about the "great responsibility which is inseparable from this high honor," he concluded, "And now, I will not longer defer the pleasure of taking you, and each of you, by the hand." (WMSH Archives.)

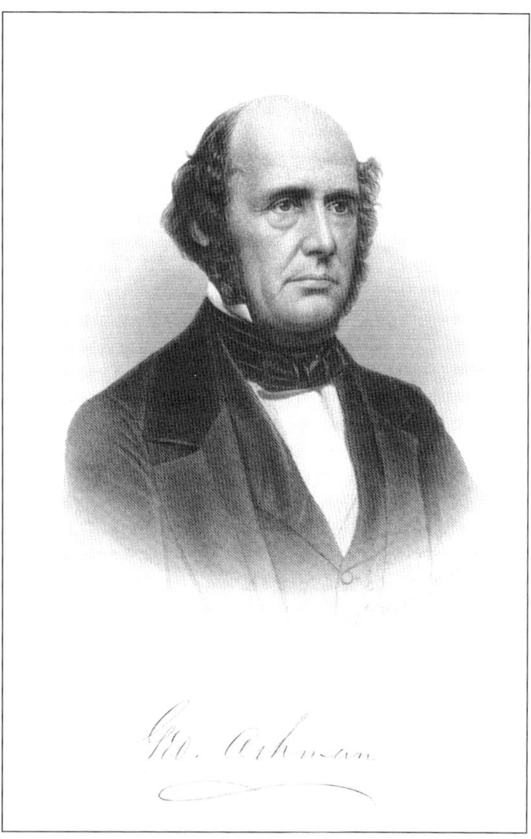

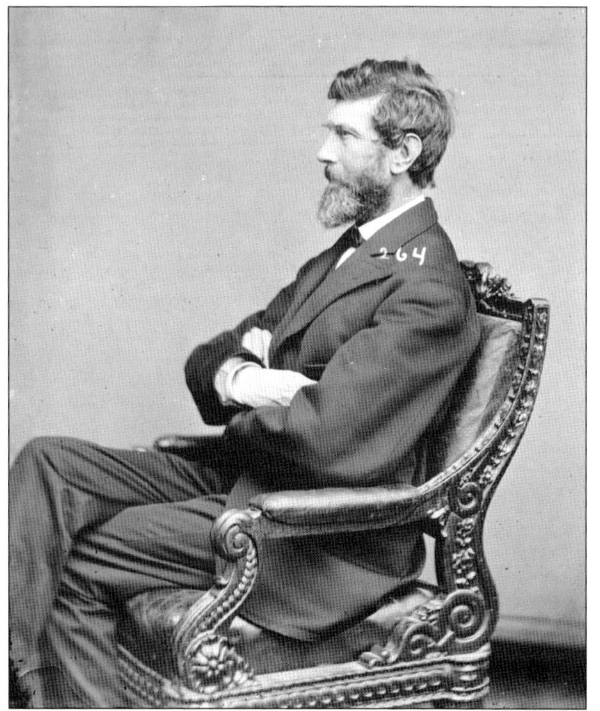

William D. Kelley of Pennsylvania noticed that Lincoln smiled and "his eyes lit up" as he addressed the delegation. Standing one inch shorter than the six-foot-four Lincoln, Kelly remarked, "Pennsylvania bows to Illinois. My dear man, for years my heart has been aching for a President that I could look up to, and I've found him at last in the land where we thought there was none but little giants." (LOC.)

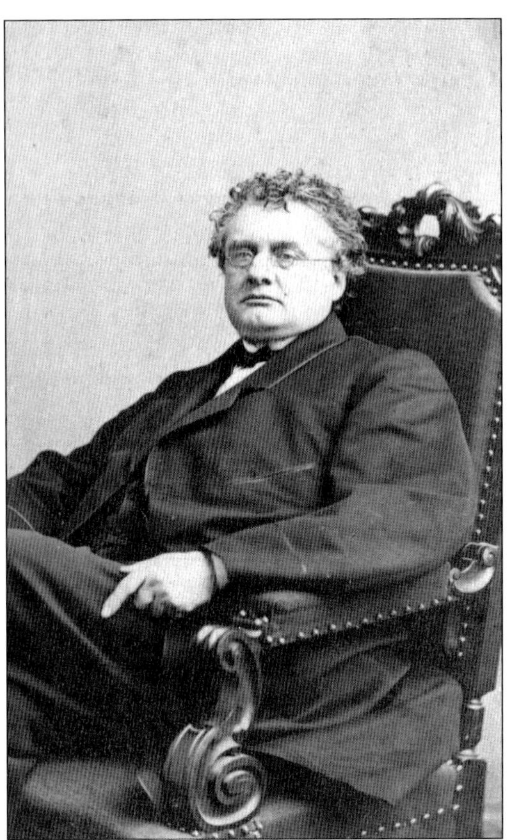

John A. Andrew of Massachusetts also took note of Lincoln's height, joking to a Boston audience that "it was no difficult matter to catch a sight of that honest and intellectual face, for he stood like Saul among his brethren, head and shoulders above every man." Andrew said that he could see Lincoln's honesty and intellect in his face and eyes. "He has a countenance which bespeaks the benignity and beauty of a noble soul." (LFFC.)

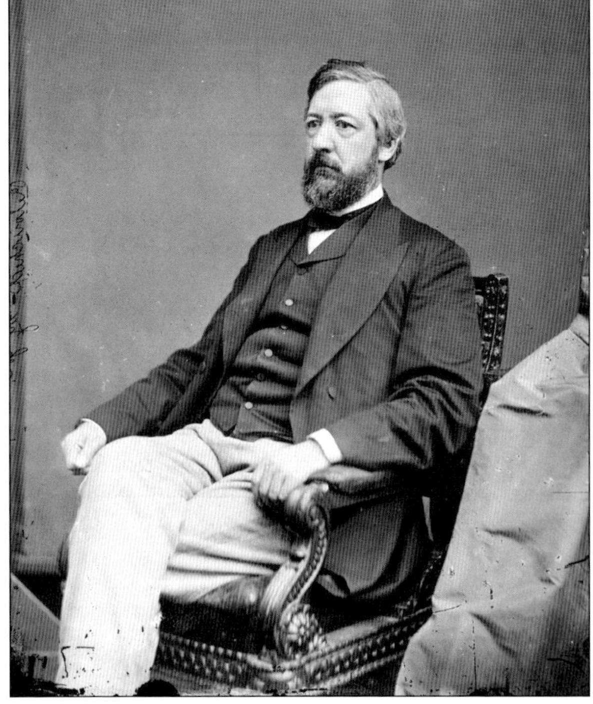

James G. Blaine, a rising politician from Maine, reported that Lincoln was "a very awkward looking man," though "you realize at once that it is the awkwardness of genius rather than any proof of the lack of it." Blaine added that Lincoln "was a far better looking man" than his pictures would have people believe, and that Mary Lincoln "is a very ladylike and quite good looking person." (LOC.)

George Opdyke, a wealthy New Yorker, took particular notice of Lincoln's home. It was "handsome, but not pretentious," and the parlors were "neatly, but not ostentatiously furnished." Everything about the home "had a look of comfort and independence," wrote Opdyke. "The library I remarked in passing, particularly, and I was pleased to see long rows of books, which told of the scholarly tastes and culture of the family." (LOC.)

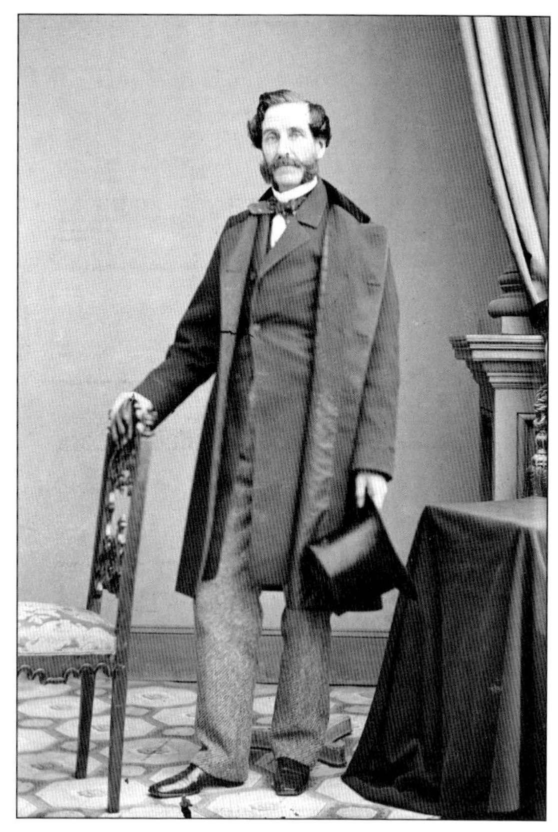

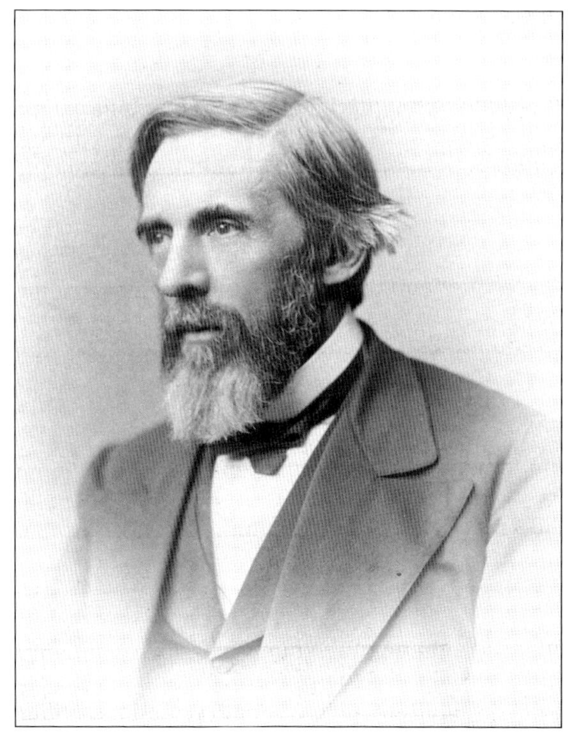

The committee felt relieved after meeting Lincoln. George S. Boutwell of Massachusetts said, "Why, sir, they told me he was a rough diamond. Nothing could have been in better taste than that speech." Another New Englander added, "I was afraid I should meet a gigantic rail-splitter, with the manners of a flatboatman, and the ugliest face in creation; and he's a complete gentleman." (Groton Historical Society.)

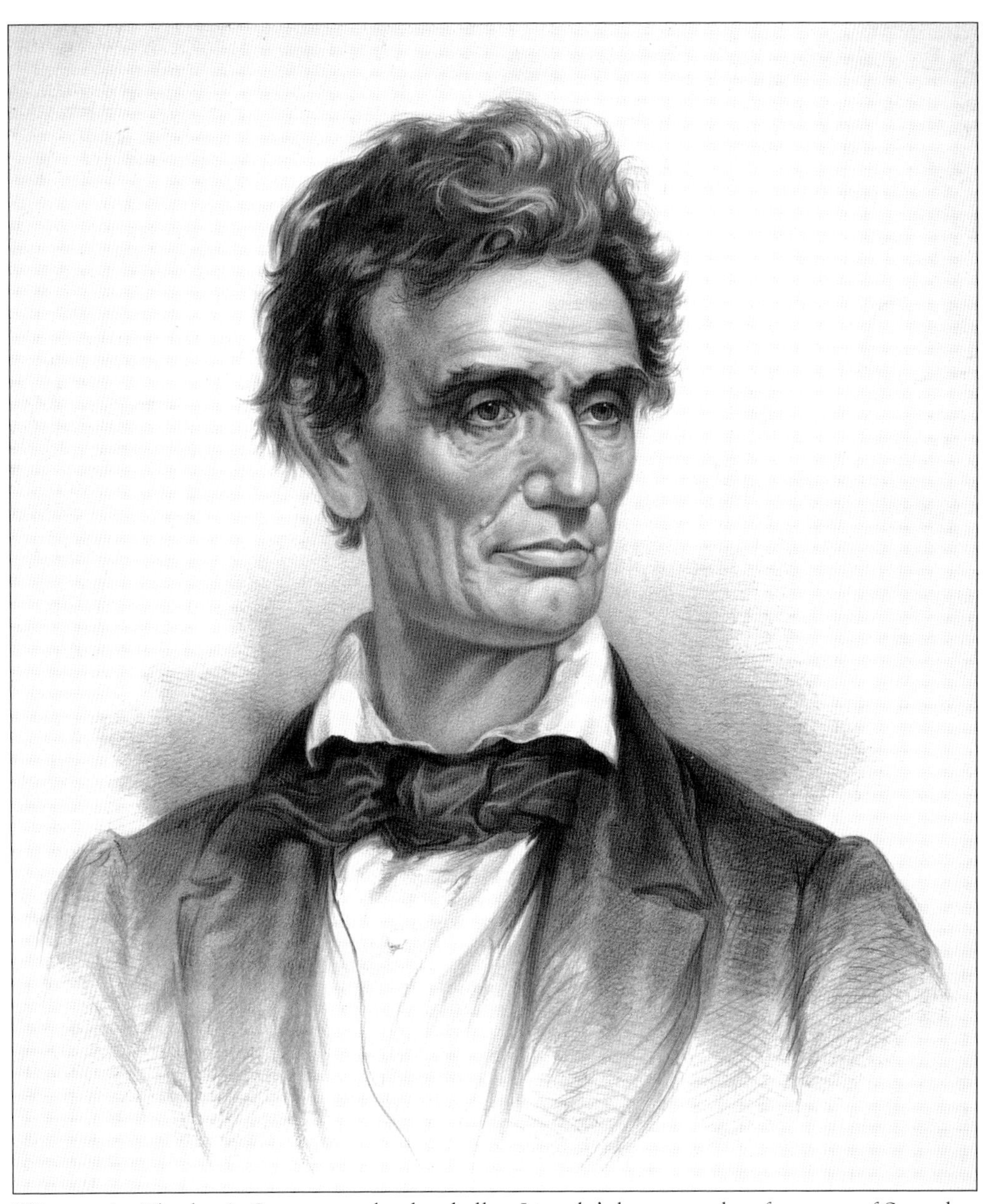

When artist Charles A. Barry rang the doorbell at Lincoln's home on the afternoon of Saturday, June 3, 1860, he was greeted by a small boy who said, "Hello, Mister, what yer want?" Barry replied that he had come all the way from Boston to see Lincoln. Then the small boy shouted, "Come down, Pop; here's a man from Boston." Lincoln came down the stairs, shook Barry's hand, and joked, "They want my head, do they?" Lincoln added, "Well, if you can get it you may have it, that is, if you are able to take it off while I am on the jump; but don't fasten me into a chair. I don't suppose you Boston folks get up at cock-crowing as we do out here. I am an early riser and if you will come to my room at the State House on Monday at seven o'clock sharp, I will be there to let you in." When Barry's portrait was published in Boston, the governor of Illinois, mayors of Chicago and Springfield, and some 60 others attested that "Mr. Barry's portrait of 'Honest Abe' is a correct and striking likeness." (LOC.)

When *New York Times* editor Henry J. Raymond visited Lincoln's home in the summer of 1860, he heard Mary Lincoln shouting out an upstairs window, "Abraham! Abraham! come and put this child to bed!" Newspapers circulated this story widely, joking that Raymond did not know "whether Mrs. L. meant herself or the baby by the expression 'this child.' " (LOC.)

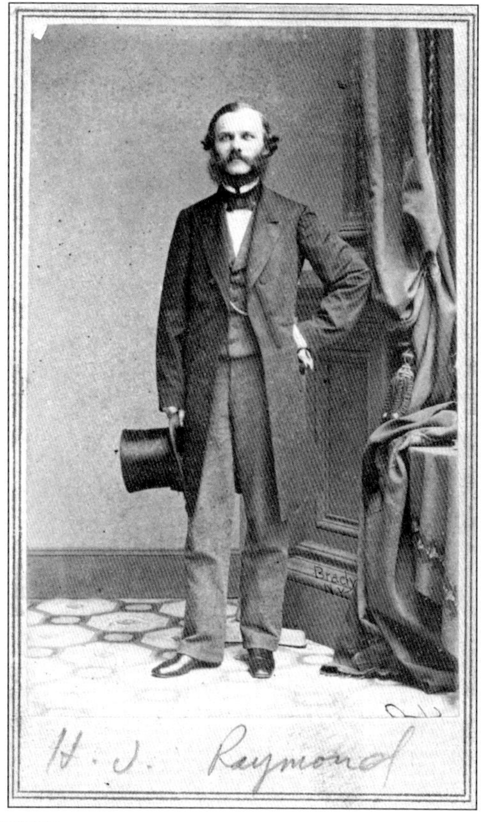

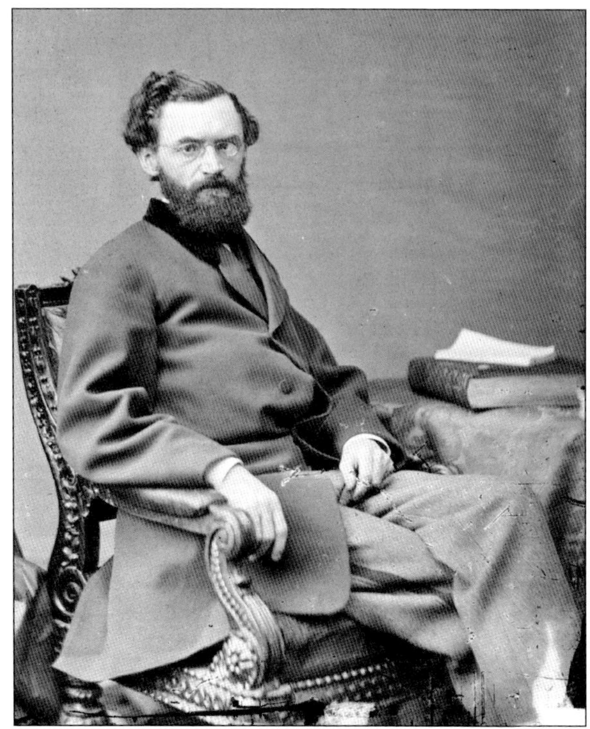

On July 24, German immigrant Carl Schurz returned to Springfield to speak at a Republican rally. Lincoln invited Schurz to dinner at his home, and they conversed about the campaign. "He was in the best of humor, and we laughed much," Schurz later recalled. After dinner, a brass band began playing in front of the house, and several Wide Awake clubs escorted Lincoln and Schurz to the state house, where Schurz delivered a rousing campaign speech. (LOC.)

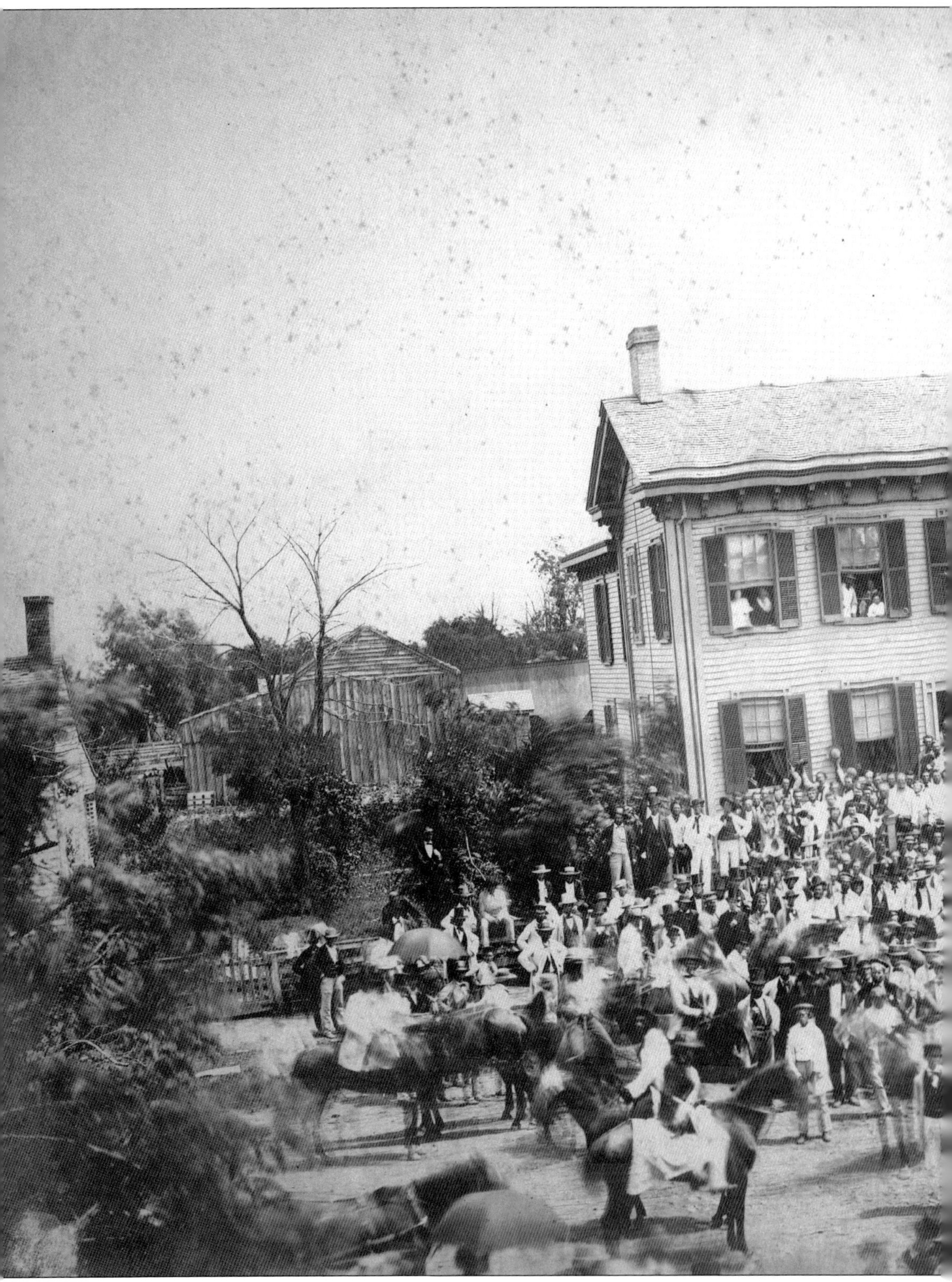

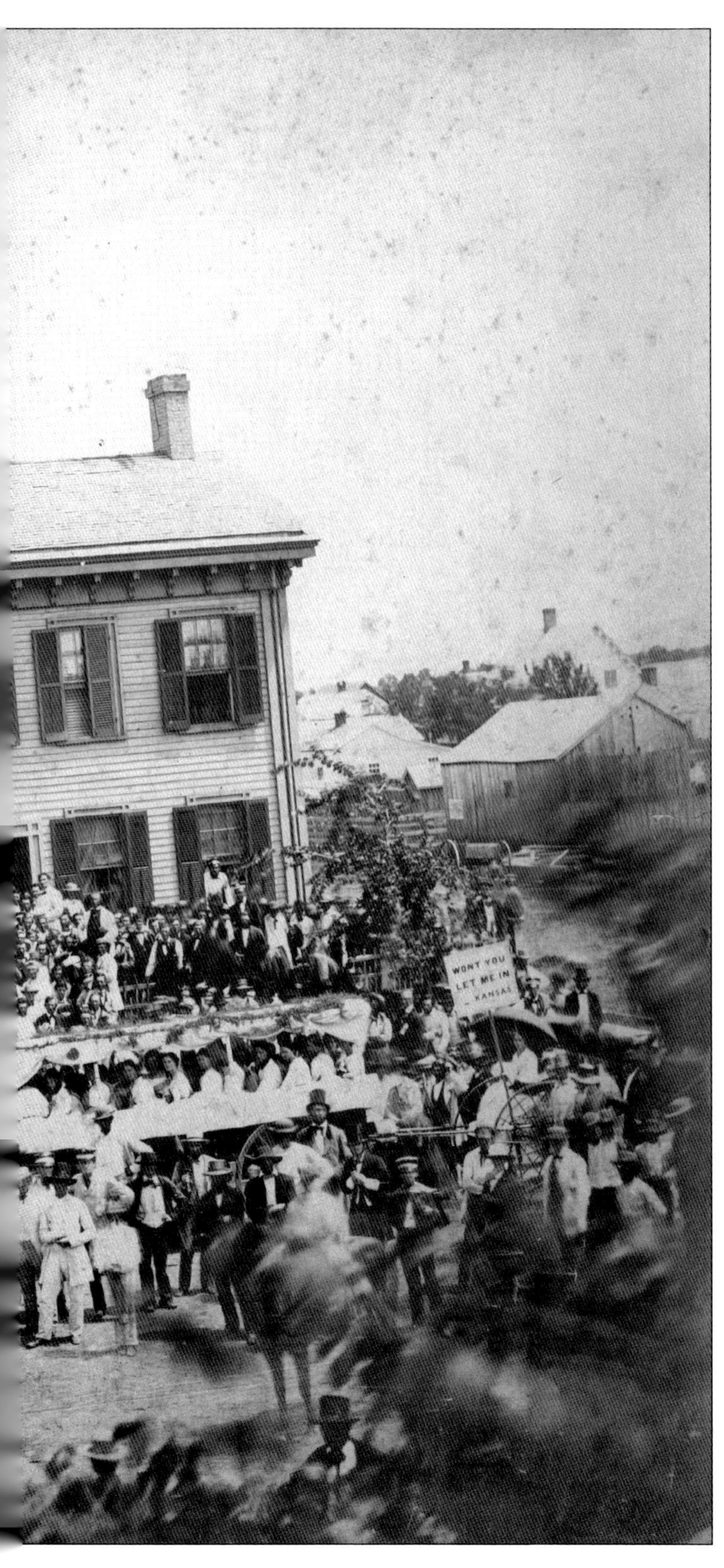

An estimated 80,000 people converged on Springfield for the Republican rally on August 8. A 12-mile-long parade went past Lincoln's home, and Lincoln stood in his yard in a white suit watching. In this image, a float carrying 33 women dressed in white passes his home. "Those waiting to shake hands with Mr. Lincoln stood in a line blocks long to wait their turn," remembered one woman who had witnessed the scene. One man told Lincoln, "I came all the way from Chicago to shake hands with the next president and I'm not going away without doing so." Lincoln gave the man his hand and said, "God bless you." That evening, a torchlight procession illuminated the streets. When it was all over, many revelers slept on curbsides and front yards since the hotels were all full. Chicago photographer William Shaw captured the scene as the parade went by. Afterward, Shaw developed this photograph in Lincoln's cellar, while Lincoln carefully observed the process. (HL.)

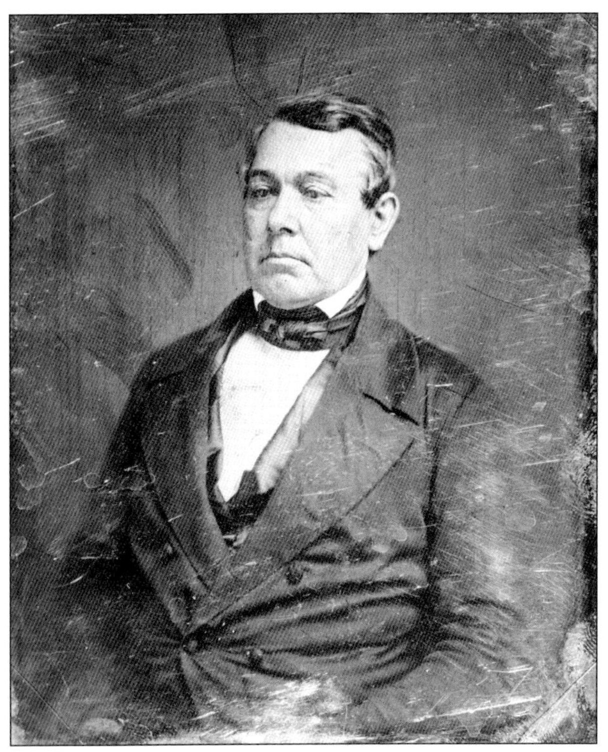

On Sunday, October 14, Abraham and Mary hosted a dinner party for several guests, including Congressman Thomas Corwin (left) of Ohio and Sen. Lyman Trumbull (below) of Illinois. Later in the evening, David Davis and Ozias M. Hatch also dropped in. Davis observed that "Mr. Lincoln looked as if he had a heavy responsibility resting on him. The cares & responsibilities of office will wear on him." Mary, by contrast, "seemed in high feather," although she was "not to my liking." Davis added, "I dont think she would ever mesmerise any one. I am in hopes that she will not give her husband any trouble." One reporter noted during the election that Lincoln "loves a good dinner, and eats with the appetite which goes with a great brain; but his food is plain and nutritious." (Both, LOC.)

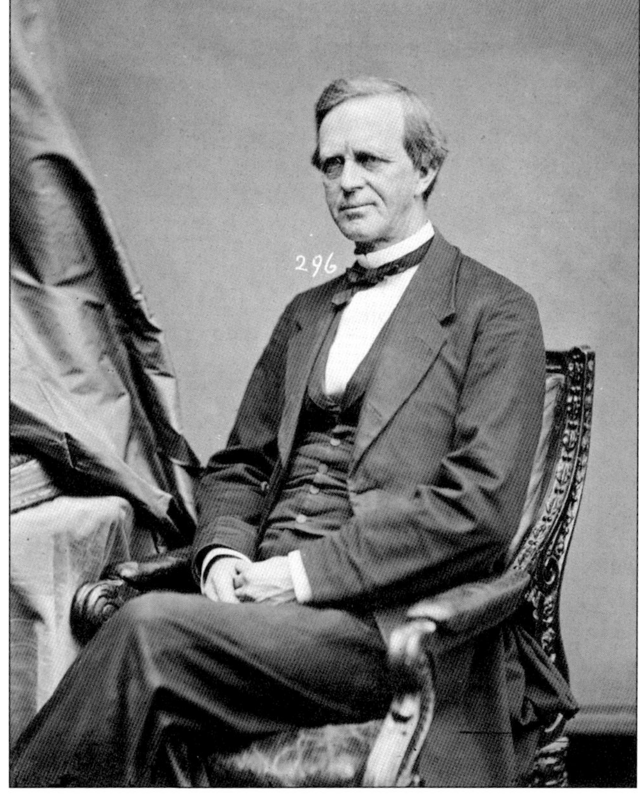

Five

Springfield White House
The Residence of the President-Elect

On November 6, 1860, Lincoln woke up early and walked to the polls to vote. Following the custom of the day, he cut his own name from his ballot so that he would not have the indignity of voting for himself. When asked by a bystander how he planned to vote, he joked, "by ballot." That night, Lincoln's private secretary, John G. Nicolay, tried to go to bed at 4:30 a.m. but "couldn't sleep for the shouting and firing guns."

People continued to flood into Springfield to meet with the president-elect. On November 20, journalist Henry Villard observed, "Although 'Old Abe' had been nearly tortured to death during the daytime, the people gave him no rest after dark, even at his private residence. At half-past six he was once more crowded upon in his parlor, and had to undergo another agony of presentations. The whole lower story of the building was filled all the evening with well dressed ladies and gentlemen, whose comfort was, however, greatly diminished by the constant influx of an ill-mannered populace." Often, Mary Lincoln would hear callers ask each other, "Is that the old woman?" Willie and Tad, however, "seemed to enjoy the fuss hugely." Whenever they heard cheering outside, they "always responded to [it] by their juvenile yells."

Some guests did not know when they had outstayed their welcome. On New Year's Day, when one visitor gave "evidence of staying indefinitely," Lincoln had to ask a group of young men to take him home.

On February 6, 1861, the Lincolns hosted a farewell reception at their home. The party lasted from 7:00 p.m. until midnight, and the house, according to a woman from Missouri, was "a grand outpouring of citizens and strangers" and was "thronged by thousands up to a late hour." According to a local girl, "At nine o'clock the street was lined with visitors and many could not get in at all." Henry Villard noted that it was "a success in every respect, with the exception of a slight jam created by the limited dimensions of the building. Every room both on the first and second floor was densely packed with a fashionable multitude."

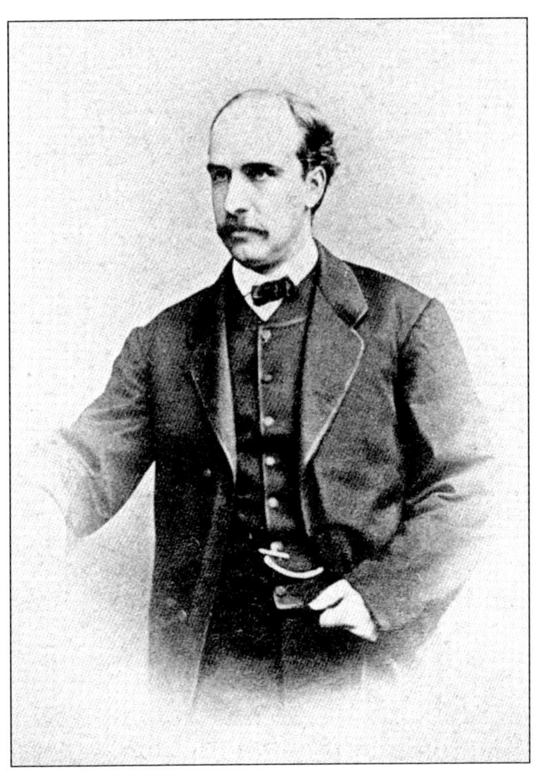

German-born journalist Henry Villard traveled to Springfield from November 1860 until February 1861 to cover the president-elect. During this time, he grew to admire Lincoln, although he noticed by mid-December that Lincoln's appearance "has somewhat changed to the worse . . . he looks more pale and careworn than heretofore." Still, Villard noted, "the vigor of his mind and the steadiness of his humorous disposition are obviously unimpaired." (University of Chicago.)

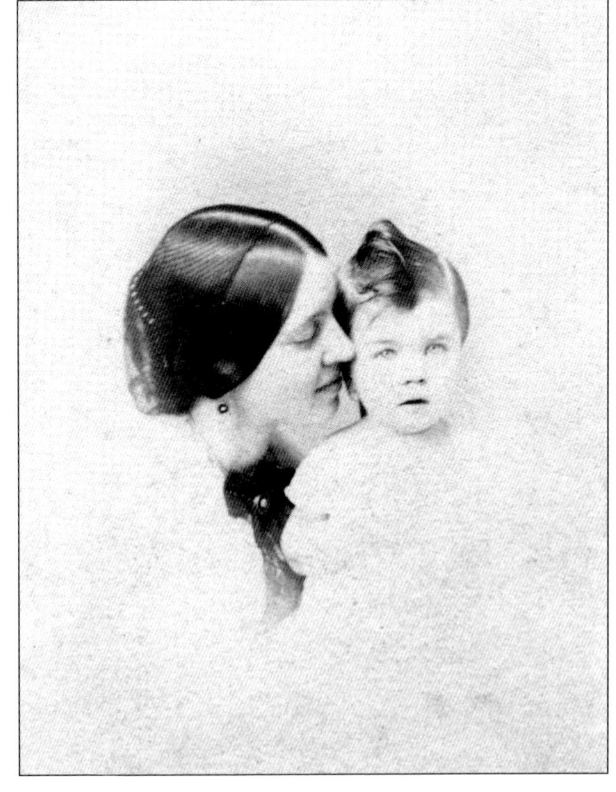

In mid-November, Ada Bailhache (pictured here with her son Arthur around 1863), daughter of Springfield editor Mason Brayman, spent a "very pleasant" evening at the Lincolns' home. She wrote her mother on November 20, "Mrs. L. is just as agreeable as ever," and "Mr. L. has not altered one bit he amused us nearly all the evening telling funny stories and cracking jokes. I could hardly realize that I was sitting in the august presence of a real live President." (HRFA.)

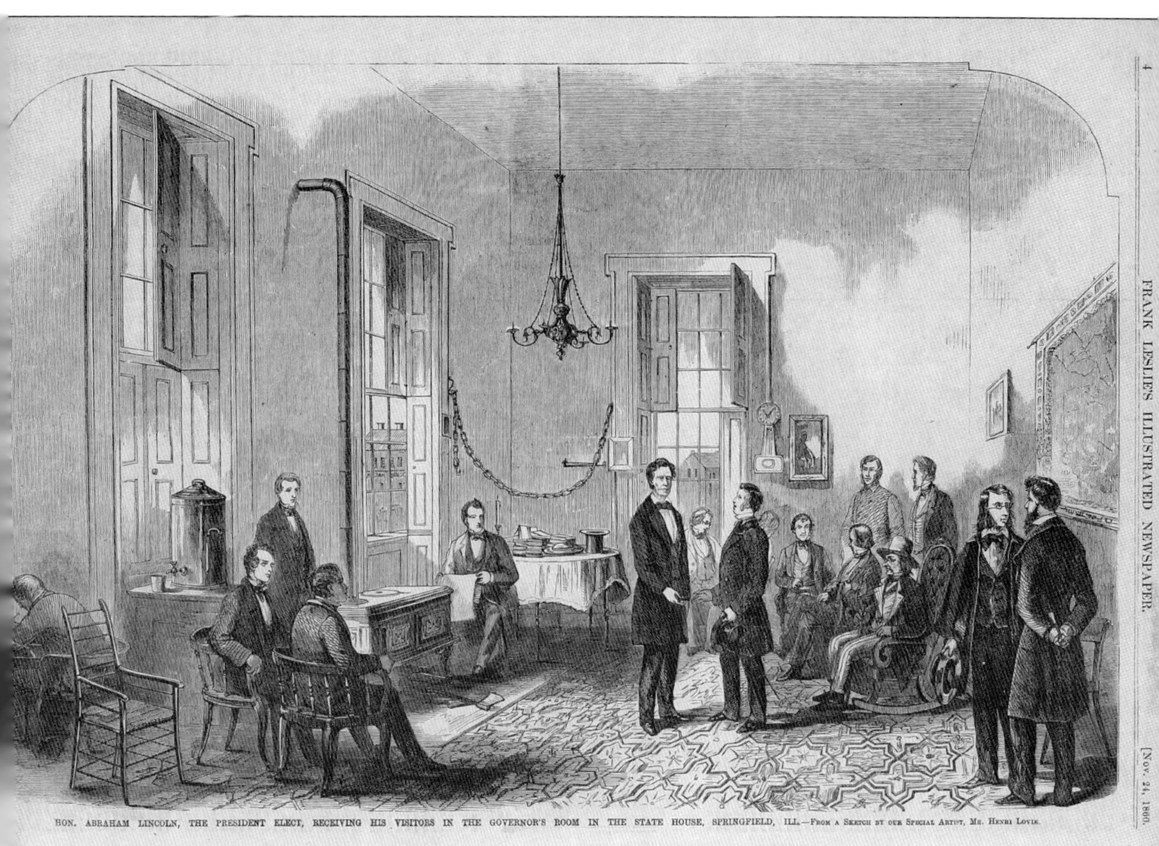

The day after he won the election, Lincoln left his home and walked to the state house, according to one journalist, "as though nothing of importance had happened," although on this particular day, he was greeted by cheers as he walked into the city. His days became more hectic than they had ever been before. On a typical morning, he rose early and took his breakfast at 7:00 a.m. (he liked eggs and toast). After spending about half an hour with his family, he walked to the state house, where he had been setting up shop in the governor's room (pictured here) since he won the Republican nomination in May. He worked from 8:00 to 10:00 a.m., sifting through his mail, and from 10:00 a.m. to 12:00 p.m., he greeted callers. At noon, wrote journalist Henry Villard, Lincoln "retires from the public gaze, and spends his time at home until 3 o'clock, when he returns to the State House, to reopen the levees, which are then continued until half-past 5." Lincoln then sought "relief at his private dwelling" until 7:00 p.m., when he returned to work with his private secretary. (LFFC.)

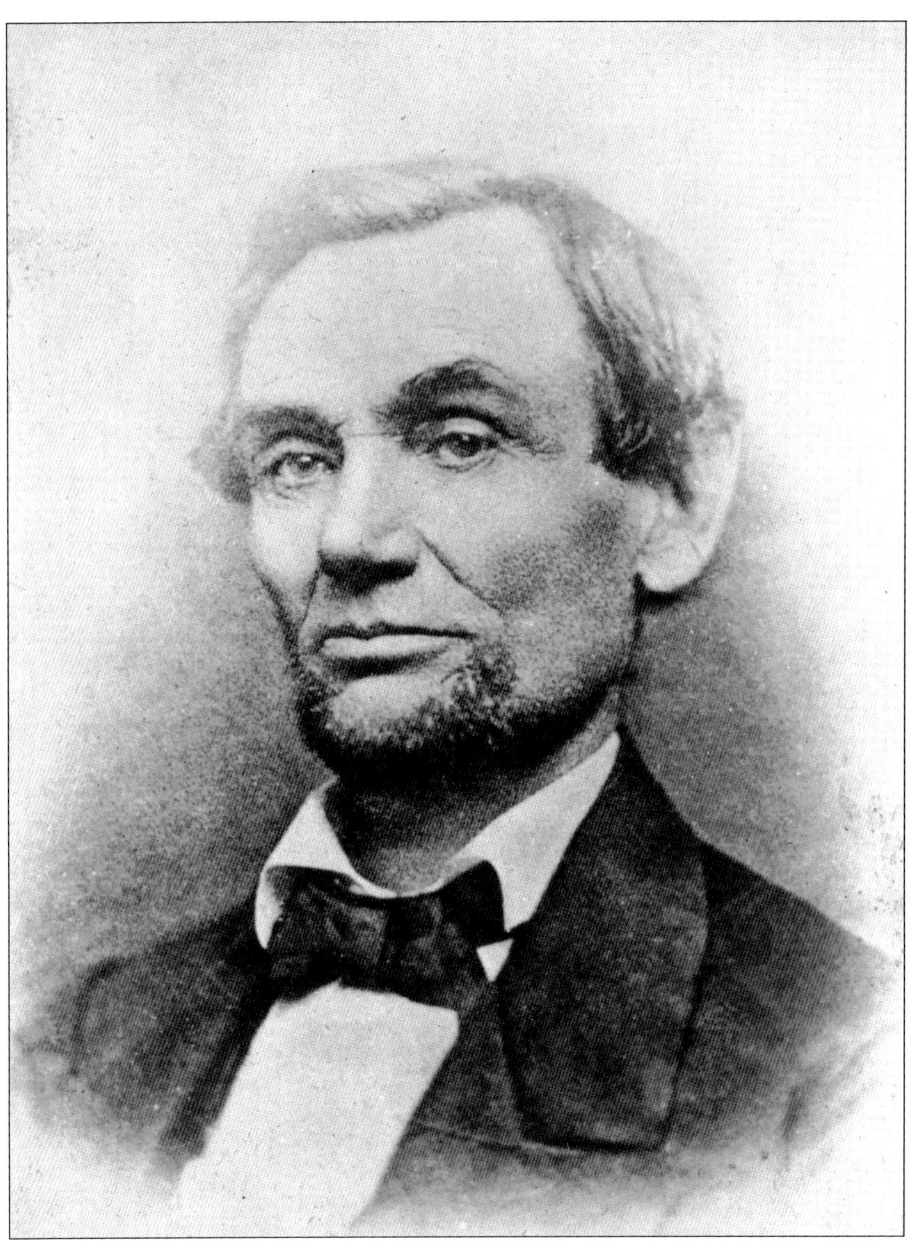

"The pressure of place seekers from both at home and abroad continued unabated," observed Henry Villard. Lincoln was able to easily get rid of the "common herd of solicitants of second class post offices, consulships, clerkships, &c.," but the self-important "distinguished men" who came to Springfield to give advice regarding Cabinet appointments could be relentless. If unsuccessful at the state house, "they will call at his private residence," Villard wrote. And if denied in their first attempt, "they never fail to make a second, third, &c., &c., one, until their wishes are . . . gratified by the object of their obtrusiveness." According to Villard, "Abraham knows there is no safety for him from this infliction, either in his office or his house, and hence he has been looking out for other places of retreat, to which the irrepressible impudence of distinguished strangers would not follow him." At times, he hid in the studio of a sculptor or a newspaper office. This portrait was made by Samuel G. Alschuler of Chicago on November 25, 1860. (LOC.)

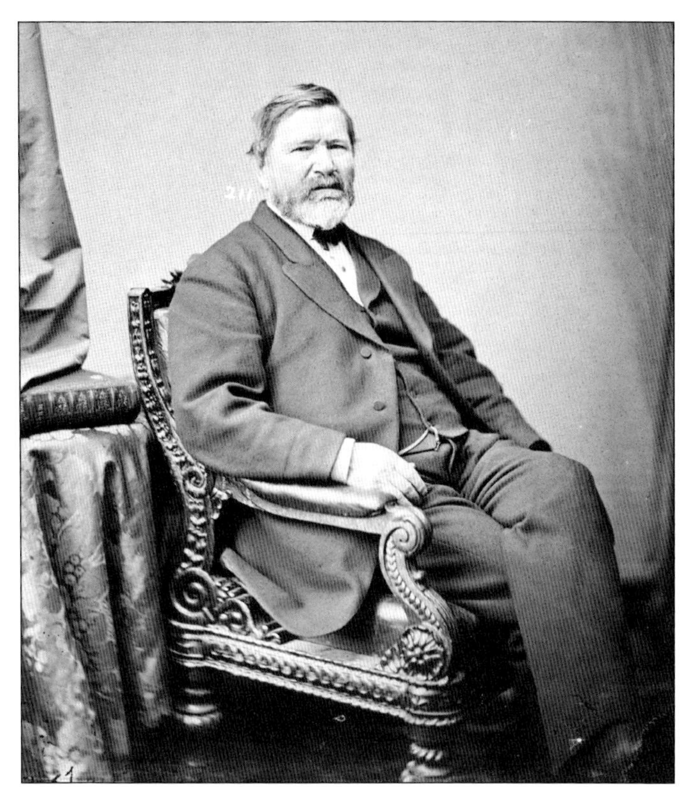

On November 19, the city of Springfield held a jubilee to celebrate Lincoln's election. Upon their arrival from Ohio, Robert C. Schenck (right) and Donn Piatt (below) found the city "drunk with delight." The Lincolns invited the two Ohioans to supper at their home. "It was a plain, comfortable frame structure, and the supper was an old-fashioned mess of indigestion, composed mainly of cake, pies and chickens, the last evidently killed in the morning, to be eaten, as best they might, that evening," recalled Piatt many years later. (Both, LOC.)

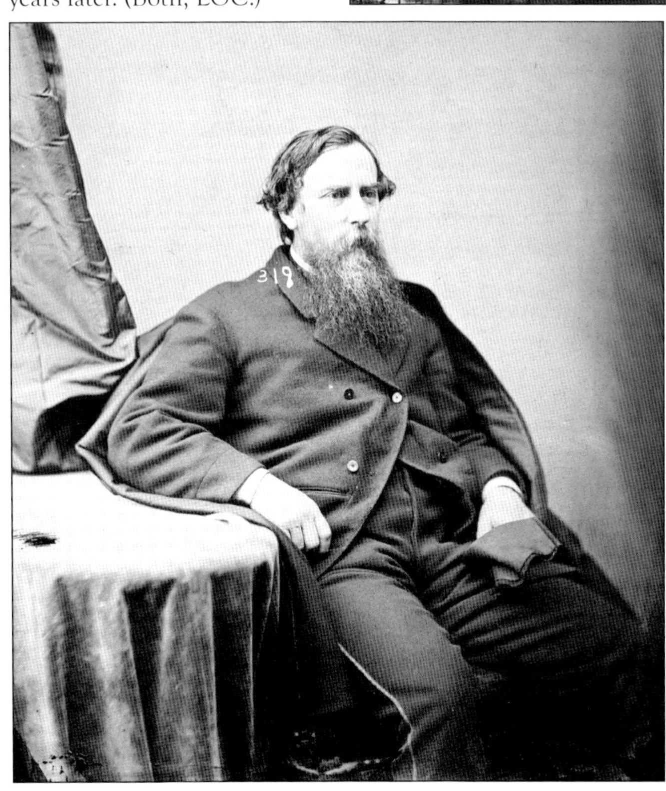

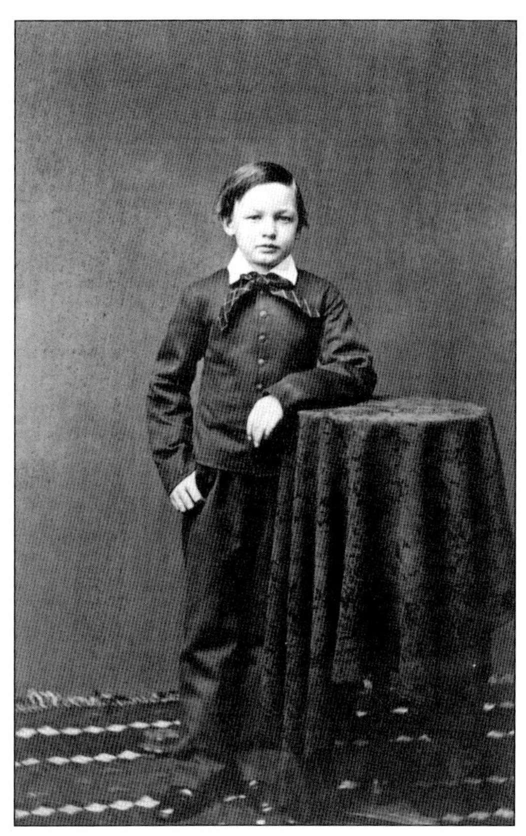

After supper, Donn Piatt remembered, "We sat, far into the night, talking over the situation. Mr. Lincoln was the homeliest man I ever saw. His body seemed to me a huge skeleton in clothes. Tall as he was, his hands and feet looked out of proportion, so long and clumsy were they. Every movement was awkward in the extreme." Lincoln sat with one leg thrown over the other, swinging his top foot like a pendant. While the men were talking, Willie (left) and Tad (below) "clambered over those legs, patted his cheeks, pulled his nose, and poked their fingers in his eyes, without causing reprimand or even notice." (Both, LFA.)

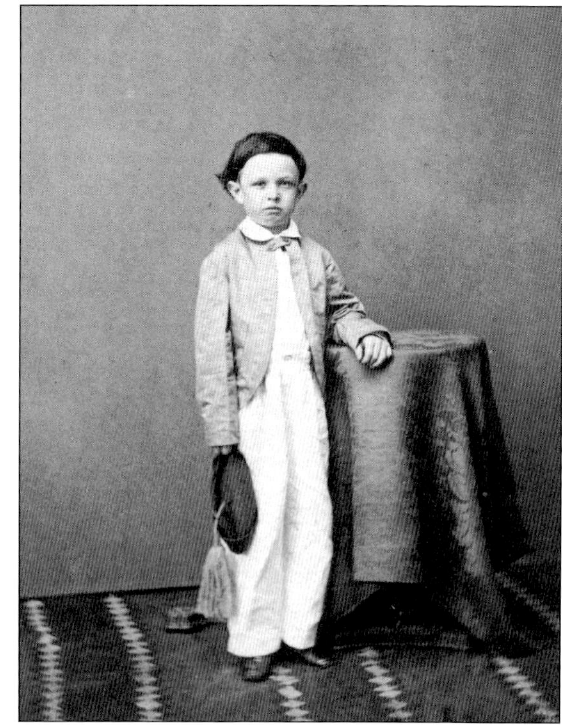

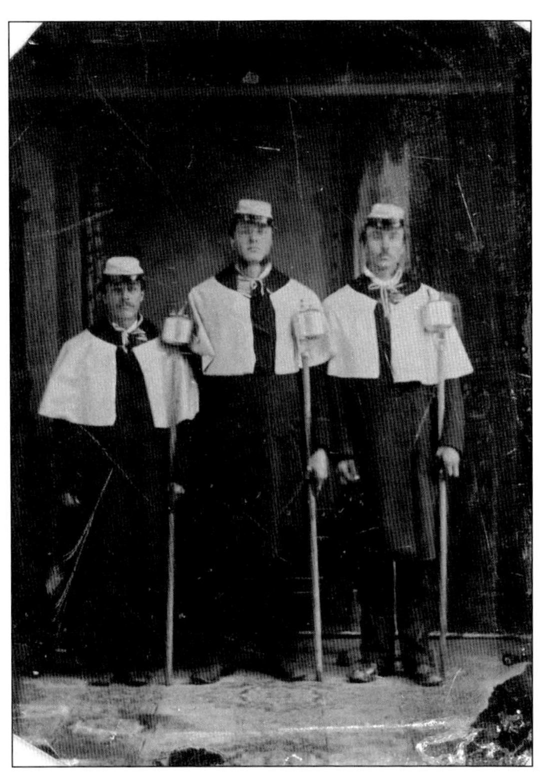

On November 20, a group of Wide Awakes gathered torches blazing outside of Lincoln's home. One enthusiastic member of the crowd called upon "Old Abe to come out and show his honest face." Lincoln stepped outside and thanked them for "the kindness and compliment of this call" and for their votes. "I rejoice with you in the success which has, so far, attended that cause," he continued. "Yet in all our rejoicing let us neither express, nor cherish, any harsh feeling towards any citizen who, by his vote, has differed with us. Let us at all times remember that all American citizens are brothers of a common country, and should dwell together in the bonds of fraternal feeling." (Right, JW; below, LOC.)

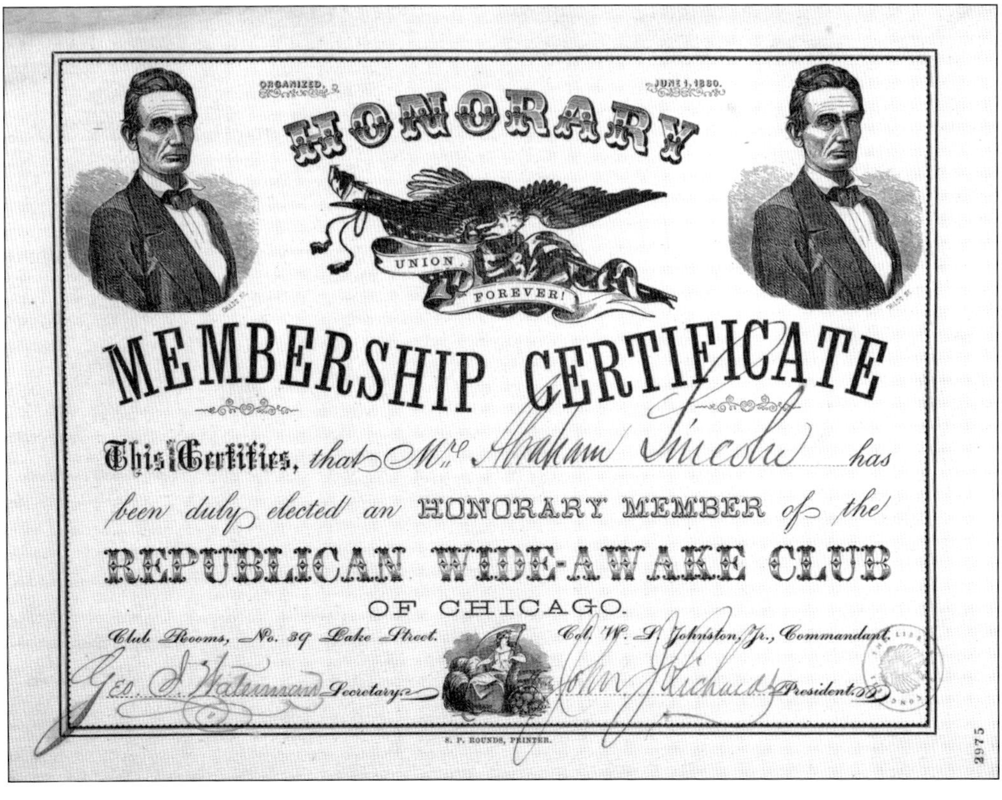

ORGANIZED, JUNE 1, 1860.

HONORARY

UNION FOREVER!

MEMBERSHIP CERTIFICATE

This Certifies, that Mr. Abraham Lincoln has been duly elected an HONORARY MEMBER of the

REPUBLICAN WIDE-AWAKE CLUB

OF CHICAGO.

Club Rooms, No. 39 Lake Street. Col. W. L. Johnston, Jr., Commandant.

Geo. S. Waterman Secretary. John J. Richards President.

S. P. ROUNDS, PRINTER.

2975

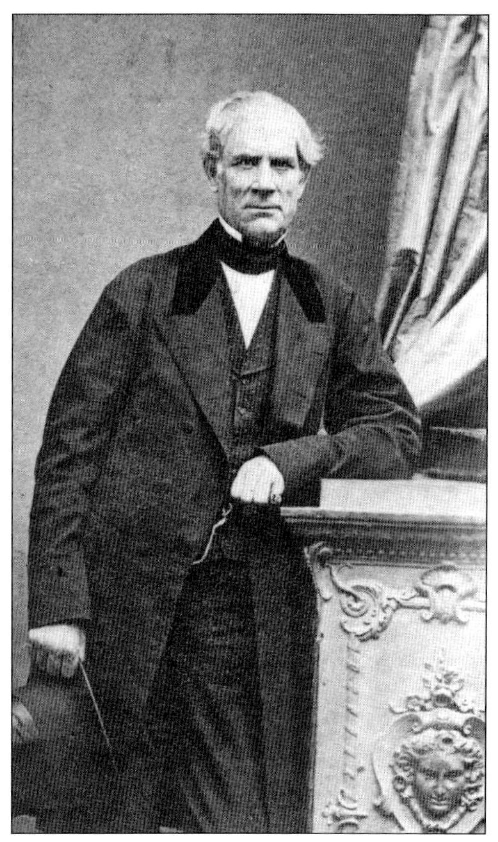

On Thursday, December 20, Thurlow Weed (left), the editor of the *Albany Evening Journal* and a close ally of William H. Seward's, called on Lincoln at his home to propose compromises with the South. According to Henry Villard, "He flashed up like a meteor, moved some brief hours on this narrow stage, and was heard no more." Weed had come in on an early morning train and, after breakfast, went to Lincoln's home. Their interview lasted from 9:00 a.m. until 3:00 p.m., and at some point during the day, Lincoln's old friends Leonard Swett (below) and David Davis also joined the meeting. Swett later stated that Lincoln and Weed "took to each other." (Left, LFFC; below, GBC.)

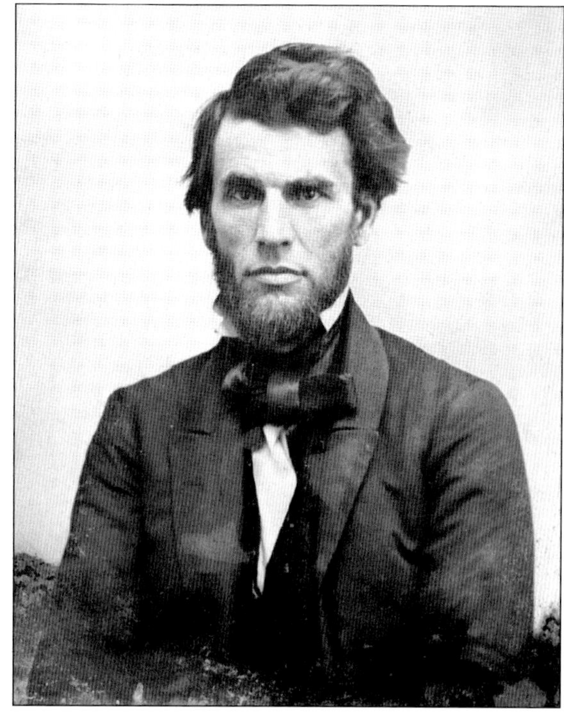

On December 30, Lincoln welcomed Edward Bates (right) of Missouri and Simon Cameron (below) of Pennsylvania to his home, where he received them, in Villard's words, "with his customary artless Western heartiness." Bates went on to serve as Lincoln's attorney general. Cameron, a highly corrupt politician, would serve as secretary of war for Lincoln's first 10 months in office. (Both, LOC.)

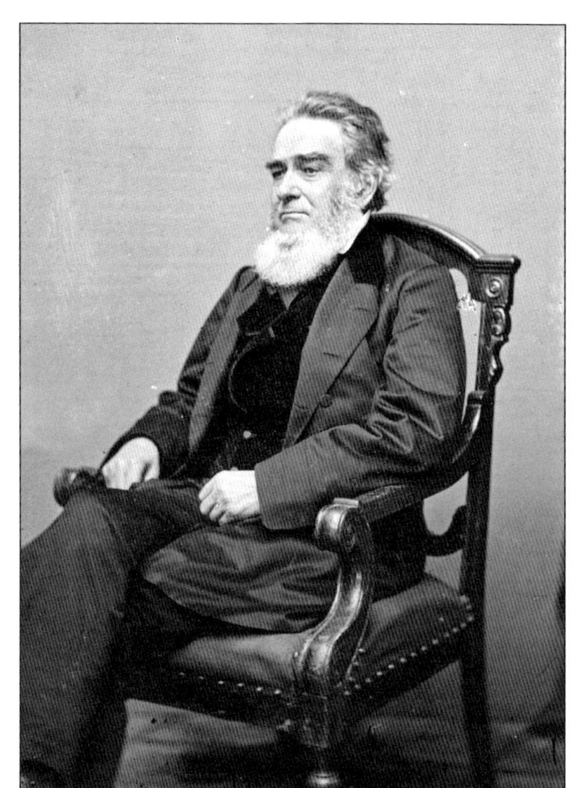

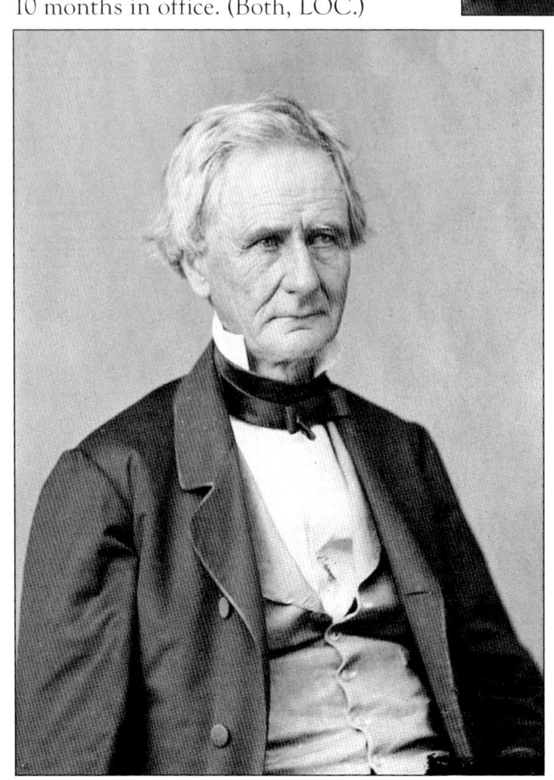

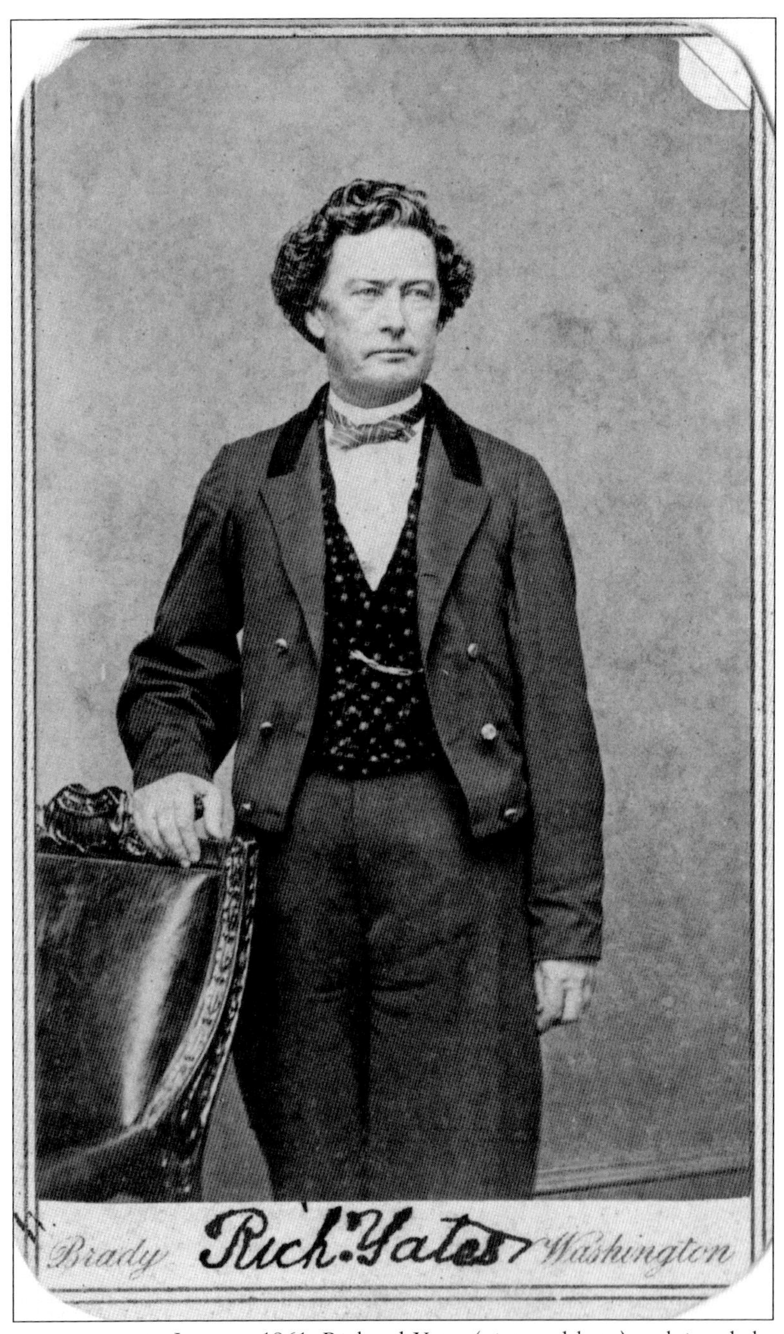

Upon his inauguration in January 1861, Richard Yates (pictured here) reclaimed the governor's room at the state house. For a time, Lincoln and John G. Nicolay worked out of Joel Johnson's hotel, across the street from the Chenery House. He also met more visitors at his home. A New York newspaper correspondent observed that the "Springfield White House" appeared "more modest" than many other houses in the vicinity and that "No one would suspect it of illustrious associations. Yet it is unequivocally at this writing the most notable building and important centre in Springfield, for since Governor Yates took possession of the Executive chamber at the Capitol, Mr. Lincoln is only to be seen at 'his warm but simple home.' " (LFA.)

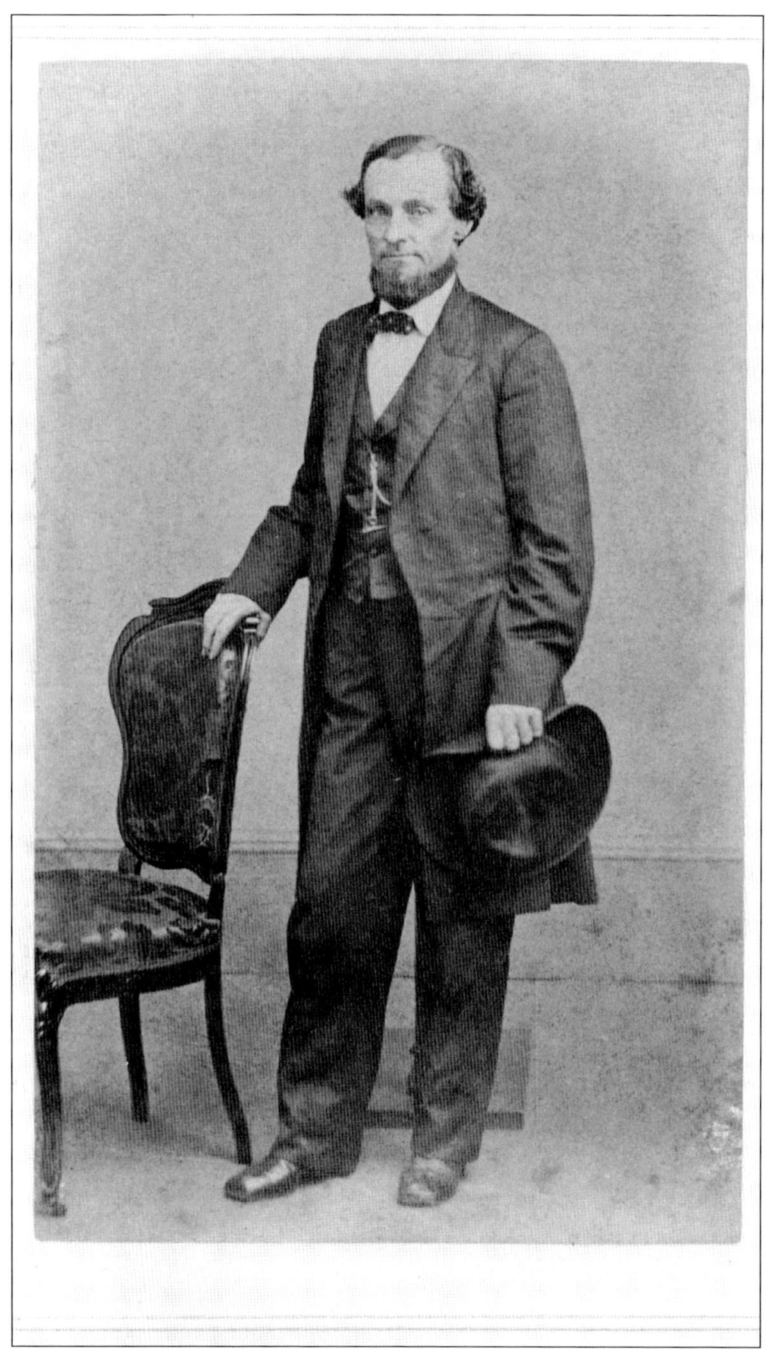

In January, Lincoln began assembling "historical and other researches" to write his inaugural address. According to William H. Herndon, Lincoln had to borrow many of these sources because, "aside from his law-books and the few gilded volumes that ornamented the centre-table in his parlor at home," Lincoln had "comparatively no library." Eventually, the home and the state house became too busy for him to write, so Lincoln holed himself up in a "dingy, dusty, and neglected . . . small counting-room" on the third floor of his brother-in-law Clark M. Smith's (pictured here) grocery store on the south side of the public square. (ALPLM.)

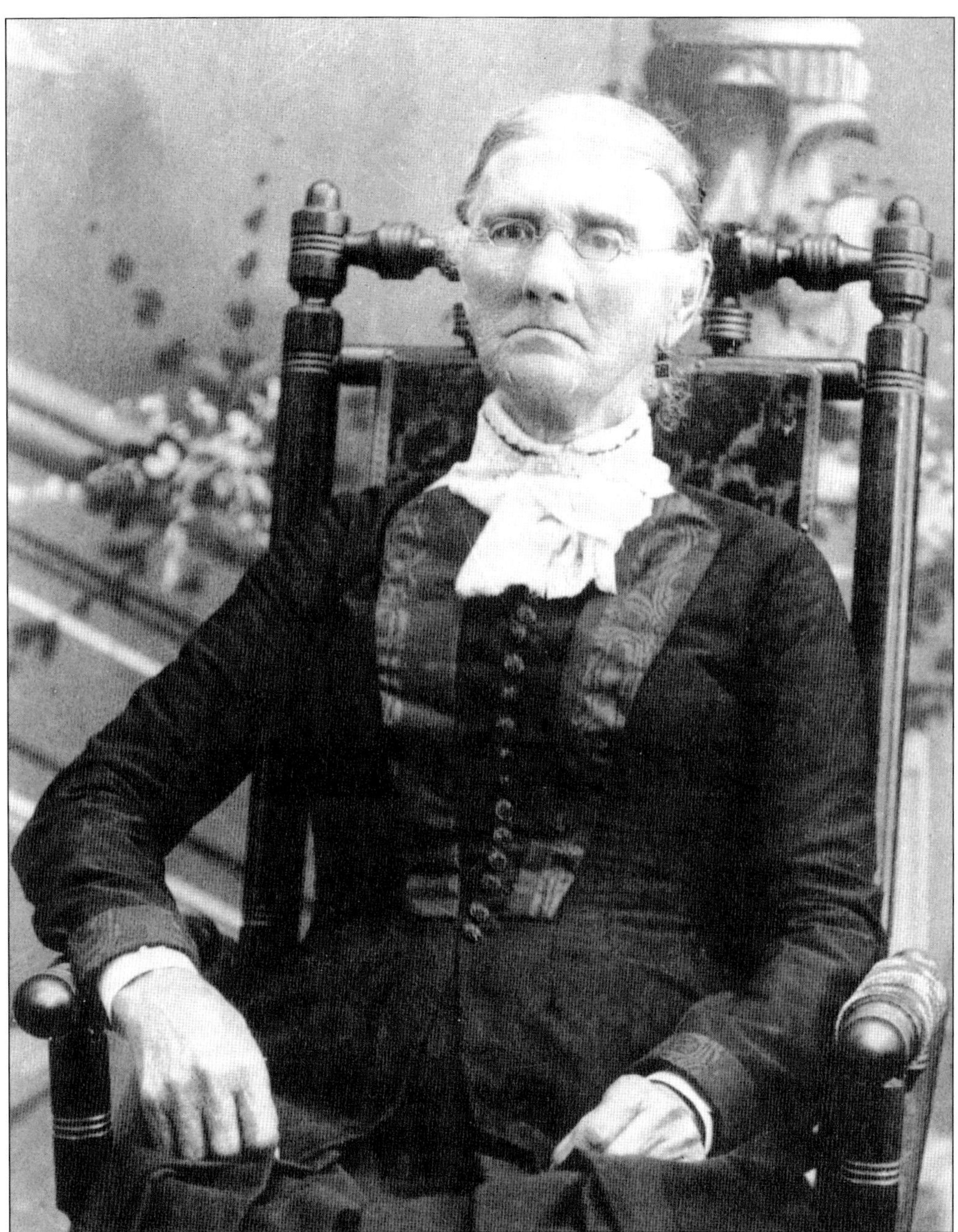

One of the last people to visit Lincoln before he departed for Washington was his old friend Hannah Armstrong. Lincoln had wrestled Hannah's husband, Jack, back in New Salem days and had served as a lawyer for her son Duff when he was accused of murder. Hannah recalled, "the boys got up a story on me that I went to get to sleep with Abe," but "I replied to the Joke that it was not every woman who had the good fortune & high honor of sleeping with a President." She said, "This stopt the sport—cut it short." In Springfield, Armstrong talked to Lincoln for some time. As she was about to bid him goodbye, she had a feeling "that I should never see him again—that they would kill him." Lincoln smiled at her and jokingly said, "If they Kill me I shall never die an other death." They then said goodbye, never to see each other again. (ALPLM.)

On January 29, 1861, Lincoln advertised his household goods for private sale "without reserve" in the *Sangamo Journal*. About this time, neighbor Jared P. Irwin saw Lincoln cleaning out his desk and burning letters. Irwin asked if he could keep some of the letters as souvenirs, and Lincoln consented. Irwin collected about 60 pieces of private correspondence, such as this 1848 letter from Lincoln to Mary when he was in Congress. (ALPLM.)

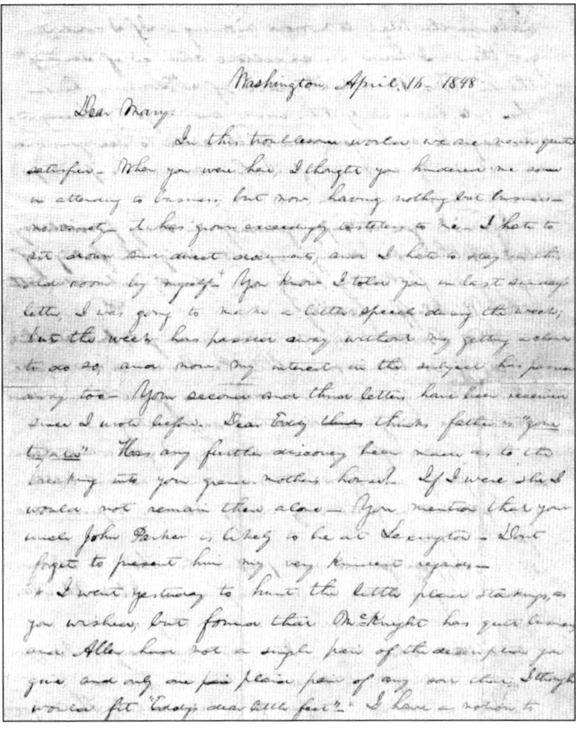

Washington, April 16 - 1848

Dear Mary:

In this troublesome world, we are never quite satisfied. When you were here, I thought you hindered me some in attending to business; but now, having nothing but business—no variety—it has grown exceedingly tasteless to me. I hate to sit down and direct documents, and I hate to stay in this old room by myself. You know I told you in last sunday's letter, I was going to make a little speech during the week; but the week has passed away without my getting a chance to do so; and now my interest in the subject has passed away too. Your second and third letters have been received since I wrote before. Dear Eddy thinks father is "gone tapila." Has any further discovery been made as to the breaking into your grand-mother's house? If I were she, I would not remain there alone. You mention that your uncle John Parker is likely to be at Lexington. Don't forget to present him my very kindest regards.

I went yesterday to hunt the little plaid stockings, as you wished; but found that McKnight has quit business, and Allen had not a single pair of the description you give, and only one plain pair of any sort that I thought would fit "Eddy's dear little feet." I have a notion to

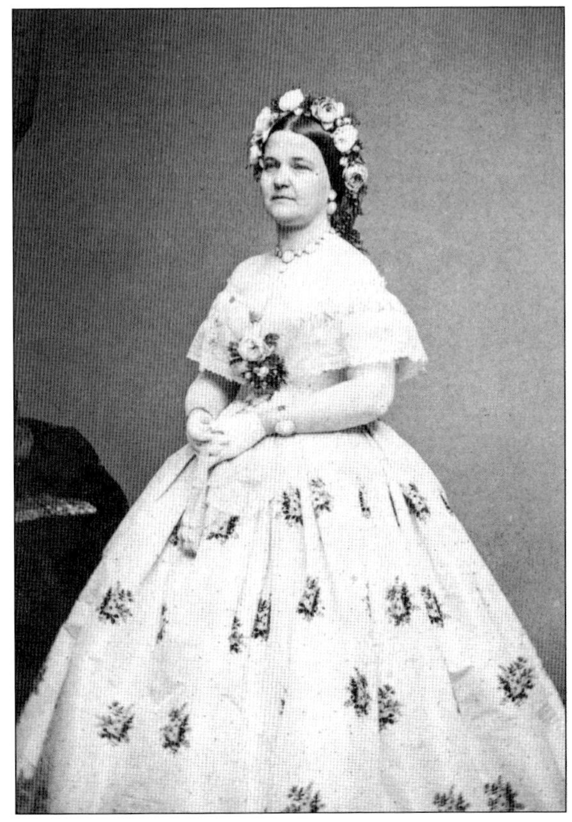

Henry Villard noted that the farewell reception on February 6 was "the most brilliant affair of the kind witnessed here in many years." The president-elect received the guests as they entered the parlor and were introduced to him. They then passed on to Mary Lincoln, "who stood near the center of the parlors, and who . . . acquitted herself most gracefully and admirably." (LOC.)

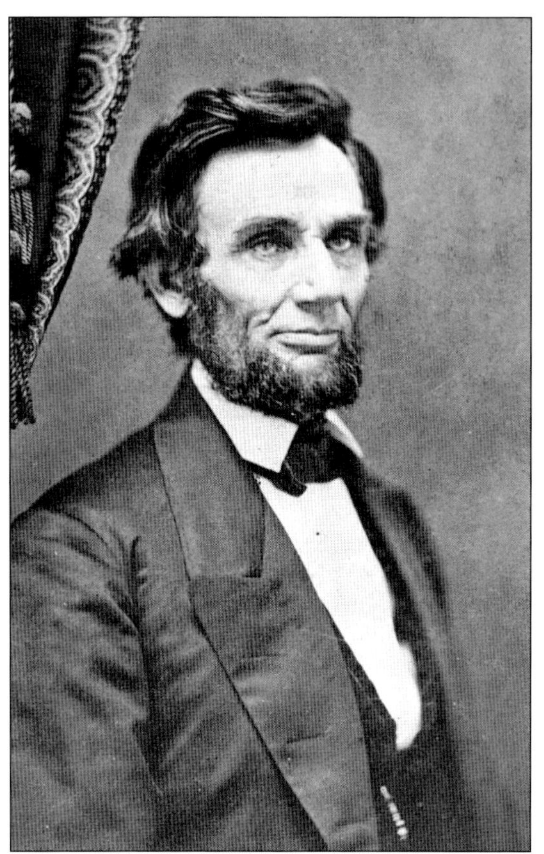

During the reception, Willie and Tad played on the sofa in the parlor behind their father. According to a journalist, Tad "was as noisy as a cub wolf," and it took "a considerable time" for Lincoln to notice him and stoop down to pick him up. Lincoln "had some of the pleasantest words for the little fellow, that can be imagined." After that, Tad was quiet. This was Lincoln's last portrait in Springfield, made by Christopher S. German on February 9, 1861. (LOC.)

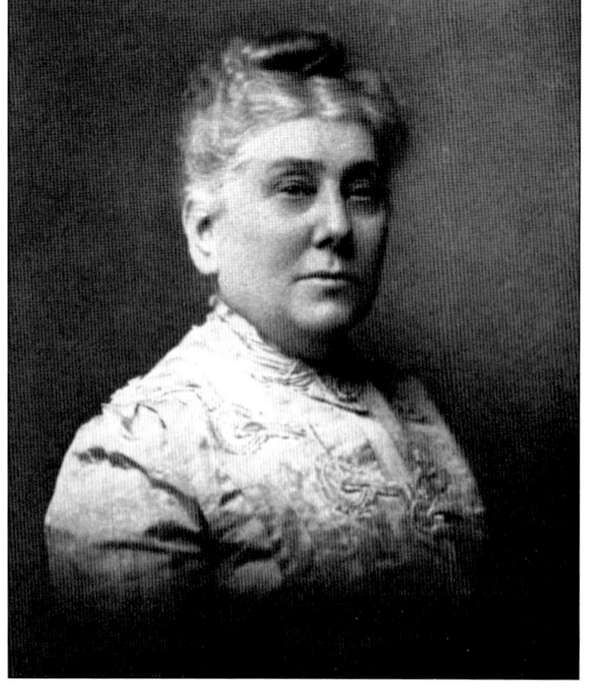

One attendee, 19-year-old Anna Ridgely (pictured here later in life), had a change of heart about Lincoln after seeing him at the reception. In November 1860, she had been "disappointed" in Lincoln's election because he had no "knowledge of state affairs" and lacked "any polish of manners." But now, she wrote, "Mr. L really looked handsome to me. His whiskers are a great improvement and he had such a pleasant smile I could not but admire him." (Google Books.)

One attendee had never seen "such a crowd" at a private home. "It took about twenty minutes to get in the hall door," she wrote. While she was standing near Lincoln, Robert "came up, and in his humorous style," shook his father's hand, saying, "Good evening Mr. Lincoln!" In response, "his father gave him a gentle slap in the face." (LFA.)

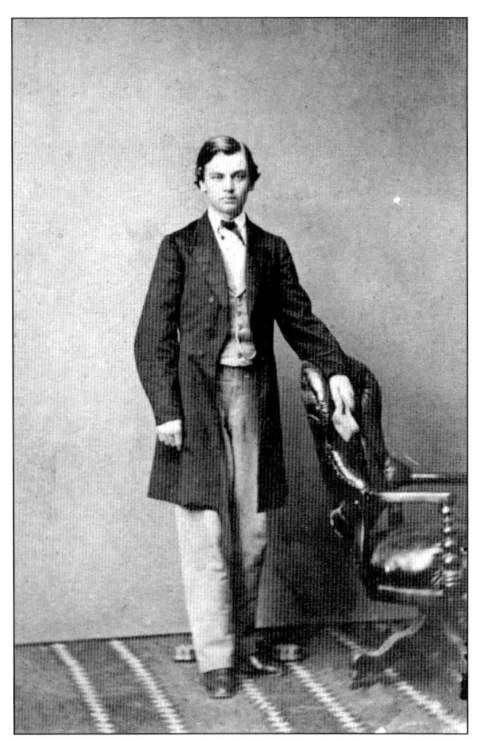

On Friday, February 8, the Lincolns moved out of their home and relocated to the Chenery House, a five-story hotel located at the corner of Washington and Fourth Streets in Springfield. The building, which had opened in 1855, boasted "eighty single rooms for gentlemen, numerous parlors, reception rooms, and suites for families"—in total, 130 guest rooms. The Lincolns occupied rooms on the second floor facing Fourth Street. (SVC.)

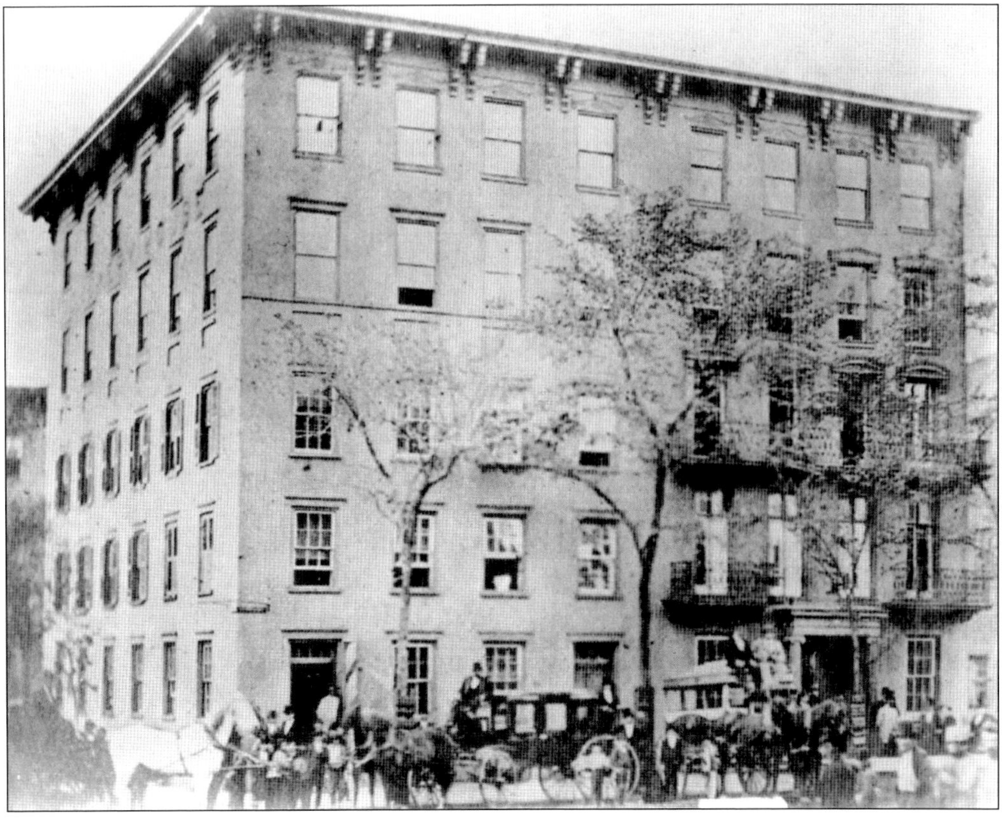

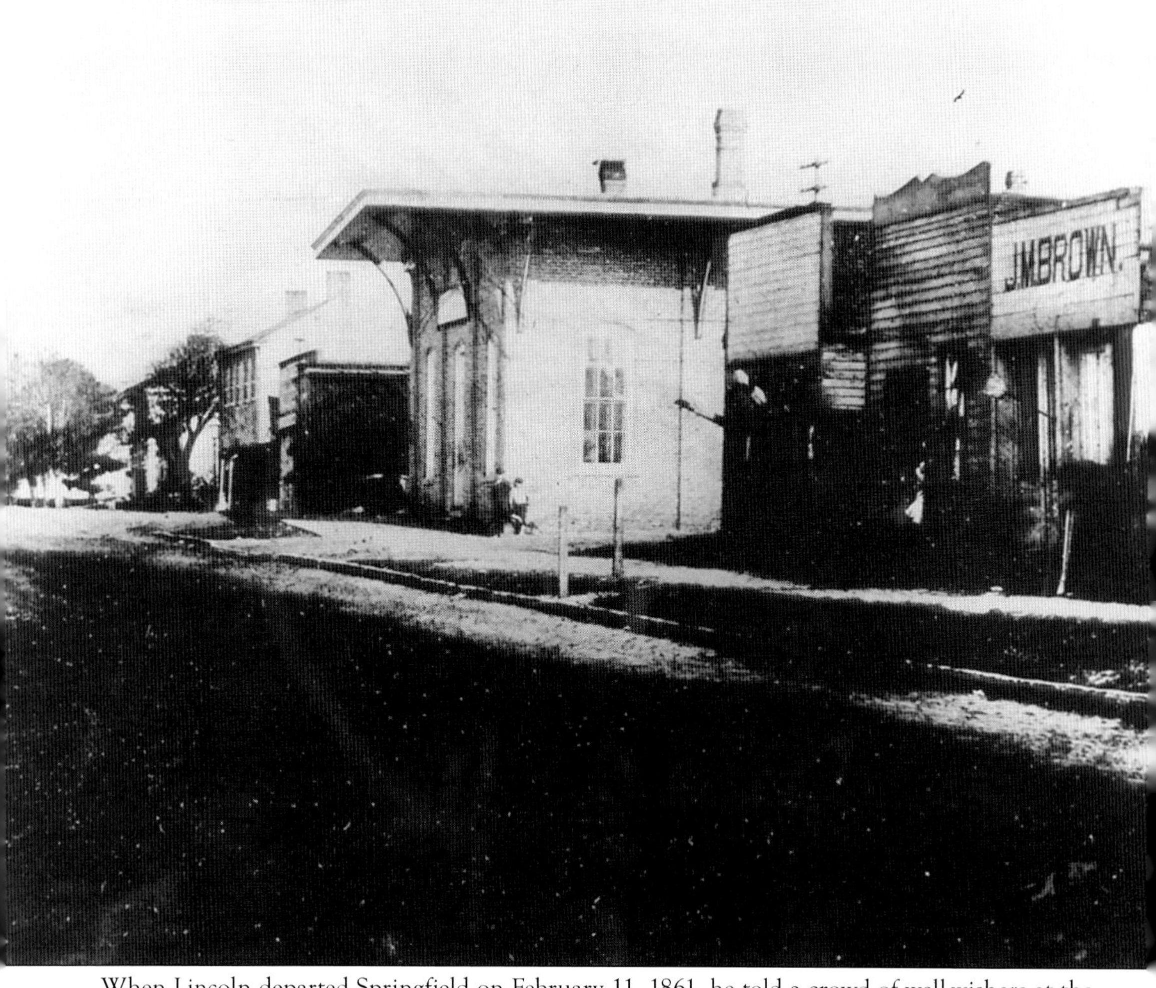

When Lincoln departed Springfield on February 11, 1861, he told a crowd of well-wishers at the depot (pictured here), "Here I have lived a quarter of a century, and have passed from a young to an old man." He was leaving, he said, "not knowing when, or whether ever, I may return" and "with a task before me greater than that which rested upon Washington." Trusting in God for guidance and assistance, he concluded, "Let us confidently hope that all will yet be well. To His care commending you, as I hope in your prayers you will commend me, I bid you an affectionate farewell." He then boarded a train bound for Washington, never to return to his home of 17 years. (ALPLM.)

Six

My Present Tenant is a Dead Beat

From Rental Property to Private Museum

A new sort of tourist came to Lincoln's home during the Civil War. Thousands of Union soldiers tramped through Springfield on their way to the front, and many took a moment to see where their commander in chief had lived. But not all were impressed by what they saw. Cyrus Cummings of the 2nd Illinois Light Artillery thought "it is nothing more than common, 3 or 4000 dollars would build such a house." Another soldier was "surprised to see such a plain house, and not in the best part of the city at that."

From 1861 to 1869, the Lincolns rented their home to the Tilton family. The Tiltons were generous hosts to the throngs of sightseers. When three Illinois infantrymen walked over to the house, Lucretia Tilton "invited us in [and] we had a long chat." She also "played on the piano for us," and as they departed, "she gave us some leaves and some flowers from the yard," which the soldier sent to a friend, knowing that she would be "happy to receive such curiosities." The Tiltons also made some improvements to the property. One soldier remarked, "The yard being filled with flowers and plants made it a very attractive-looking place."

Waves more came to the home following the assassination. "Many persons came to look at the house," noted Carlton Greenleaf of the 24th Michigan Infantry, who was ordered to stand guard there in April 1865. "I saw many of them shed tears. Some cursed with bitter emphasis." Eventually, Greenleaf's curiosity got the better of him. He went to the back door and "tried it gently. It yielded and I went in, holding my breath." The kitchen "looked neat and clean." Greenleaf then walked up to the front of the house (probably the parlor). He spied "an old desk, open; with pens and pencils and small articles." Snooping around, he was tempted to take a souvenir. "I had to fight the devil and all his hosts for they were all right there and urging me to help myself. But I did not do it!—believe it or not."

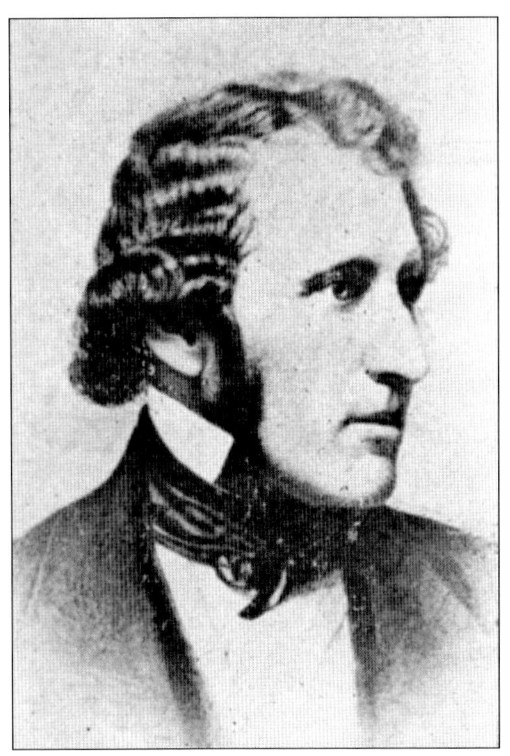

Beginning on February 11, 1861, Lincoln rented his home to Lucian Tilton, president of the Great Western Railway Company, for $350 per year. When the Tiltons decided to move out in 1869, Robert tried to persuade them to stay. "I need not say how much I regret your intention," he wrote. "The great courtesy exhibited by you and your family, towards strangers visiting this house, who must have given you so much trouble, will always be gratefully remembered." (LFFC.)

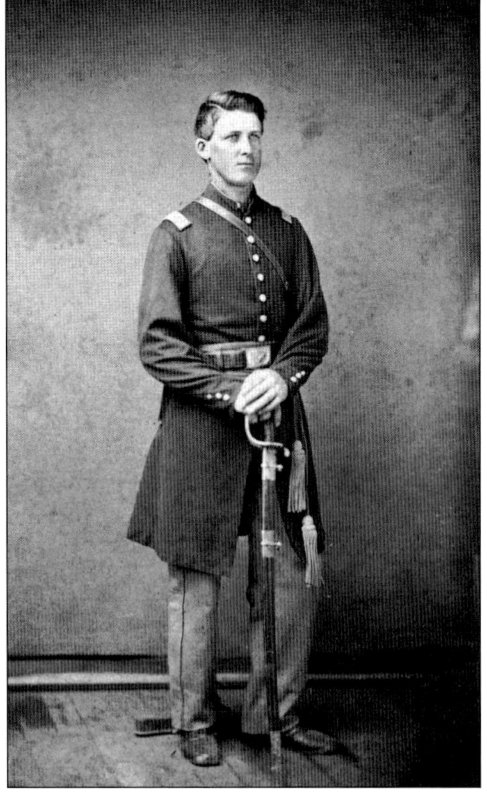

When Pvt. George Buswell of the 7th Minnesota Infantry passed through Springfield on his way to the front in December 1863, he took "a tramp around the city. Saw the home of our father Abe Lincoln, a rather plain square two story frame house. This seems like a very pleasant place." An antebellum supporter of Stephen A. Douglas, Buswell would cast his first vote for Lincoln in 1864. (HL.)

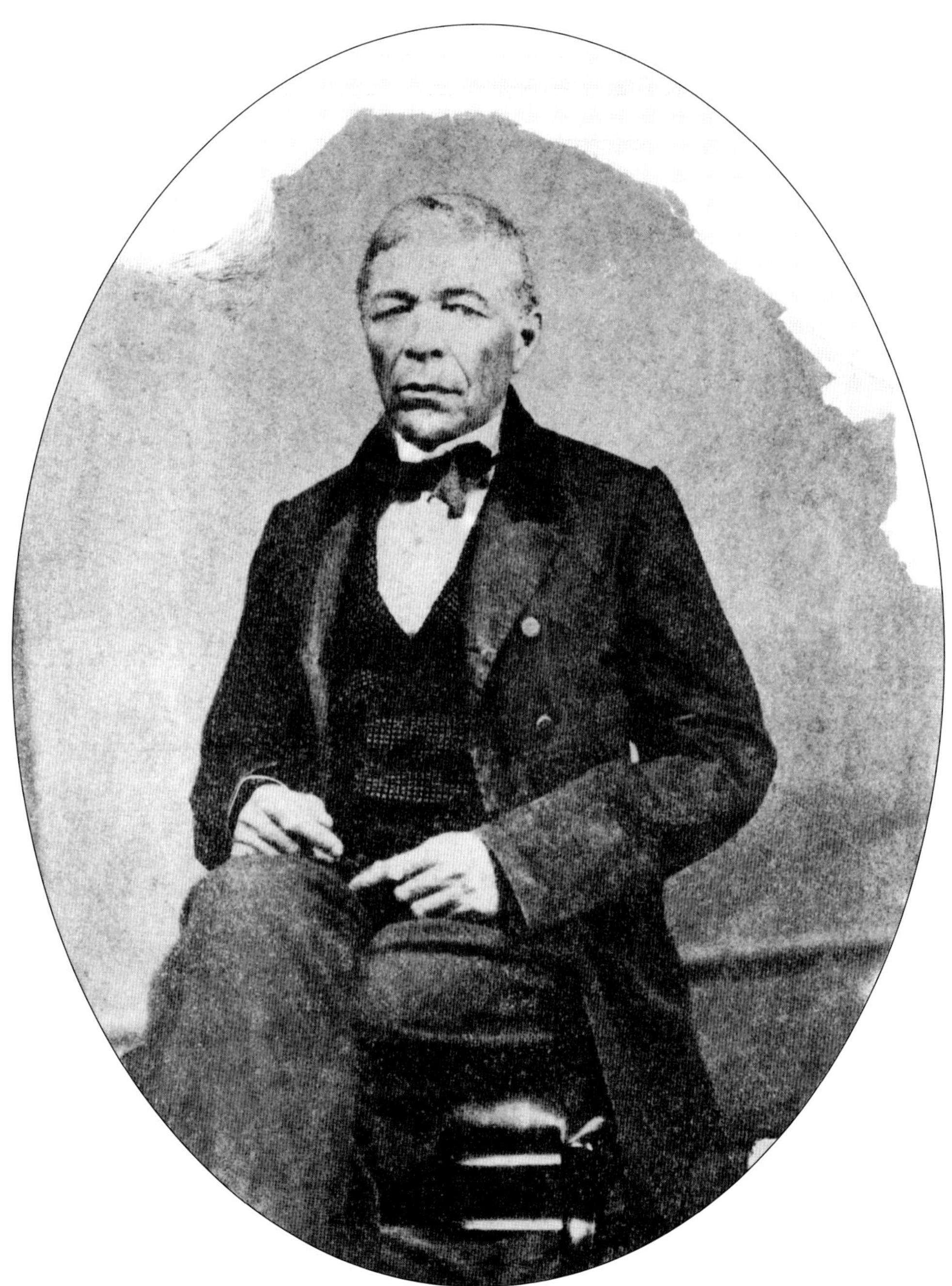

Lincoln's friend and former barber, William Florville, sent Lincoln a personal note in December 1863 updating Lincoln on life back in Springfield. Florville, who was a Haitian immigrant, thanked Lincoln for issuing the Emancipation Proclamation. He also stated that things looked promising for Lincoln's reelection in 1864. As for life in Springfield, Florville wrote, "Tell Taddy that his (and Willys) Dog [Fido] is a live and Kicking doing well." Lincoln's home "is Kept in good order. Mr Tilton has no children to ruin things." Florville added that "Mrs Tilton and Miss Tilton are verry Strong Union Ladies and do a great deal for the Soldiers who are suffering So Much for us & to sustain the Goverment." (ALPLM.)

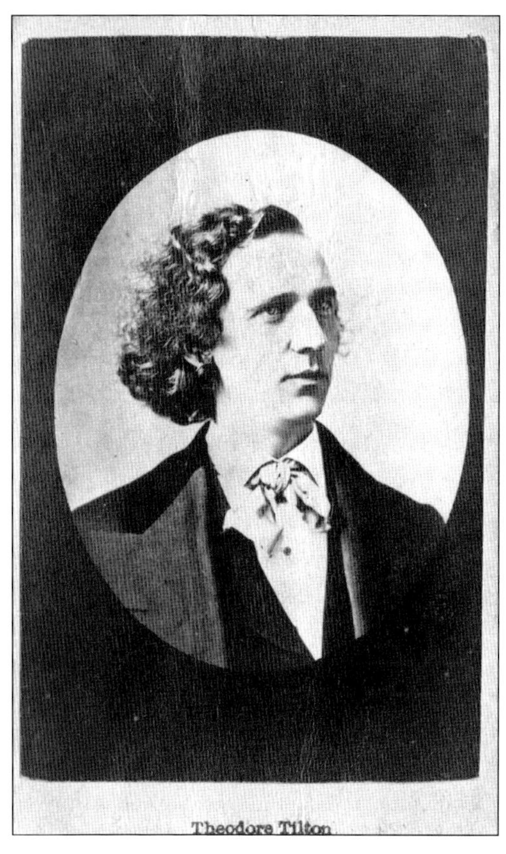

Abolitionist editor Theodore Tilton (left) of New York visited Springfield on January 4, 1865. Lt. Gov. William Bross (below) met Tilton and took him to the Lincoln home, which Tilton described in a letter to his wife the next day as "a plain, two-story, wooden building, painted brown,—looking like the residence of a man neither poor nor rich." To his surprise, Tilton found that the present occupants of the home shared his surname. They "received me with great cordiality," and Tilton remained at the home conversing with the Tiltons until dark. Before he departed, the Tiltons invited their guest to return with his family for another visit. Lucian Tilton's daughter plucked some white flowers from the garden, which Theodore Tilton sent to his wife. (Left, Boston Public Library; below, University of Illinois.)

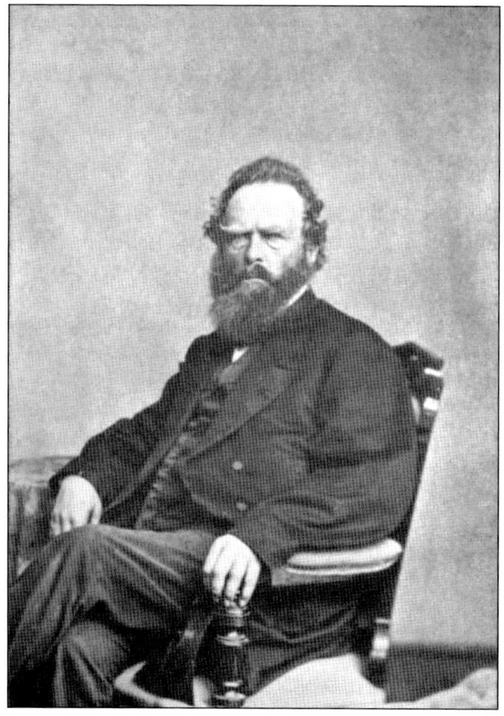

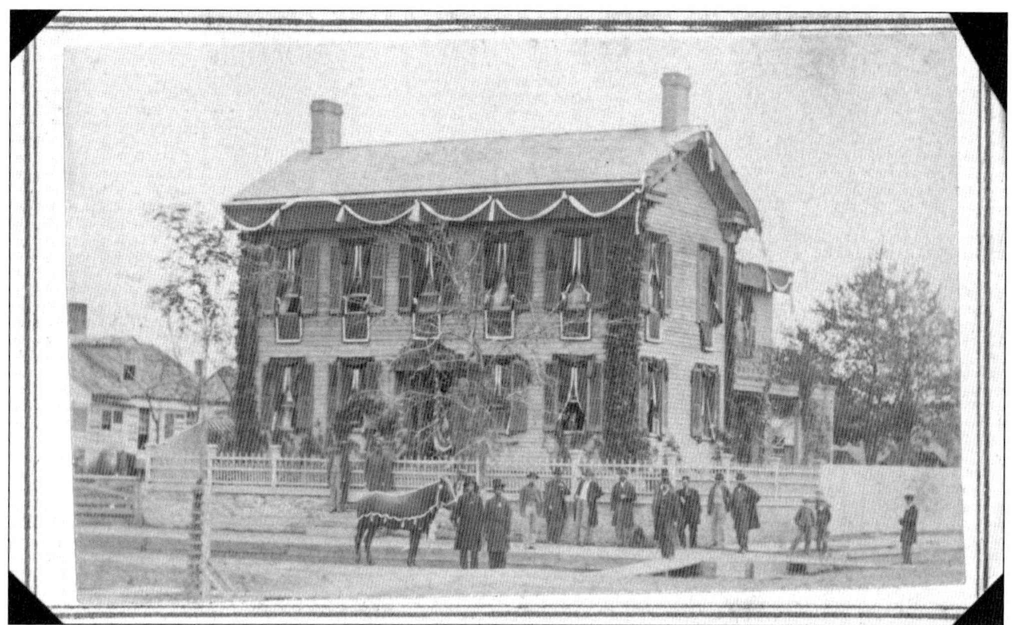

Privates Victor Wheeler and Isaac Andrews of the 146th Illinois Infantry were selected to drape the Lincoln home in mourning because of their "good work on the state building." According to news reports, their efforts won the "approbation of the chief of the citizens' committee." Another soldier, Carlton Greenleaf of the 24th Michigan Infantry, later recalled what it was like to stand guard outside Lincoln's home following the assassination: "Ah, Me! It was a long time ago and nearly all of his soldiers have followed their great Commander-in-Chief to their eternal rest. And the last ones will soon follow. And I remember as I stood there on that April day, I thought, 'here I am, a tough little soldier, with the great Civil War only a memory and a history, guarding the empty house of our great Commander who will never need again an earthly habitation, all this—and I—not yet—nineteen years of age.' " (Above, LOC; below, LFFC.)

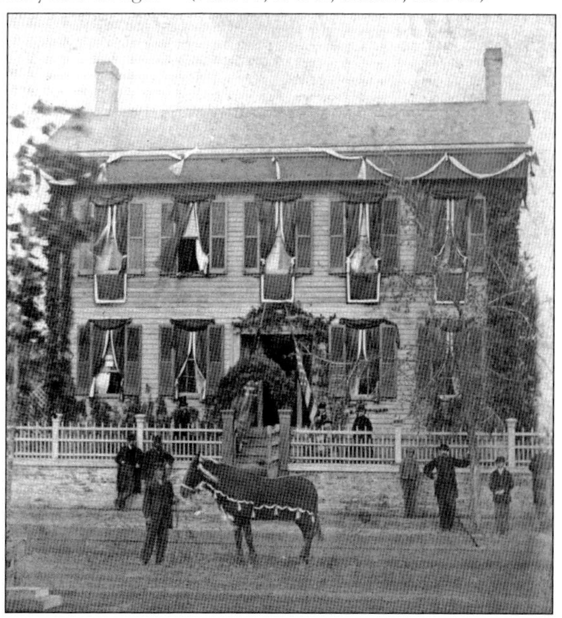

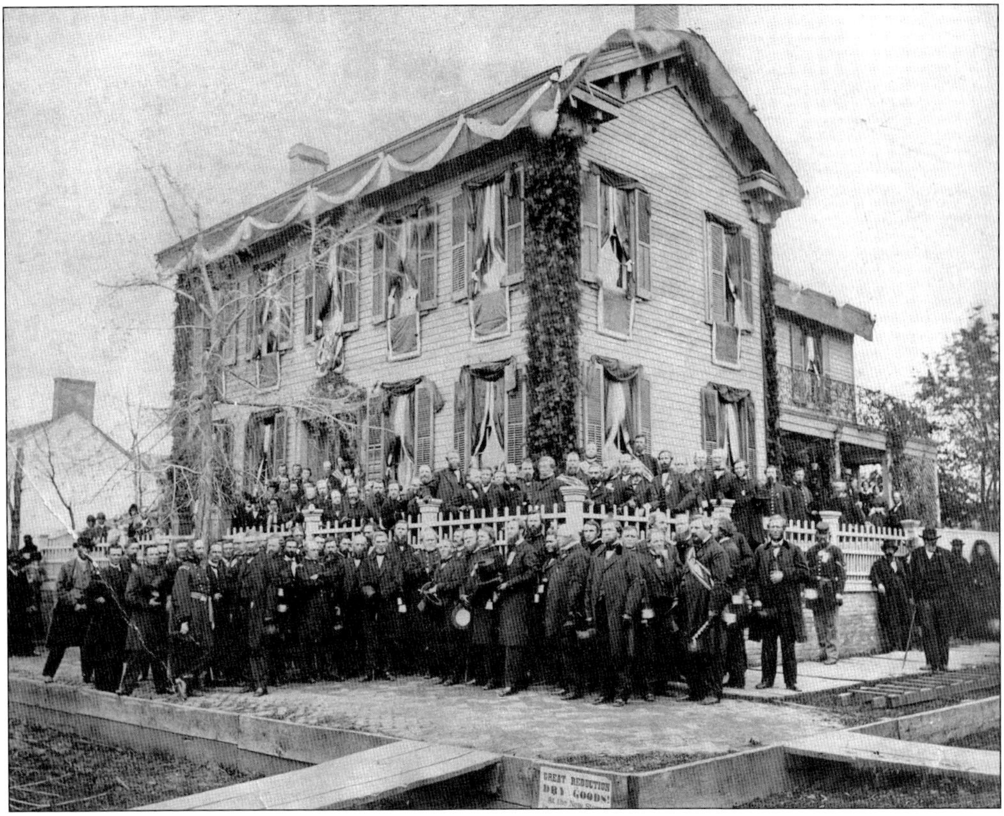

The crowds were so large outside of the home that the *Illinois State Journal* reported that it was "necessary to send for a military guard to graduate the stream of visitors." During the funeral, "thousands of persons, representing almost every State of the Union, passed through the house, viewing everything connected with it with the deepest interest." Several groups posed for photographs, like these soldiers and civilians, many of whom stood with their hats in their hands to show respect to the fallen commander in chief. According to the *Journal*, the Tiltons "kindly received all, and patiently strove to gratify their curiosity." (Above, SVC; below, LOC.)

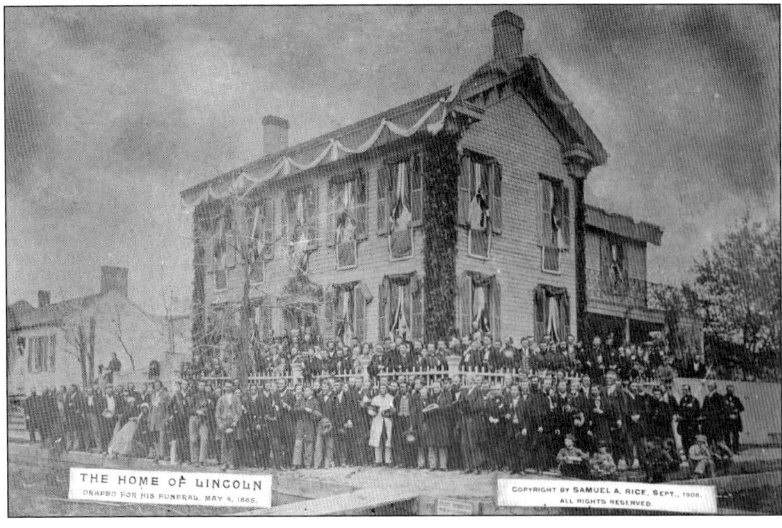

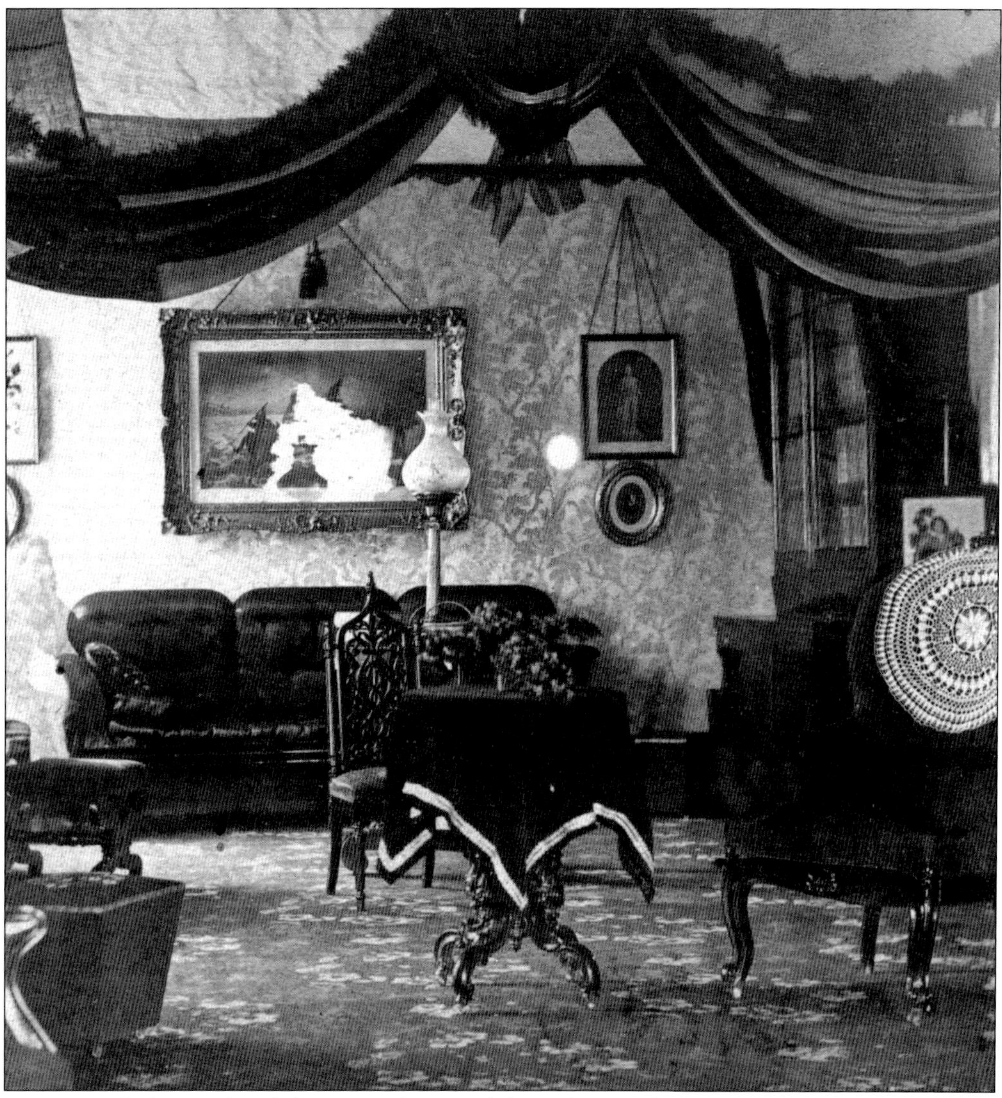

Visitors to the home placed donations for Lincoln's tomb into a box on a table in the parlor. Above them, a large American flag was draped over the folding doors that separated the two parlors. The picture of Lincoln that hung above the flag had been supplied by Chicago photographer John Carbutt and "was placed in its position by the late President's doorkeeper." Hanging on the back wall was a copy of Emanuel Leutze's 1851 painting *Washington Crossing the Delaware*. Leutze's artwork had not appeared in the engraving of Lincoln's parlor in *Frank Leslie's Illustrated Newspaper* in 1861 (see page 29), indicating that it belonged to the Tiltons. Nevertheless, Lincoln would have likely been pleased to know that it hung in his home during the war. In February 1861, he told the New Jersey State Senate that he remembered reading about the Patriots' struggle near Trenton in 1776 when he was a boy: "The crossing of the river; the contest with the Hessians; the great hardships endured at that time, all fixed themselves on my memory more than any single revolutionary event." (LFFC.)

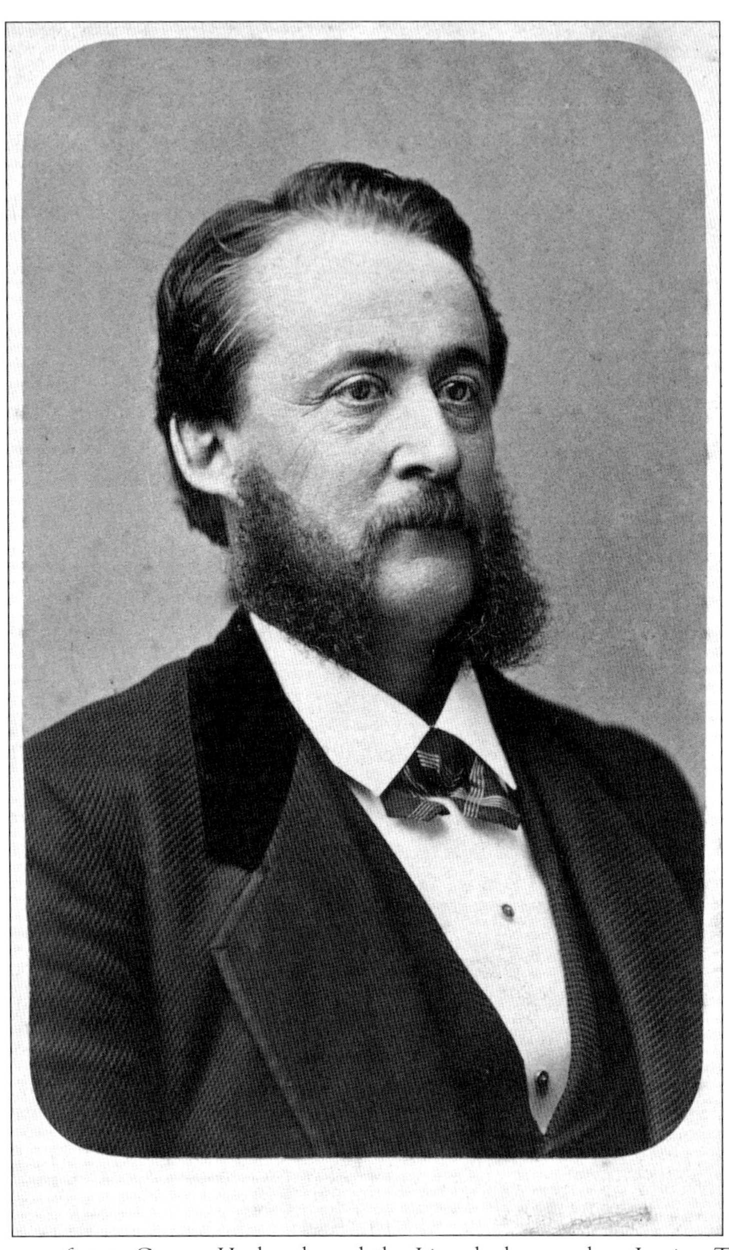

Illinois secretary of state George Harlow leased the Lincoln home when Lucian Tilton's family departed in May 1869. Robert Lincoln wanted no changes "to be made in the house of anything like a permanent character such as closing up or opening doors or windows." He further stated that he wanted "nothing done to the property except what is essential," although he did permit Harlow to whitewash the kitchen. While Harlow lived there, the house received a street number, 430 South Eighth Street, although Harlow listed his address in the city directory as "Lincoln's old home." The Harlows lost their three-year-old daughter, Kate, at the home on February 17, 1871. Harlow offered to purchase the property for $2,000 in 1877, but David Davis persuaded Robert to decline the offer because the home should either be owned by the Lincoln family or the public. Robert wrote Harlow, "I have concluded to own the house till it ruins me." The Harlows moved out in the spring of 1877. (ALPLM.)

Robert Lincoln became the full owner of the home after he purchased his mother's interest in the property in 1874. He appointed his old friend, Springfield attorney Clinton L. Conkling (pictured here), to manage the home. (ALPLM.)

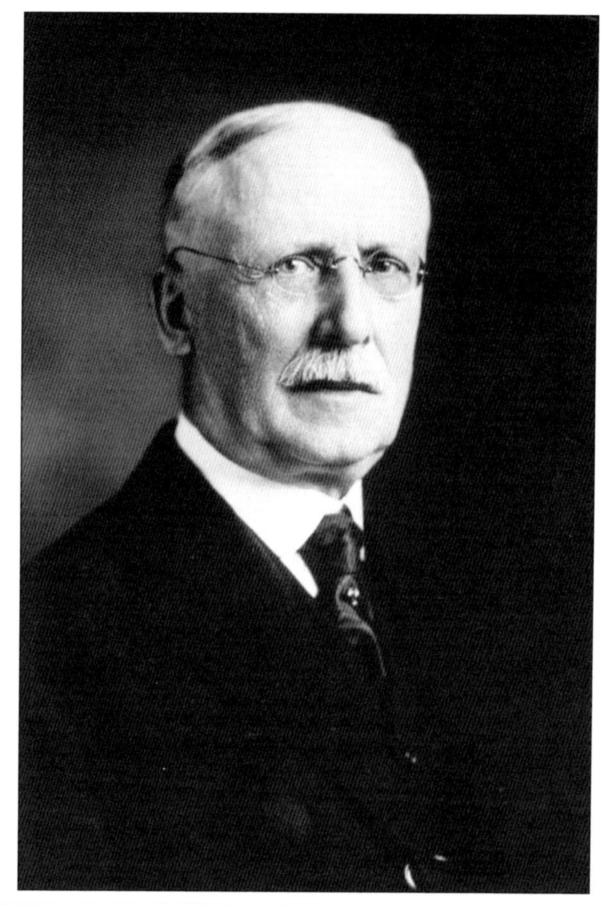

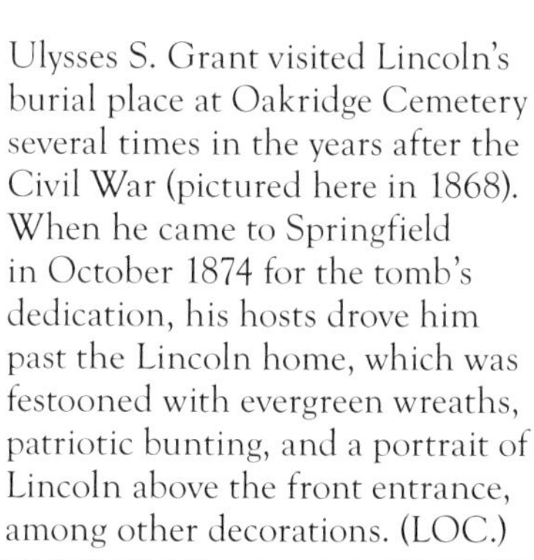

Ulysses S. Grant visited Lincoln's burial place at Oakridge Cemetery several times in the years after the Civil War (pictured here in 1868). When he came to Springfield in October 1874 for the tomb's dedication, his hosts drove him past the Lincoln home, which was festooned with evergreen wreaths, patriotic bunting, and a portrait of Lincoln above the front entrance, among other decorations. (LOC.)

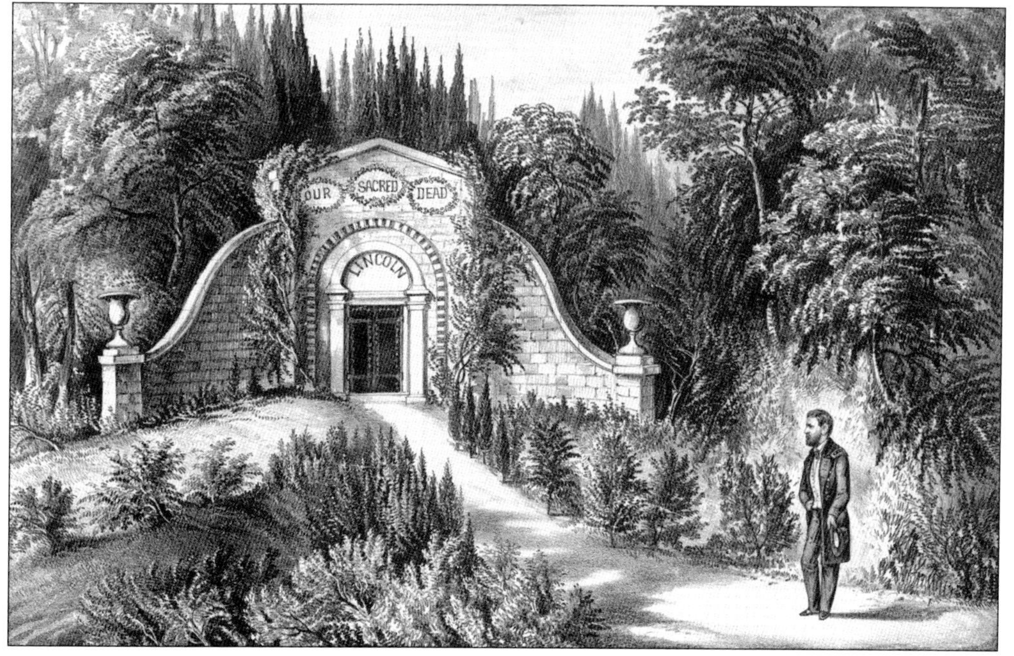

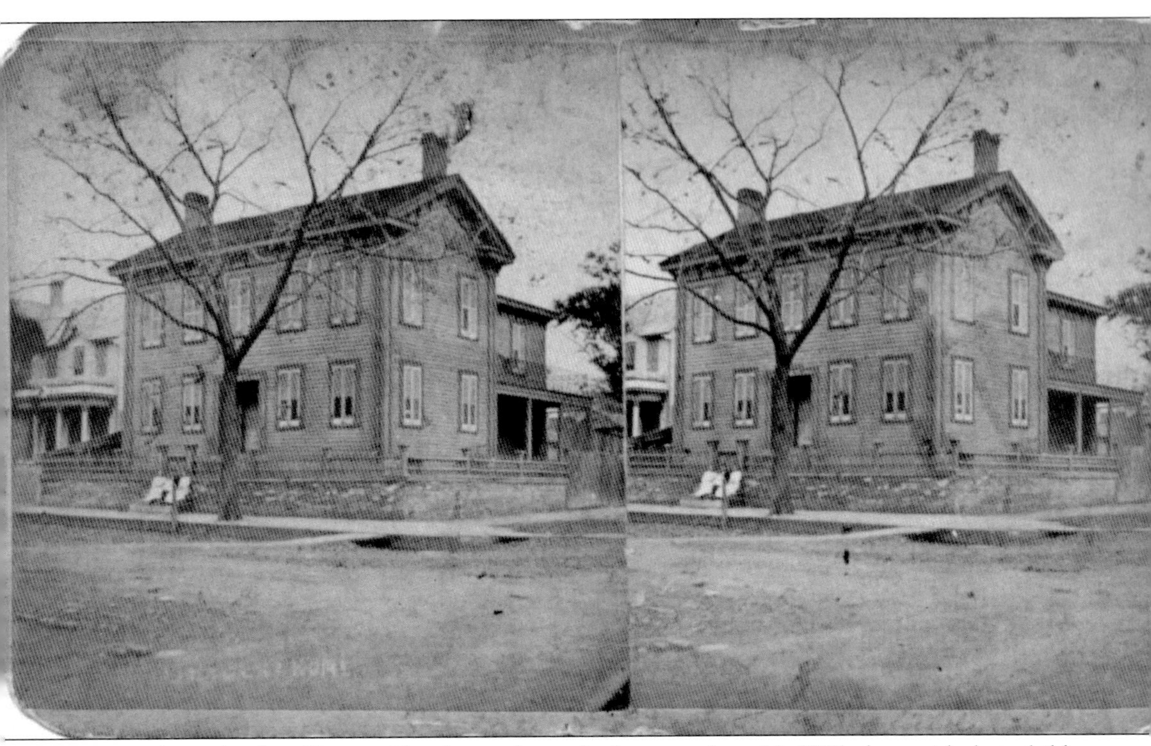

Jacob D. Akard and Letitia Akard moved into the home on June 20, 1877, along with their children, Mary Frances (8) and Edward (4), and Letitia's father, Ezra Gillman (75). Akard turned the home into a boardinghouse, but he appears to have abandoned it by late 1878, even though his lease did not end until June 1879. According to one account, the home stood "empty and vacant and became the headquarters for tramps and thieves." (SVC.)

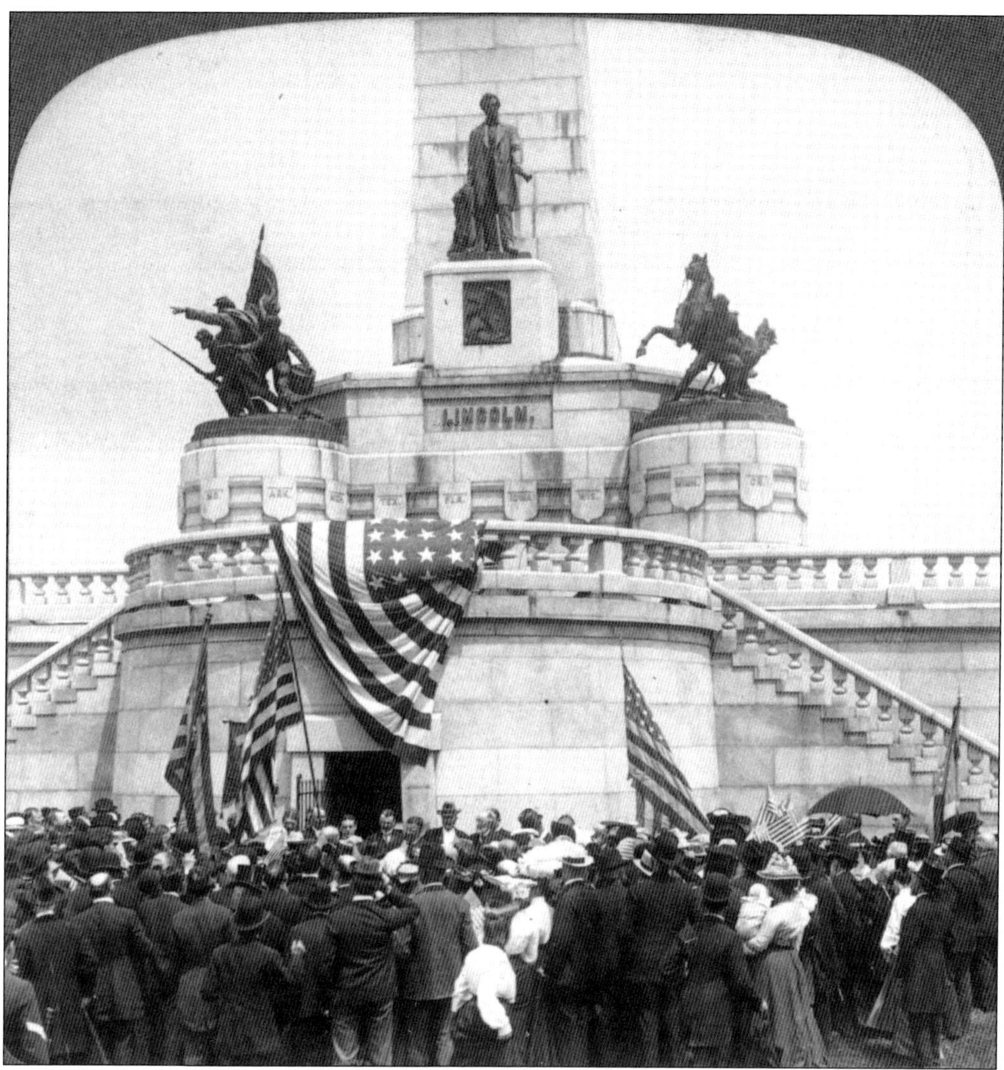

In 1879, Ozias M. Hatch, secretary of the Lincoln Monument Association, approached Robert Lincoln about transferring the home to the association "in trust as a memorial to his patriotic father." Robert was intrigued by the idea, as the house "is rapidly getting into a condition by age which will require repairs to an amount that I cannot afford." But the association had its hands full managing the Lincoln Tomb (pictured here in 1903, with Theodore Roosevelt standing near the entrance), and it also was not certain that it had the authority to accept the home. Because Robert could not afford the expense of a private custodian, he decided to rent the house as quickly as possible. On Clinton L. Conkling's recommendation, Robert rented the home to Dr. Gustav Adolph Hermann Wendlandt, who opened up his doctor's office on the first floor. (LOC.)

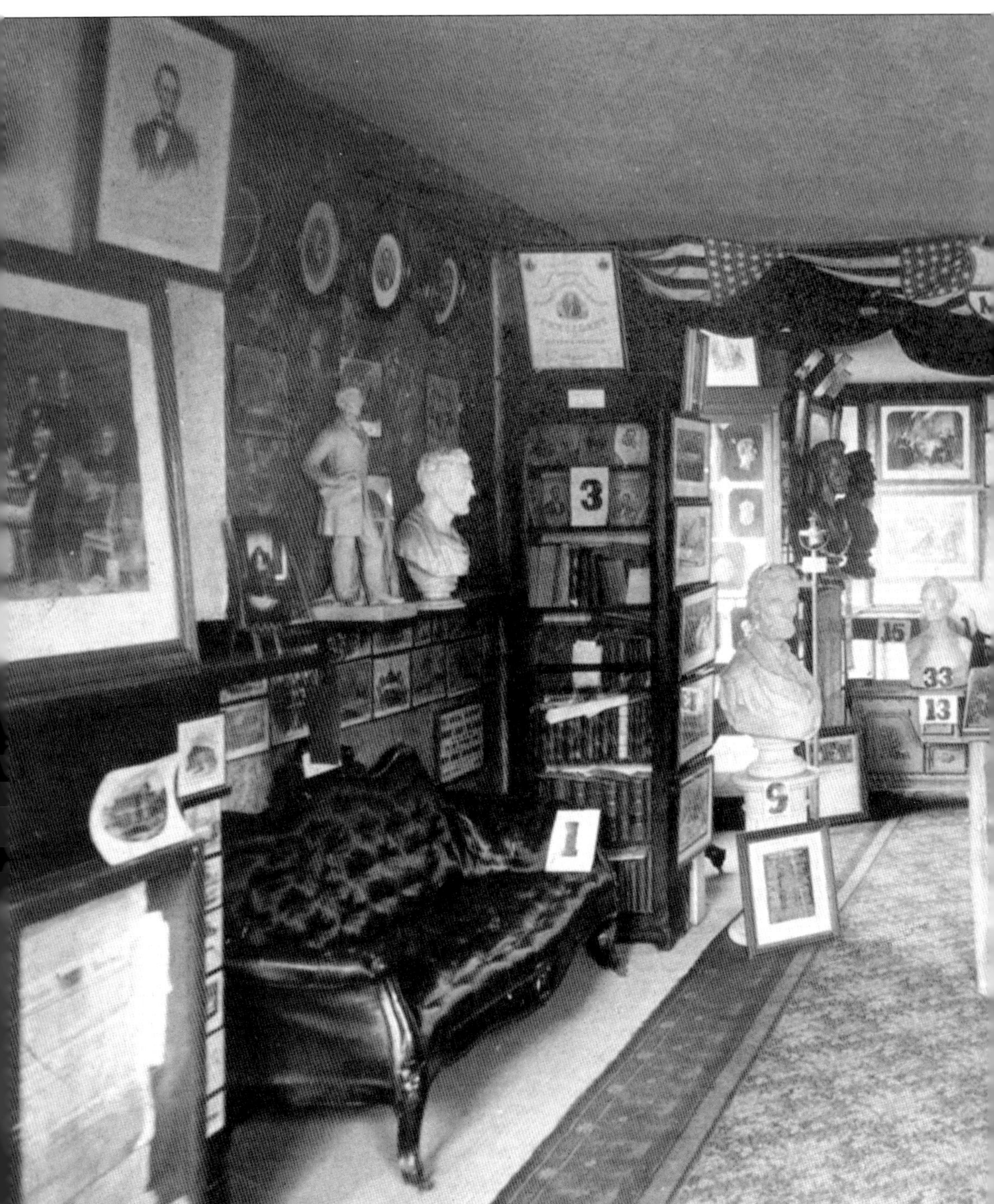

About 1882, Civil War veteran and Lincolniana collector Osborn Oldroyd moved into the Charles D. Arnold House, across Jackson Street, from which he had a view of Lincoln's home. When Dr. Wendlandt vacated the Lincoln house in the spring of 1883, Oldroyd moved in with his wife, Lida, and their daughter, Daisy. Oldroyd opened a museum on the first floor on April 14, 1884—the 19th anniversary of the Lincoln assassination. He charged admission for people to see his collection,

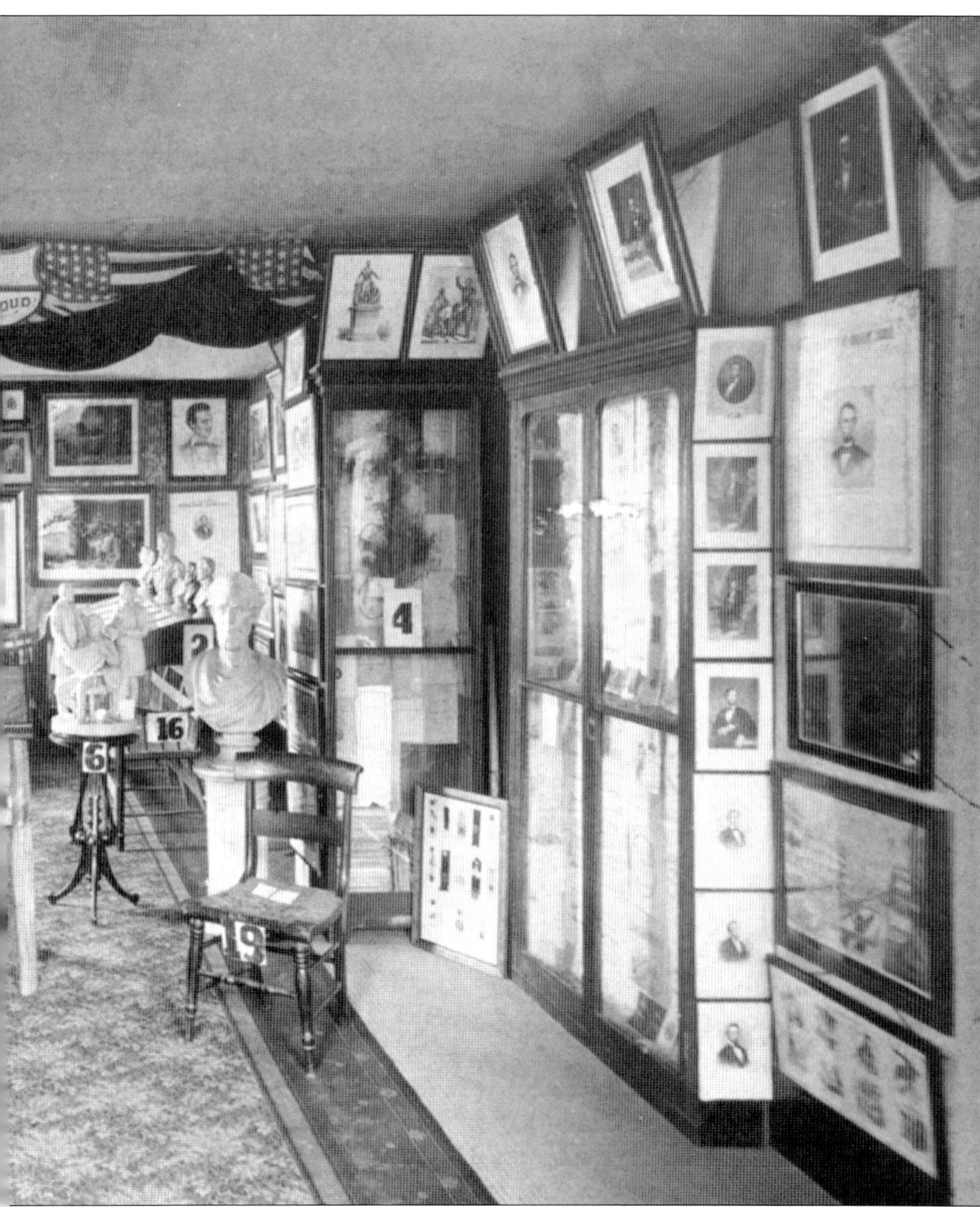

which he set up in the parlors, although he later denied ever charging a fee. He also sold books and relics, which one account said largely consisted "of cannibalized pieces of the Home and site features." Many visitors purchased cabinet cards like this one, which showed what the parlor looked like in 1885. (LIHO.)

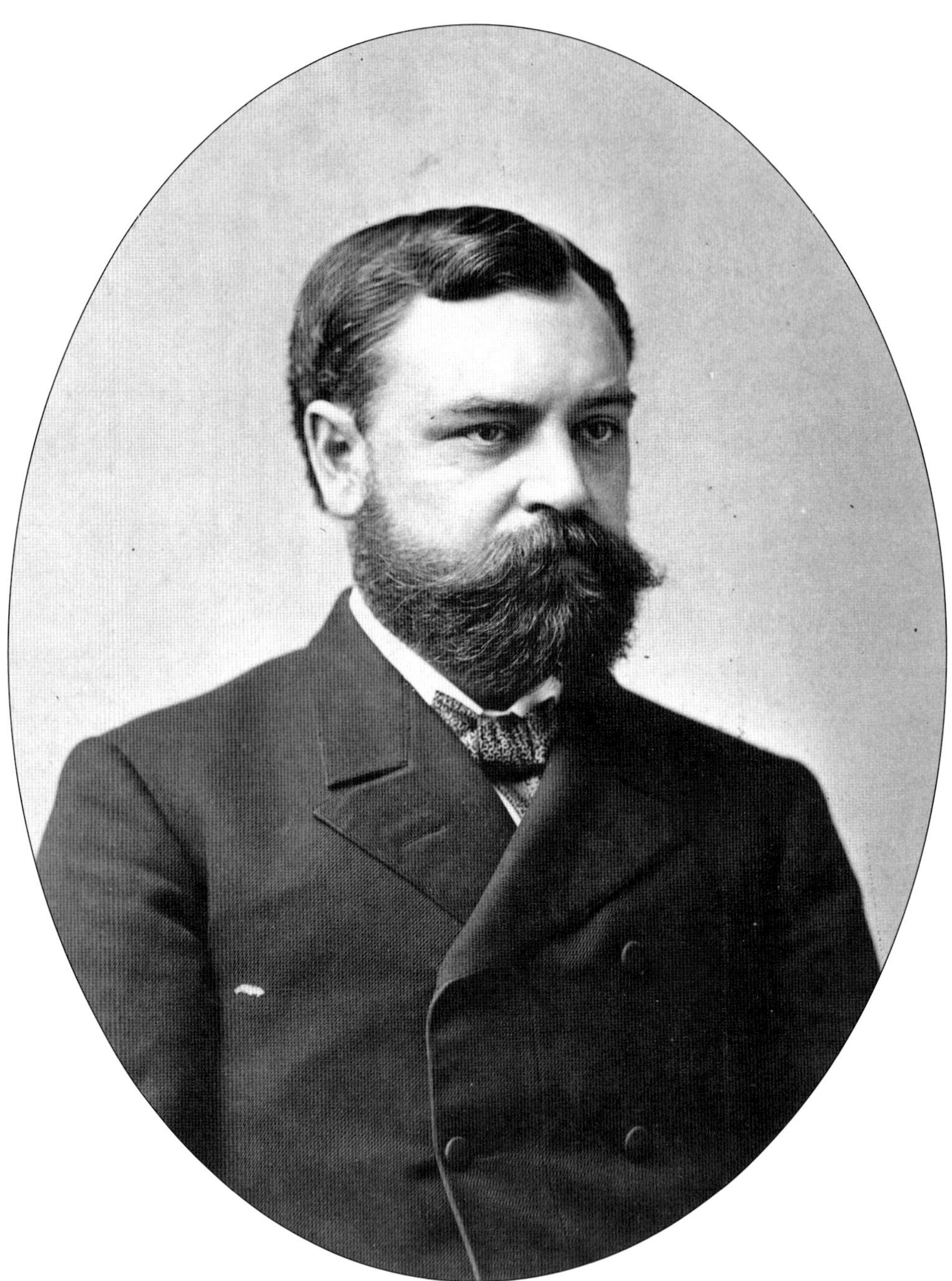

Osborn Oldroyd stopped paying rent to Robert Lincoln (pictured here in 1880) around 1885, although he continued to charge admission to see his collection on the first floor of the Lincoln home. Soon, Oldroyd began lobbying the state legislature to acquire the property. As historian Wayne C. Temple explains, Oldroyd hoped to "get the Lincoln home established as a State memorial so that he could reside there, earn a salary as the custodian, and display his collection." Robert was irked by Oldroyd's actions. "I suppose that in fact my present tenant is a dead beat and that this whole proceeding [to convey the house to the state] is expected practically to provide him with a home free of rent," he wrote to Clinton L. Conkling. (LFA.)

Seven

Keep It Open to the Public

From a State to a National Site

When the State of Illinois approached Robert Lincoln about selling the home in the spring of 1883, he replied, "I have determined not to part with the ownership of the property." The next year, when the state tried again, Robert assured them that, should he part with the property, "there would need be no appropriation for its purchase from me." After more lobbying by the state, Robert finally relented. "If the State will offer to preserve the house as an object of public interest," he wrote, "I will convey the property to the State without compensation." On June 16, 1887, Robert sold the home to the government of Illinois for $1 on the condition that the state maintain the house and keep it open to the public. Robert requested the back rent that was owed him by Oldroyd, but he never received it. Oldroyd continued to operate his museum on the first floor, while he and his family lived on the second floor. From 1887 until 1917, the home was administered by the board of trustees of the Lincoln Homestead, which hired a custodian to live on-site and manage the property.

In 1893, Gov. John P. Altgeld, a Democrat, became president of the board of trustees and fired Oldroyd, a Republican, replacing him with Herman Hofferkamp, a disabled Civil War veteran whom one local editor called "a petty Democratic politician and persistent place-seeker." Hofferkamp—who at one point placed a picture of John Wilkes Booth on the mantel in the parlor—was fired in 1897, when Republicans regained control of the state. A series of custodians continued to live in the home until Virginia Stuart Brown (great-granddaughter of Lincoln's first law partner, John Todd Stuart) retired in 1953, after nearly 30 years in service. In 1971, Pres. Richard Nixon signed a bill establishing the Lincoln Home National Historic Site, and in July 1972, the State of Illinois transferred the property to the federal government. In keeping with Robert Lincoln's wishes, the home has remained open to the public free of charge.

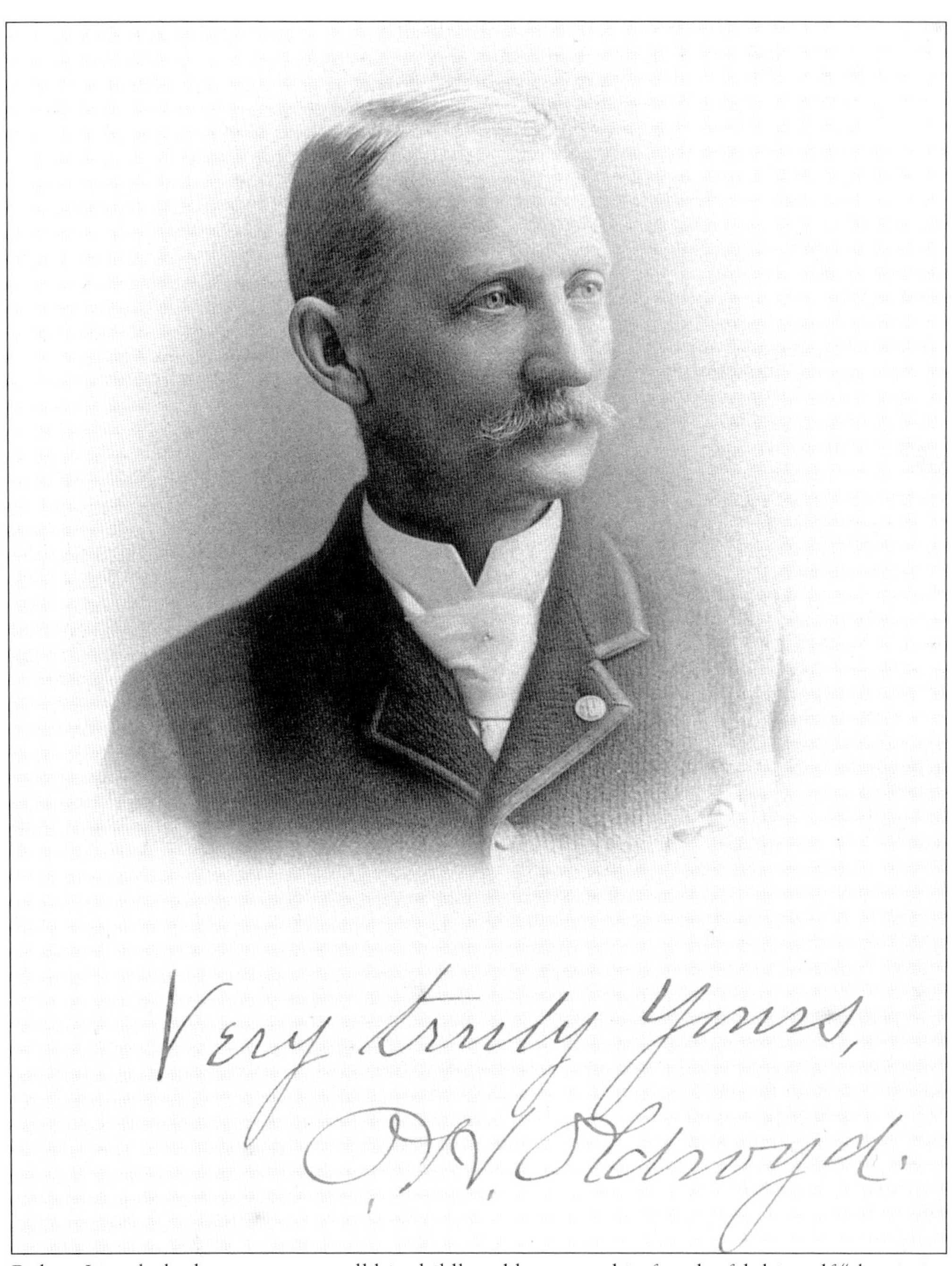

Robert Lincoln had not set out to sell his childhood home, and in fact, he felt himself "the victim of an imposition" by the State of Illinois. Nevertheless, he must have felt some relief when he signed the title over to the state, for he no longer would have to pay taxes on the property or worry about upkeep or bad tenants. In August 1887, the state hired Oldroyd as the custodian of the property at a salary of $1,000 per year. In addition to his immediate family, Oldroyd's in-laws and two brothers-in-law moved in, likely paying him rent. Oldroyd's father-in-law, William Stoneberger, died in the home in March 1888, and his mother-in-law, Josephine Stoneberger, died there that August. Funerals for each were held in the home two days after each passed. (LFFC.)

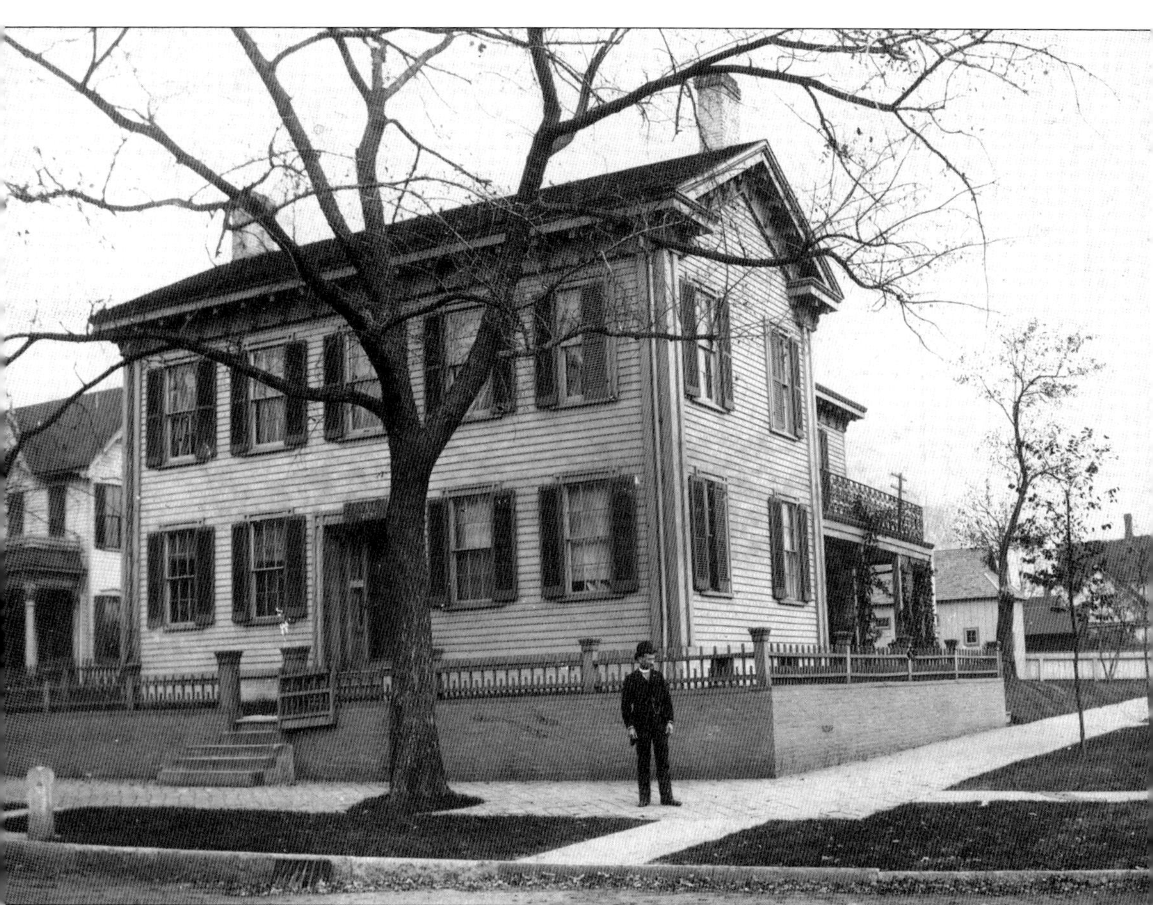

The state appropriated $2,800 for the care of the home in 1888, and Oldroyd (pictured here outside of the home) made several changes over the next year. In addition to painting, plumbing, wallpapering, and carpentry work, he resodded the yard, planted new trees, and laid a brick walkway. Oldroyd also demolished the Lincolns' barn in the backyard and replaced it with his own. He obtained a cannon from the War Department, which he placed in the backyard, calling it the Mary Todd Cannon, and also erected a 72-foot-tall flagpole in the backyard. Finally, the State of Illinois installed the home's first central heating system. Oldroyd was devastated when he was fired as custodian. In 1925, he wrote in a private letter that it "was the saddest event of my life to move out of the house." (LFFC.)

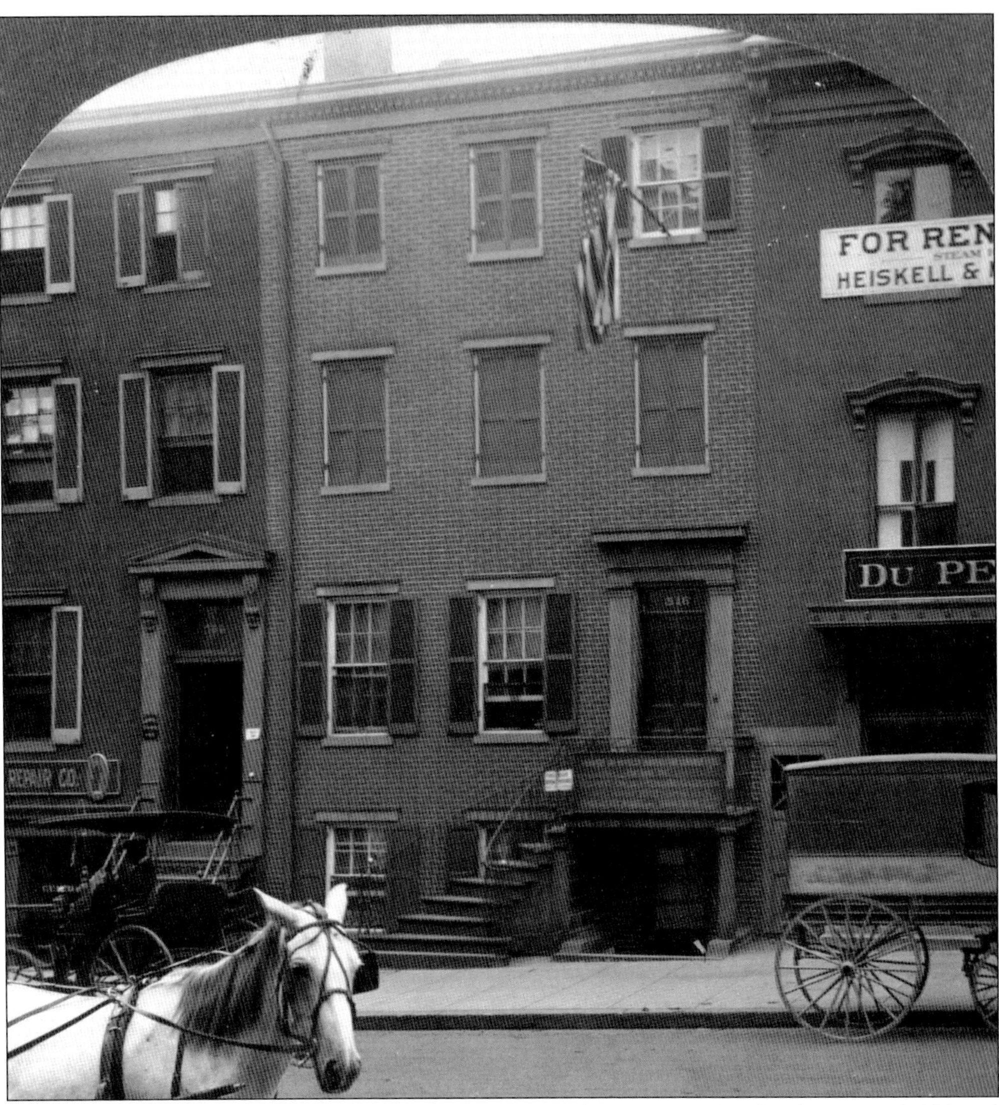

Shortly after he was fired, the Memorial Association of the District of Columbia invited Oldroyd to display his collection at the Petersen House (pictured here in 1909), the boardinghouse where Lincoln had died. Situated across the street from Ford's Theatre, Oldroyd opened his exhibit on October 17, 1893, displaying his collection on the first floor and living in the upper two. "Once more, Oldroyd began maneuvering to obtain his living quarters free of rent," writes historian Wayne C. Temple. At his urging, the US government purchased the Petersen House in 1896, and in 1926, the government paid Oldroyd $50,000 for his collection. One of the items from his collection was the original stove from the Lincolns' kitchen, which was finally returned to the Springfield home in 1959. (LOC.)

School groups have been visiting the Lincoln home for more than a century. In this image, an unidentified bevy of children visits the home around 1890. (LIHO.)

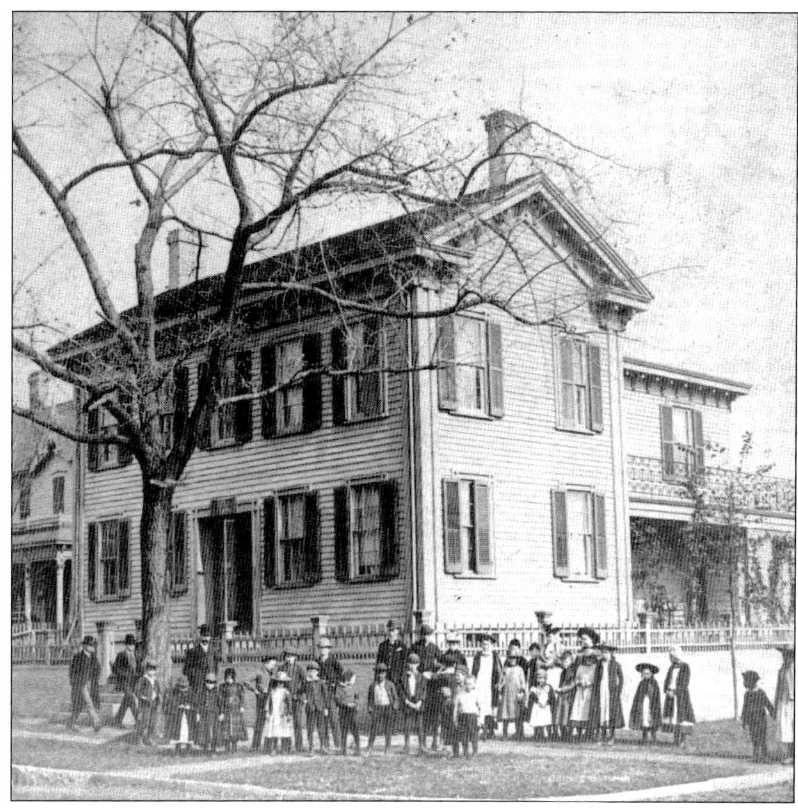

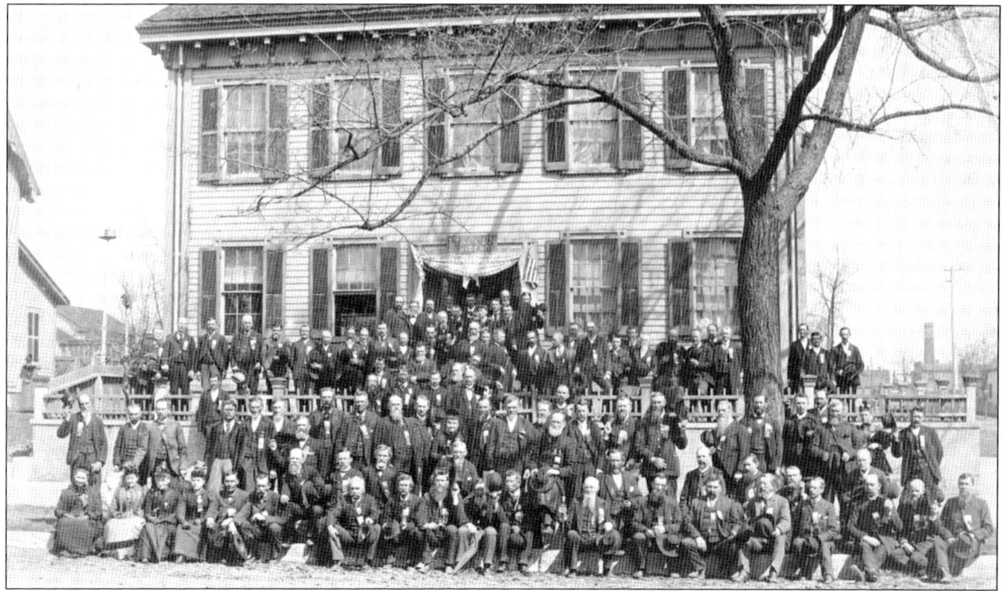

In the late 19th and early 20th centuries, veterans' groups often made pilgrimages to the Lincoln home. On October 16, 1889, for example, the Illinois Association of Ex-Prisoners of War held its 15th annual reunion there, celebrating with a flag raising. In the afternoon, local posts of the Grand Army of the Republic (GAR) and Sons of Union Veterans joined the Illinois Association of Ex-Prisoners of War in a parade to the home. (ALPLM.)

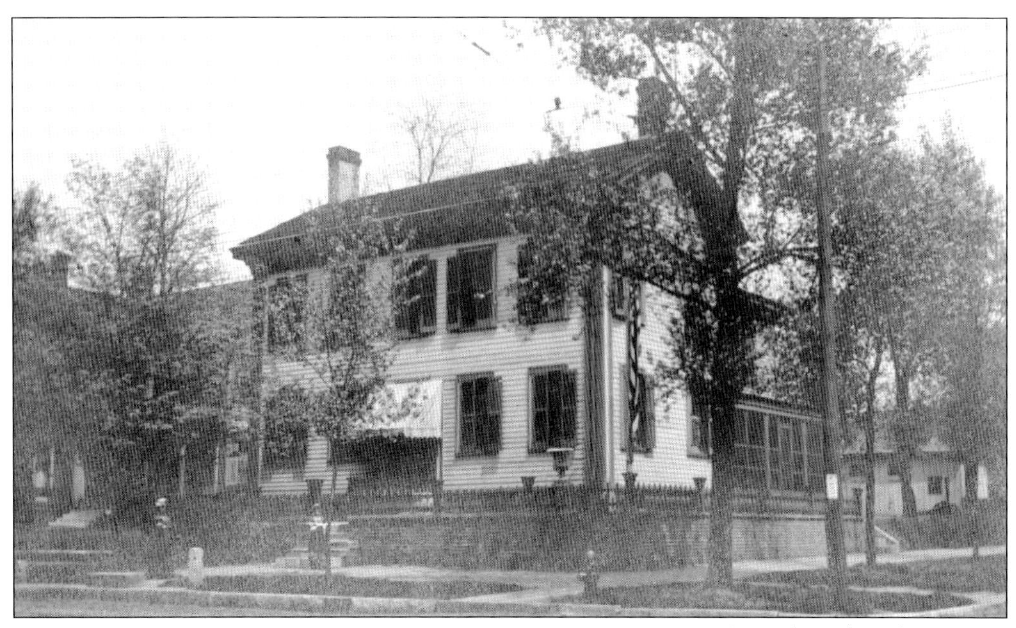

Several modern features were added to the home in the early 20th century. In 1905, an awning was installed over the front entrance. The flagpole, fire hydrant, and concrete sidewalks were added to the property by 1910. A telephone pole and wires also obstruct the view. (LFFC.)

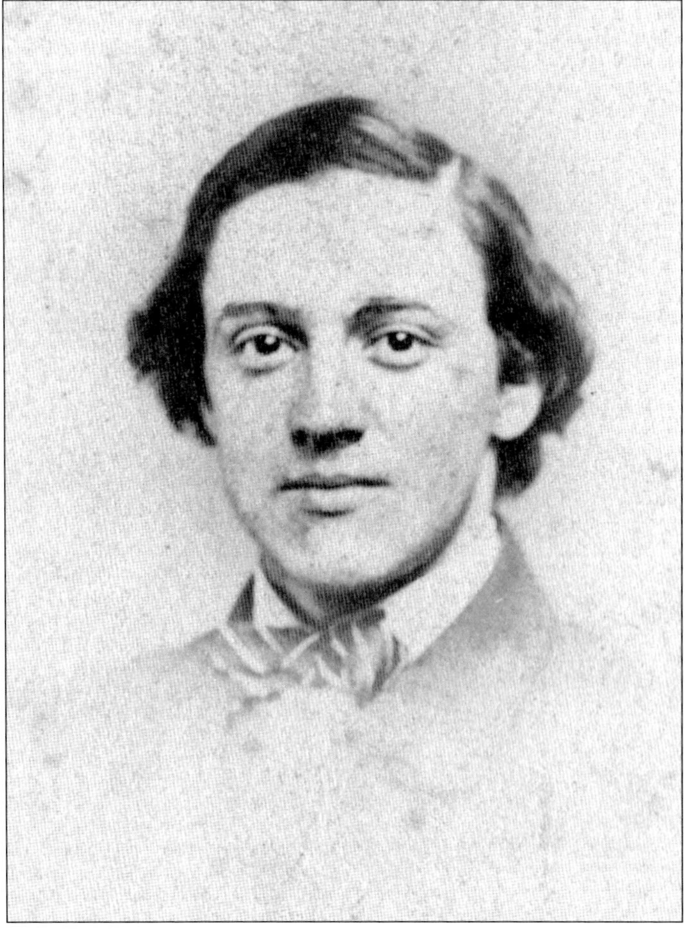

Soon after Governor Altgeld lost his bid for reelection in 1896, Robert Lincoln urged the new Republican governor to appoint a permanent custodian who was not reliant upon "political favor." Robert favored Albert S. Edwards, a nephew of Lincoln's (the son of Ninian and Elizabeth Edwards). Albert held the position until he died of a heart attack at the home on December 20, 1915. He is pictured here in the 1860s. (ALPLM.)

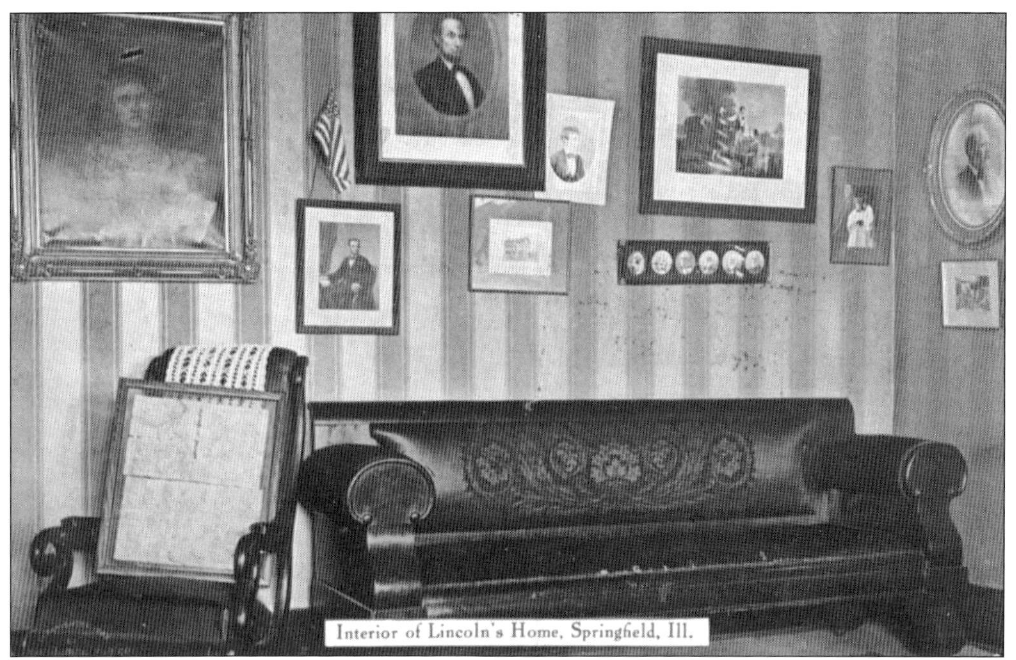

After Oldroyd removed his collection, the state purchased relics to display, but when Herman Hofferkamp was fired as custodian, he sold off those items, even though they belonged to the state. These c. 1907 images of the parlor and sitting room show some of the artifacts and artworks that were on display for visitors to see. (Both, LOC.)

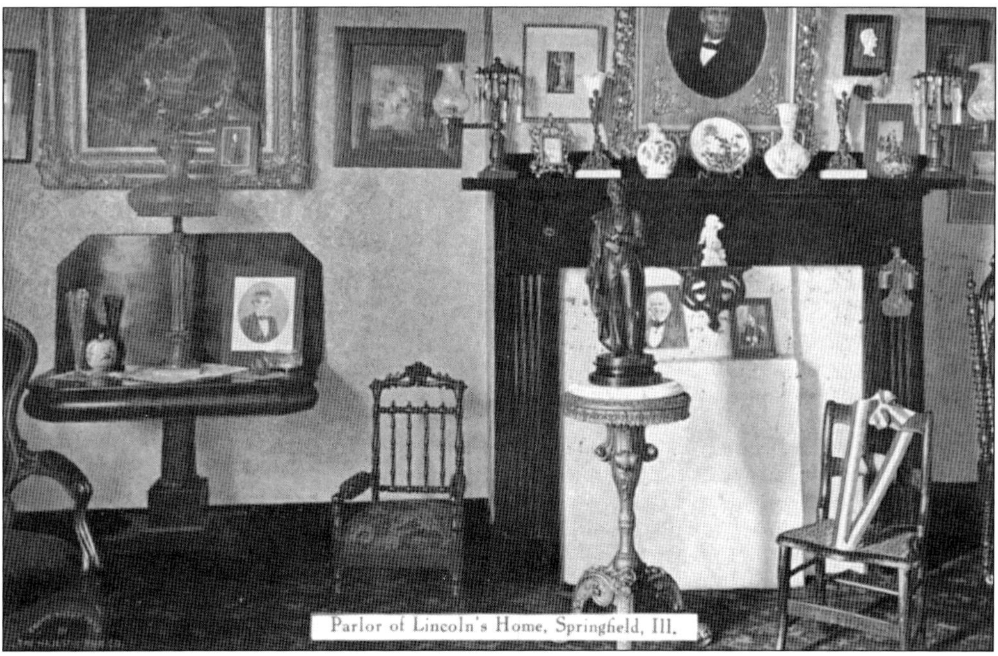

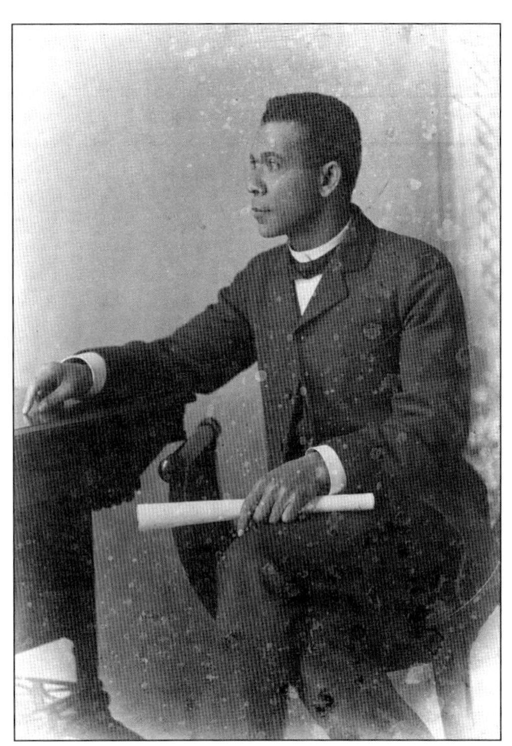

On August 8, 1903, Booker T. Washington, the president of the Tuskegee Institute, visited the Lincoln home and signed the guest registry (pictured below). Five years later, on August 15, 1908, Springfield erupted in violence against the city's black residents. Newspapers nationwide reported that an arsonist attempted to burn the Lincoln home by throwing a flaming torch against it. According to one report, shouts of "Let's burn it down!" and "Here's where Lincoln lived; he freed the negroes" could be heard in the street. When a man with a torch approached the house, custodian Albert Edwards "opened the door and stood on the porch," causing the torchbearer to retreat. "The mob again set up a great howl, cursing Lincoln, cursing the home and threatening its destruction at some future time. Then the mob turned and went away." (Left, LFFC; below, ALPLM.)

THE HOME OF LINCOLN.

No.	NAME.	RESIDENCE.	REMARKS.

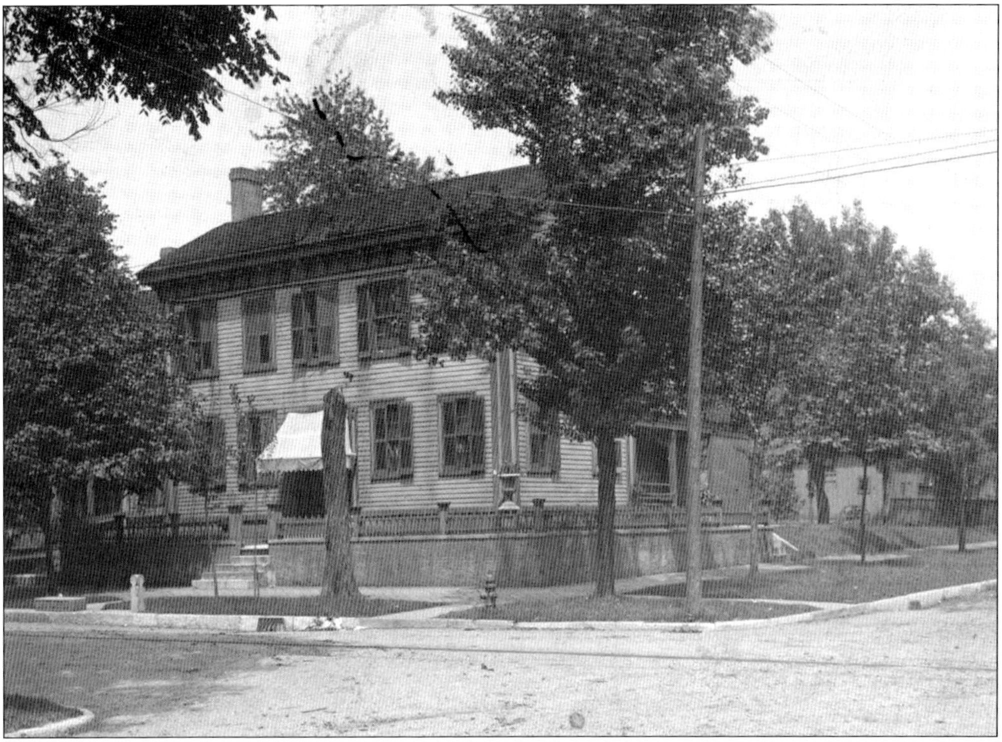

The Lincoln Elm in front of the home (on the left side of this picture) was destroyed by a thunderstorm on August 17, 1906. While newspapers at the time reported that it had been planted by Lincoln before his departure for Washington, the Illinois State Museum conducted testing on the stump in 1947 and determined that it had been planted around 1844 or 1845. (SVC.)

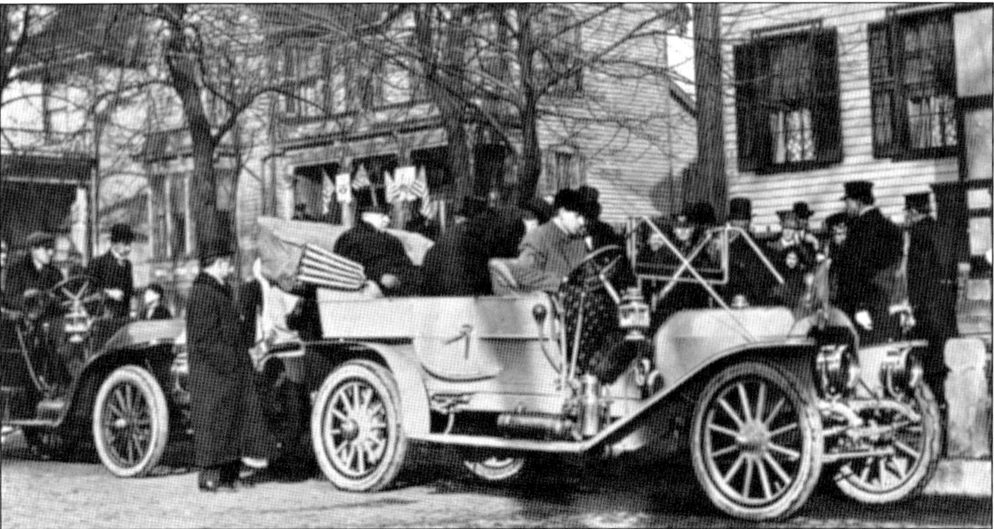

Pres. William Howard Taft came to Springfield in 1911 to commemorate the 50th anniversary of Lincoln's departure from the city. After speaking to a joint session of the state legislature and visiting several sites, Taft made his way to the Lincoln home. "I wish to walk upon the floors that Lincoln trod," he told Josephine Edwards. Historian Wayne C. Temple wrote, "Taft became the first President to tour the entire residence of the Lincolns." (SVC.)

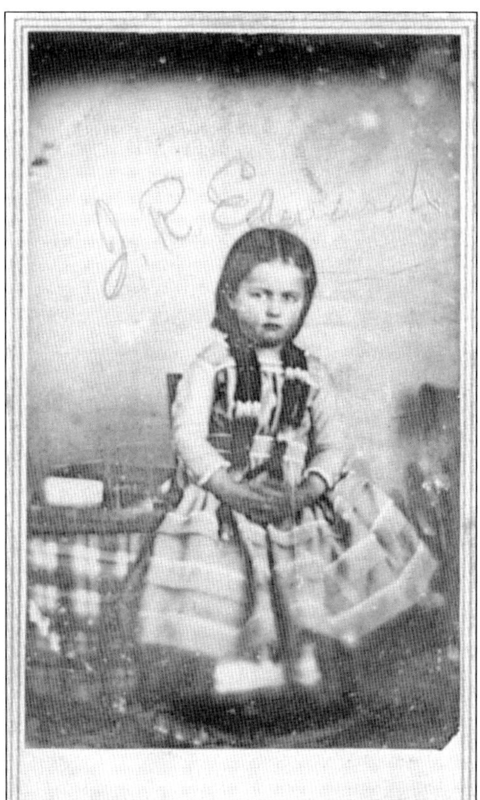

Albert Edwards's widow, Josephine Remann Edwards (pictured here as a little girl and as a young woman in the 1860s), became the custodian of the home in 1915 when her husband died. She was assisted by her two daughters, Mary Edwards Brown and Georgie H. Edwards. As a child, "Little Josie" had been a playmate of the Lincoln boys, and Abraham would carry her on his shoulders on the streets. Much to the delight of tourists, Josephine would share childhood memories of the Lincoln family. During her tenure, the state abolished the board of trustees and placed the home under the jurisdiction of the Department of Public Works and Buildings. Josephine died in the home on October 4, 1918, and her funeral was held in the front parlor two days later. Her daughter Mary Brown then took over as custodian. (Both, ALPLM.)

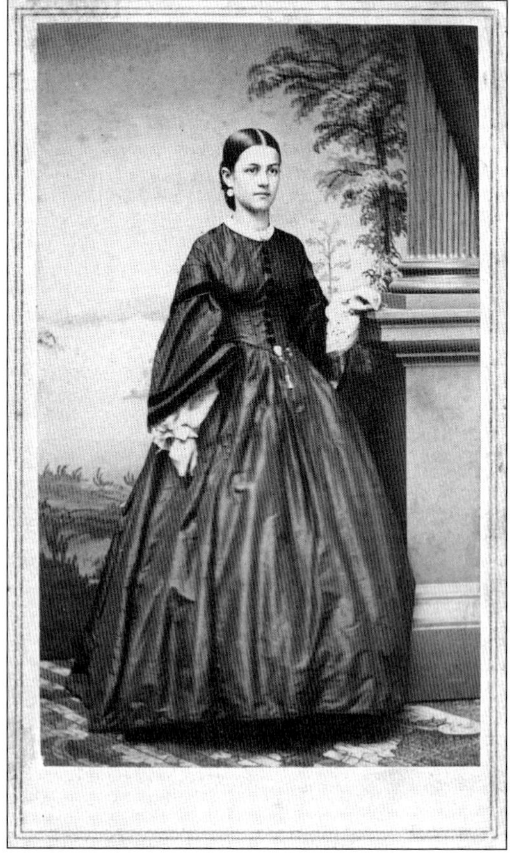

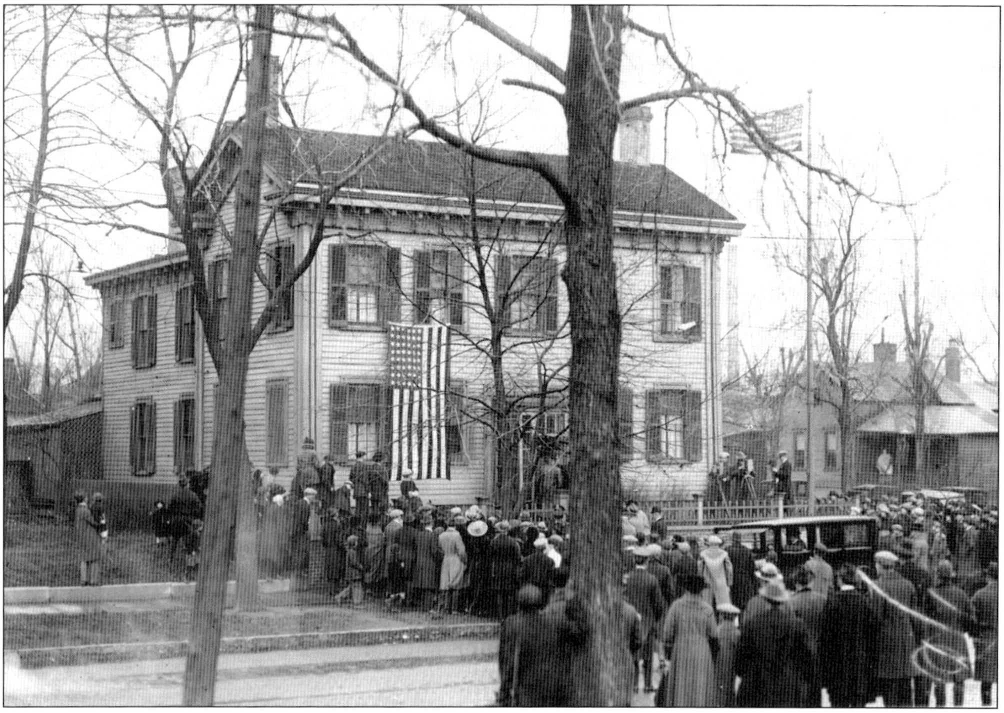

When former French prime minister Georges Clemenceau visited the home in December 1922, one newspaper reported that "he inspected the Lincoln relics with deep interest." Much to his delight, Mary "Mamie" Brown, the custodian of the home from 1918 to 1924, presented him with a penholder made from wood from the floor. "You must come again when you have more time," Mary Brown said as he was preparing to leave. "Yes, on my next trip," he replied with a smile. (JW.)

Not until the late 1920s did Virginia Stuart Brown, who served as custodian from 1924 to 1953, model the downstairs after the *Frank Leslie's Illustrated Newspaper*'s drawings (see pages 29–30) so that visitors could see the living spaces "exactly as they were during" Lincoln's time. Herbert Hoover visited the home in June 1931 when he came to Springfield for the rededication of Lincoln's tomb. This image of Hoover shows a "storm shed" that had been built in 1918 to protect the front entrance in wintertime. (SVC.)

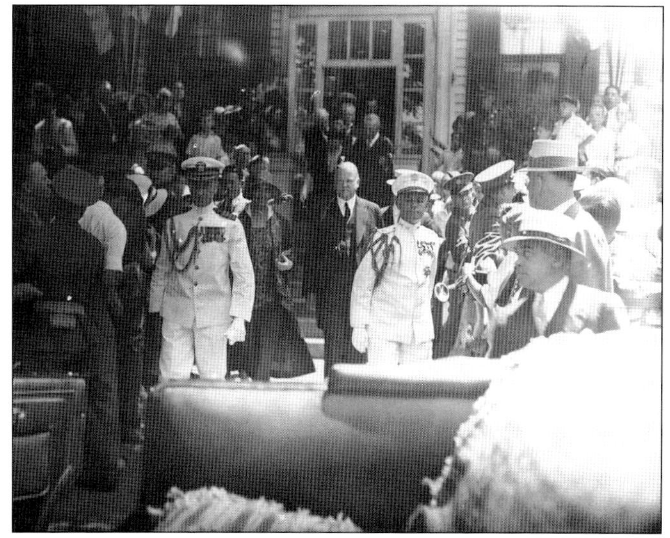

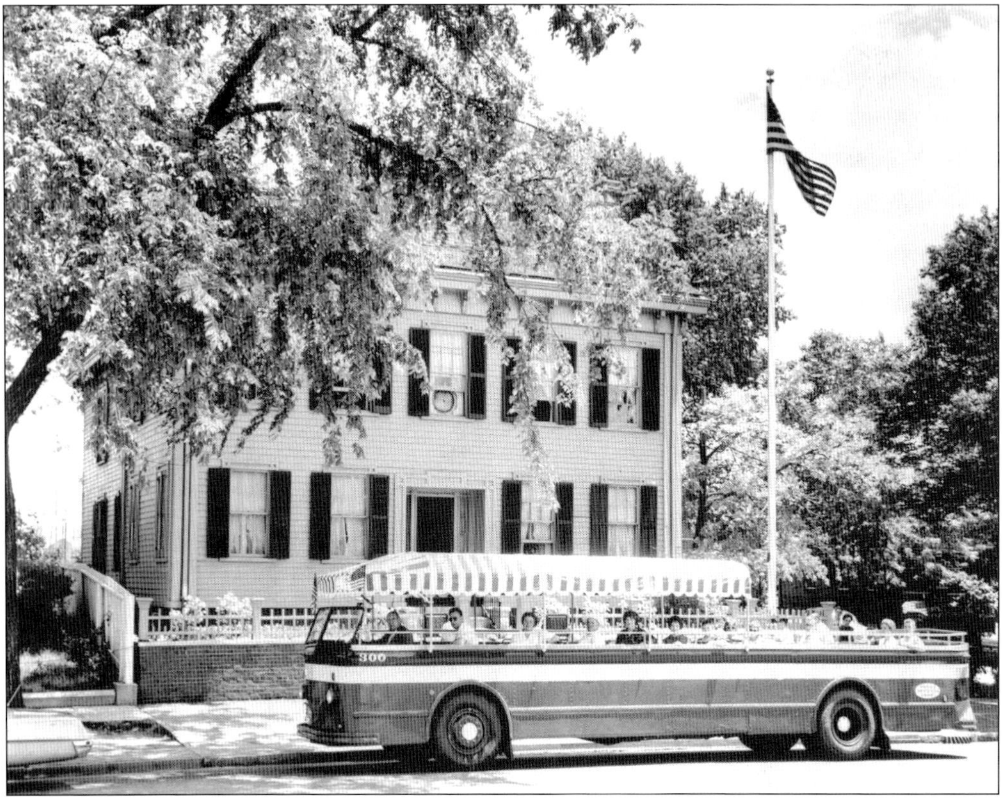

In the 1930s, the Abraham Lincoln Association raised funds to assist the state in restoring Lincoln's bedroom. Following World War II, custodian Virginia Stuart Brown encouraged the state to open the entire home to the public. Pictured here is a tour bus going by the home in the 1940s. (LIHO.)

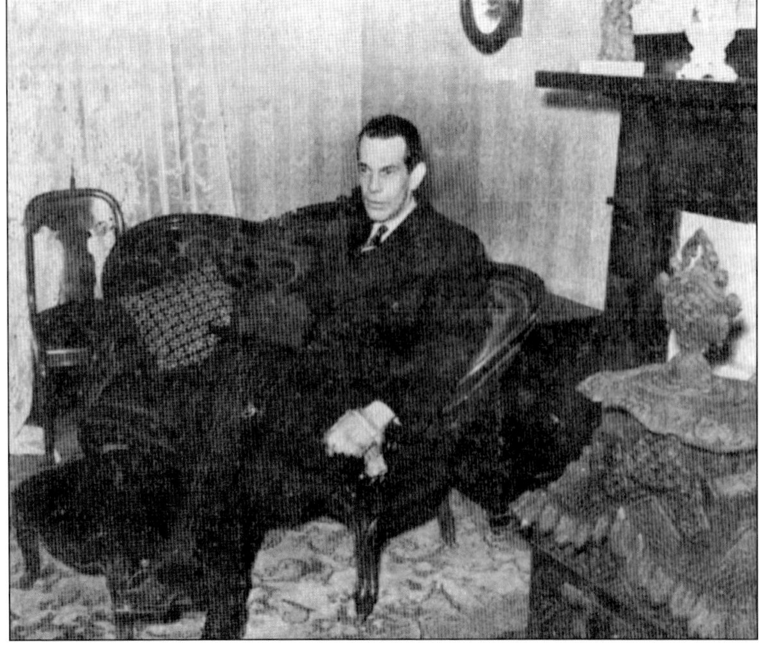

Actor Raymond Massey, who portrayed Lincoln on the stage and on screen from the late 1930s until the early 1960s, visited Lincoln's home on March 24, 1940. At the invitation of the mayor of Springfield, Massey stepped into the railed off portion of the double parlors and took a seat. He said his visit was "an inspiration, and an emotional experience." (SVC.)

Like many Chicago families, Edward and Florence DeMichaels drove their two children, Robert and Eileen, down to Springfield to see the Lincoln home around 1951. Robert, who passed away in 2021, was the uncle of the author of this book. Eileen, who is now 85 at the time of this writing (November 2025), is the author's mother. (JW.)

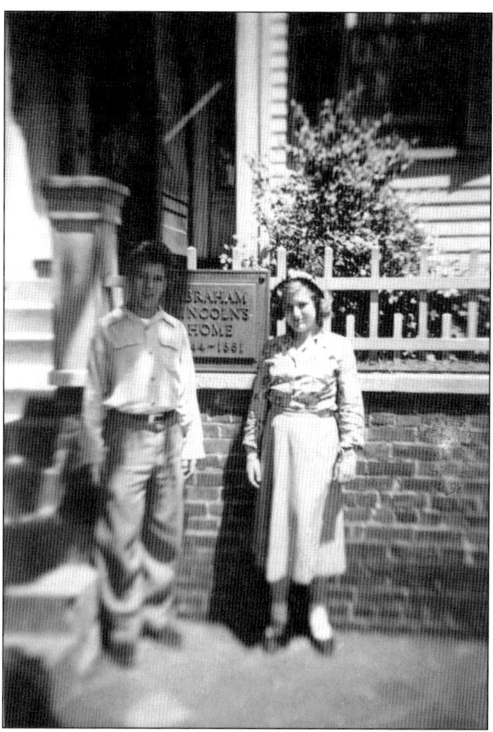

Two days after receiving the Democratic nomination for president in July 1952, Adlai Stevenson II (the great-grandson of Lincoln's friend Jesse W. Fell) "invoked the spiritual aid of Lincoln," writes a biographer. Shortly before midnight, "he quietly visited Lincoln's home and for an hour sat alone in his rocking chair, drawing strength for the staggering task." The *Chicago Tribune* mocked Stevenson's wit, calling him "Adlai the side-splitter"—compared with Lincoln as "the Railsplitter." In this image, Stevenson (right) stands at the Lincoln Tomb around 1950. (ILSOS.)

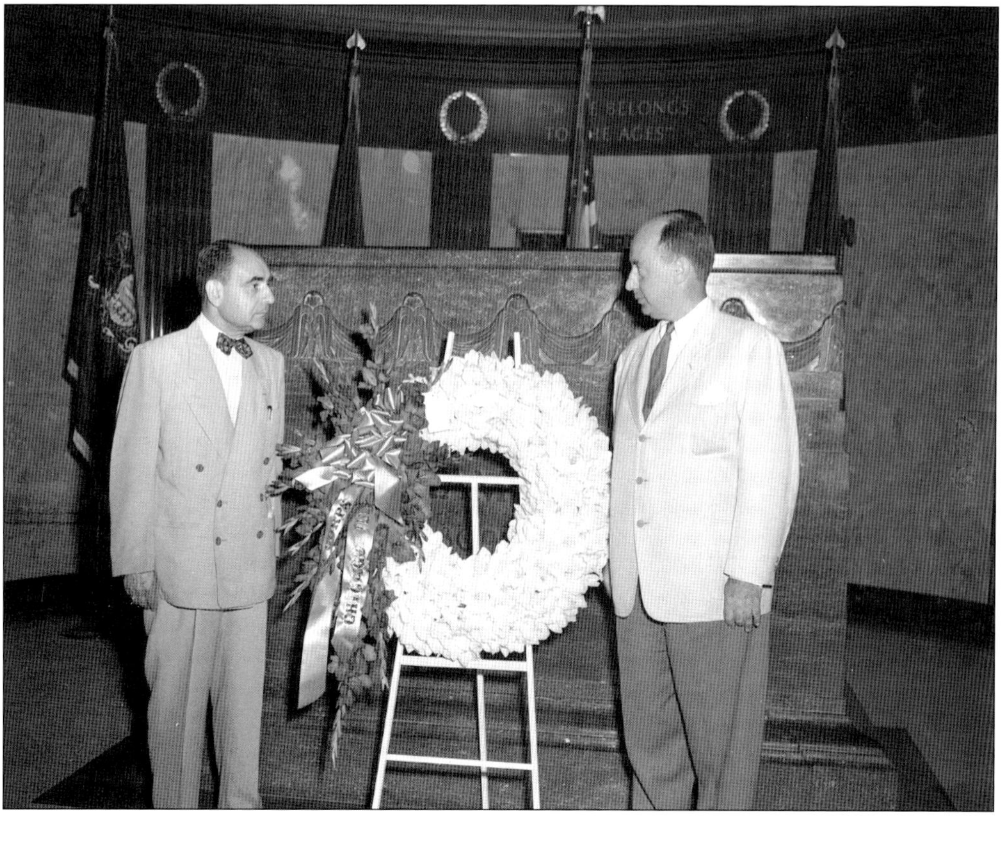

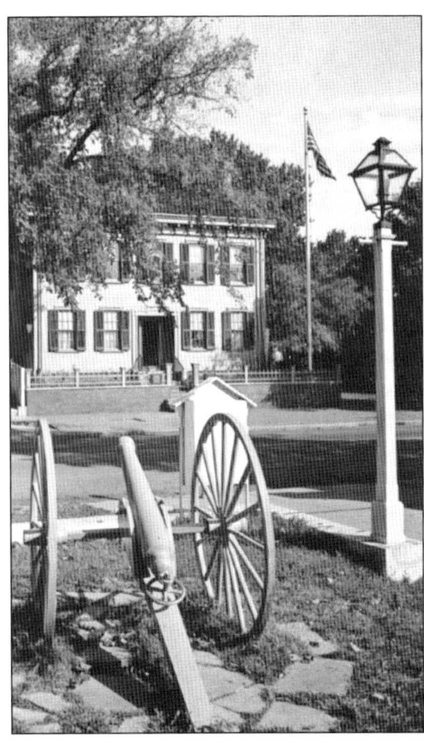

In the 1950s, the state restored the home, reopening it to the public on February 12, 1955. For the first time, visitors could tour the second floor. The final custodian, Kathleen A. Bradish (the only custodian not to live in the home), had been a tour guide at the home since 1941. She retired in 1958. In the 1960s, a cannon faced the home from across the street. (SVC.)

In 1962, Illinois Bell Telephone Company produced *Appointment with Tomorrow*, a 33-minute educational film about a high school student who travels to Lincoln sites and learns about the Illinois state government. This image is from the Mercury Studio Collection. (SVC.)

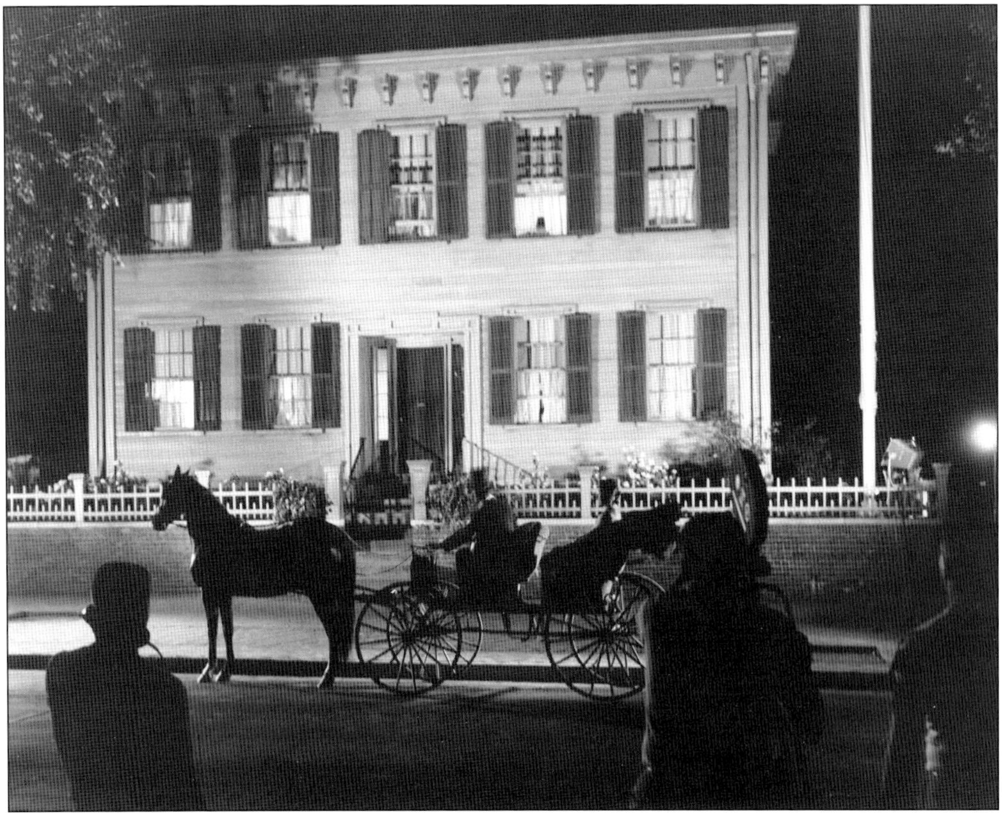

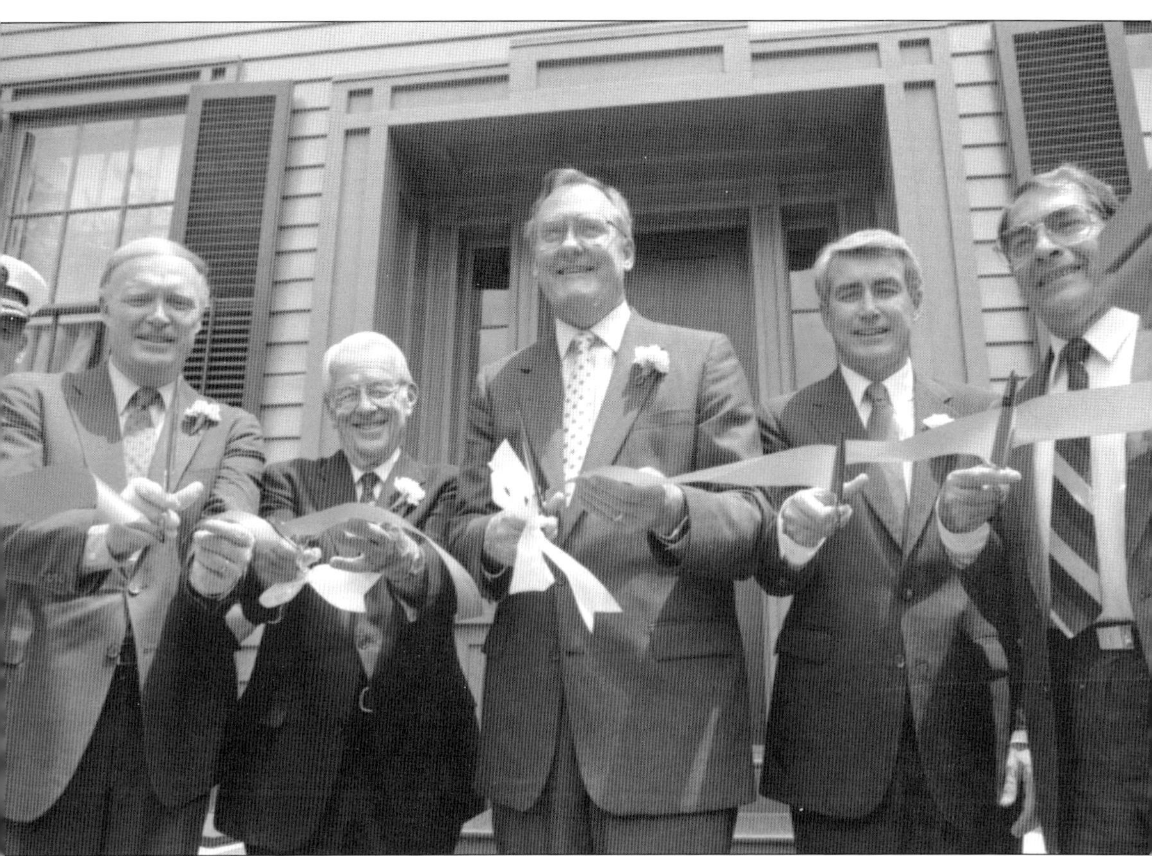

"We didn't have any money," Jim Edgar later recalled of when he married Brenda Smith in 1967, "so we went to Effingham, the Ramada Inn, for our first night." On their way to St. Louis, Edgar said, "No, that's too far. Let's go to Springfield," because he was intrigued to go to see the Lincoln sites for the first time. "So we went to Springfield . . . and the highlight of our honeymoon was we went to Lincoln's home." Edgar is pictured here (second from right) at the reopening of the home in 1988 after a lengthy renovation. Edgar went on to serve as governor of Illinois from 1991 to 1999, and on nice evenings, he would walk his dogs in Lincoln's neighborhood. Sadly, Governor Edgar died in September 2025, after a long battle with cancer. The author of this book is grateful to have had a lengthy conversation with him about Lincoln around two weeks before his passing. He was excited to know that this book was in progress, and the author is honored to include him in it. (LIHO.)

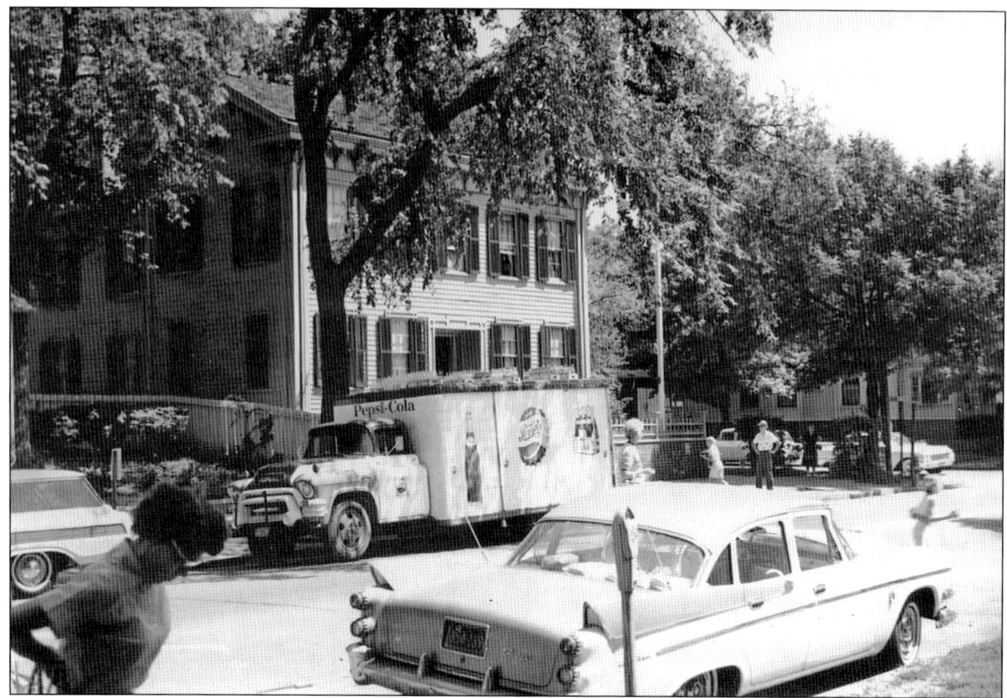

In *Land of Lincoln: Adventures in Abe's America* (2007), journalist Andrew Ferguson recalls visiting Lincoln's neighborhood in the 1960s. Although the city had taken steps to try to reduce traffic near the home, it was "a living neighborhood, still knitted into the city's warp and woof. People came and went, moved in and out, raised their children and opened shops, tore down a house here and put up a new one there." But "the neighborhood had grown shabby by the 1960s; even I, Lincoln-sozzled and young though I was, could see that," wrote Ferguson. "Next door to the Lincoln home was a bookshop whose disarranged shelves held every Lincoln title imaginable, and a glorious souvenir store in which my brothers and I dawdled for what seemed like hours. . . . On the gift shop's porch a spectacular row of battle flags flew—including Old Glory and the Stars and Bars, welcoming tourists of every inclination." (Both, SVC.)

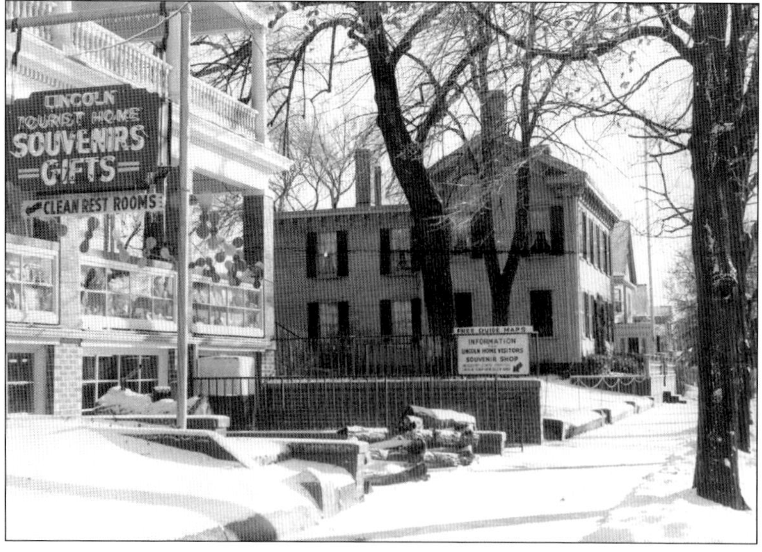

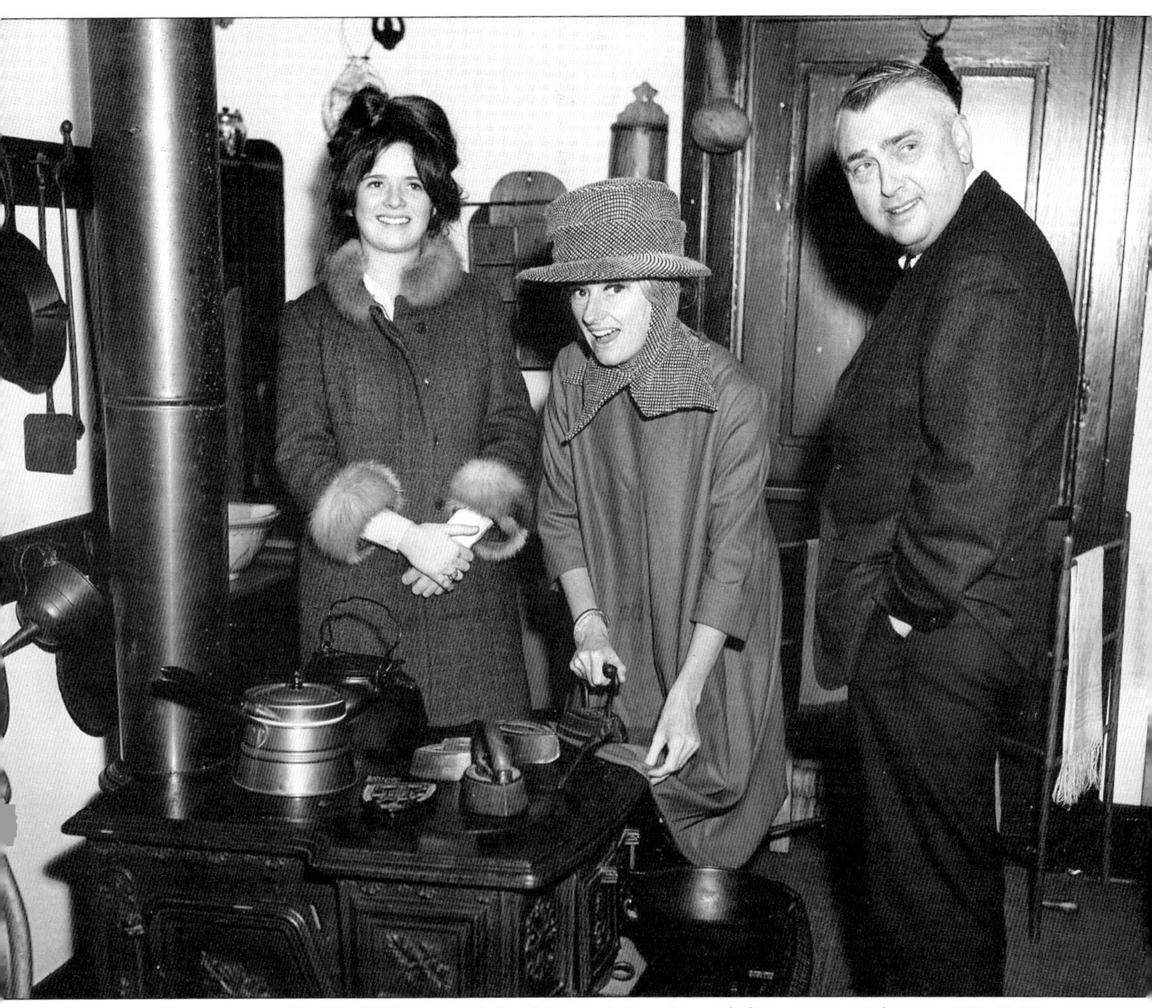

Actress and comedian Phyllis Diller stands looking at Mary Lincoln's stove on February 12, 1966. "Honestly, I didn't know it was Lincoln's birthday. Not until last night at the dinner table when someone mentioned it. I'm not lying. It just never occurred to me," she said after her visit. Diller had previously visited Springfield in 1961, after which she told her manager "that the next time I flew over Springfield, I wanted to stop and take another look at the Lincoln Home. I'm doing a Lincoln Room in my new home and I want the furnishings to be as close to the originals as possible. Sound crazy? Well, what can you expect?" Her manager remembered that request and arranged for this 1966 visit during a trip from Los Angeles to Chicago to New York City. "I love Springfield—and that home. And this is a wonderful day to be here," she said. During her visit, Diller acquired several souvenirs and antiques, including gifts from the famous collector of Lincolniana King V. Hostick. Years later, when Joan Rivers asked Diller in 1993 to name a famous person she had had an affair with, Diller deadpanned, "Lincoln." (SVC.)

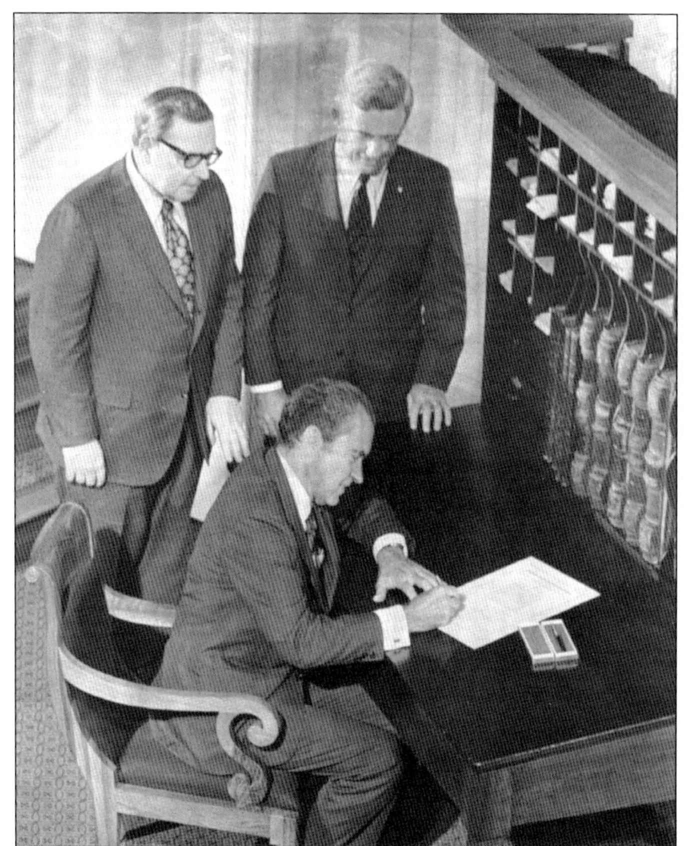

On August 18, 1971, Pres. Richard Nixon visited the Old State Capitol in Springfield, where he signed a bill into law establishing the Lincoln Home National Historic Site. Standing by him are Gov. Richard Ogilvie (left) and Congressman Paul Findley (right). The site was formally established on October 9, 1972. (SVC.)

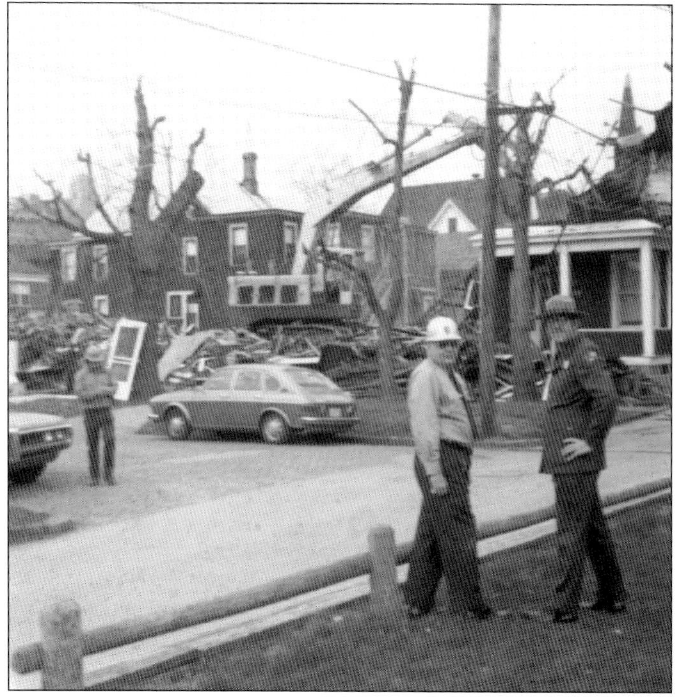

Following the creation of the Lincoln Home National Historic Site, the National Park Service had post–Civil War buildings demolished to remove anachronistic structures from the neighborhood. This 1974 photograph shows some of the demolition in progress. (LIHO.)

William Bartelt, one of the foremost scholars of Lincoln's time in Indiana, worked as a seasonal park ranger at the Lincoln Home National Historic Site during the summers of 1973 and 1974. He is pictured here ringing the Lincolns' doorbell. (Bill Bartelt.)

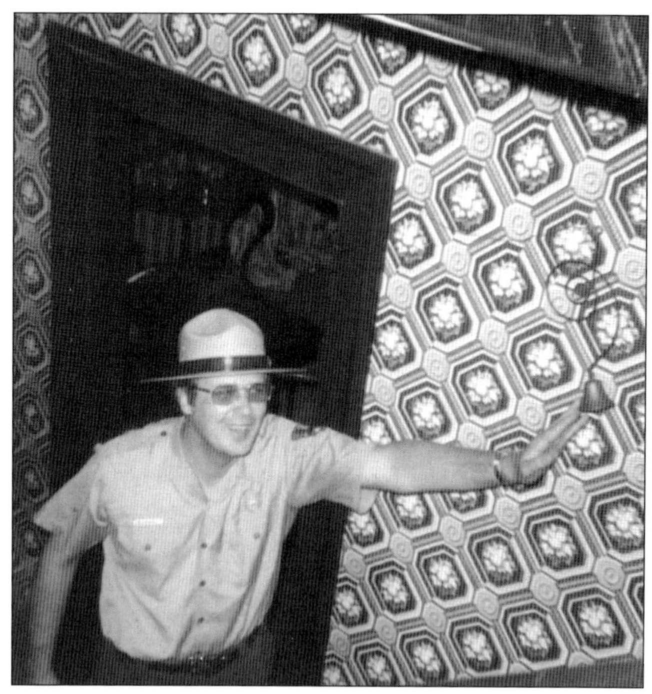

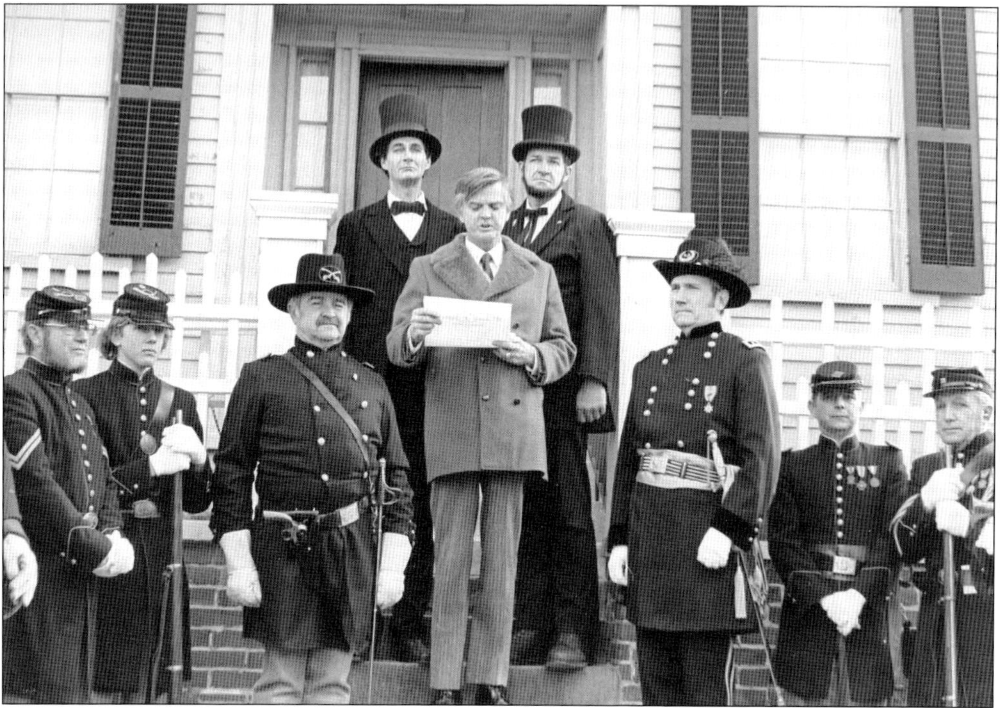

Lincoln scholar Wayne "Doc" Temple (third from right) is pictured here dressed as a general in the Illinois militia and an officer of the 114th Illinois Volunteer Infantry on January 23, 1976, as Gov. Daniel Walker reads a proclamation dedicating Lincoln's post road to New Salem. Behind the governor stand two Lincoln presenters, one with a beard and one without. Doc passed away at the age of 101 in 2025. (Alan E. Hunter.)

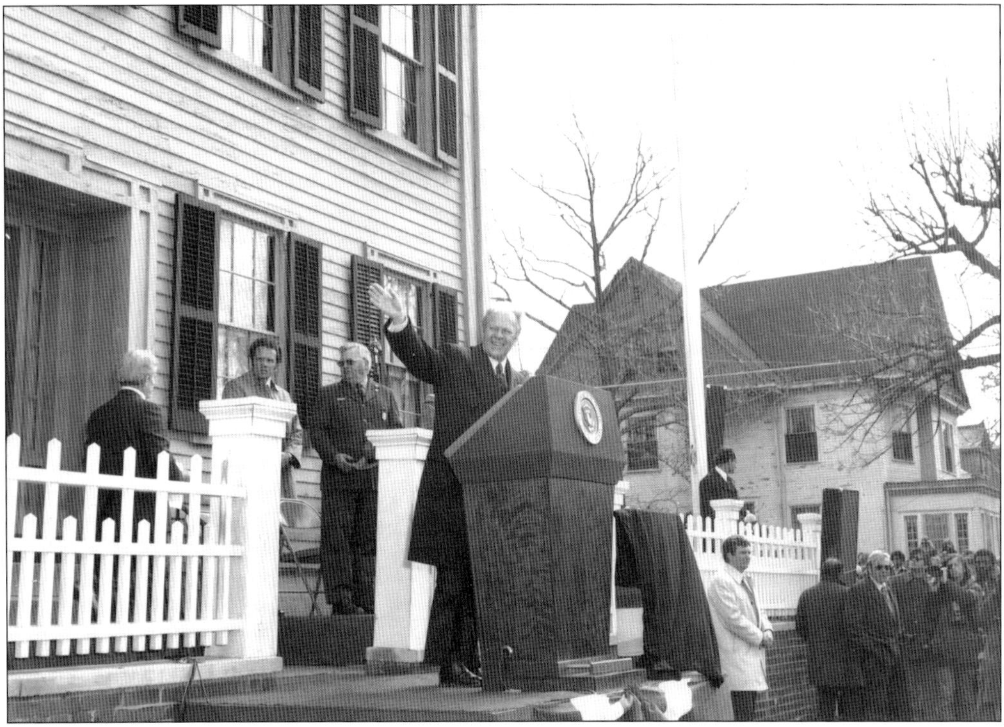

On March 5, 1976, Pres. Gerald Ford spoke at the unveiling ceremony for the cornerstone of the Lincoln Home's new visitor center. In making his remarks, Ford, a former National Park Service ranger, alluded to Lincoln's second inaugural address: "It is to Abraham Lincoln that we owe the opportunity to observe our national bicentennial at peace among ourselves and with all nations." (LIHO.)

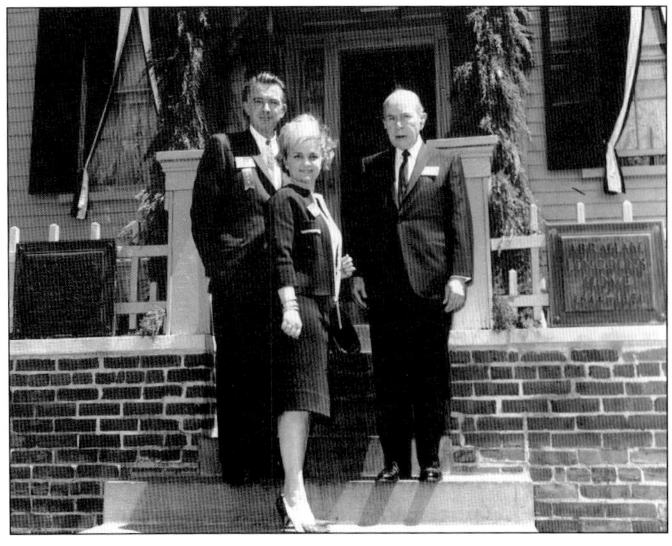

Robert Todd Lincoln Beckwith (at right), the great-grandson of Abraham Lincoln and the last known descendant of Lincoln, visited the home in 1976, bringing with him rare Lincoln family heirlooms worth $100,000 to donate to the state. When one reporter marveled at a set of knives that featured Henry Clay, Beckwith's longtime companion, Margaret Fristoe, said, "We've spread our butter every morning with these for many, many years." (LFFC.)

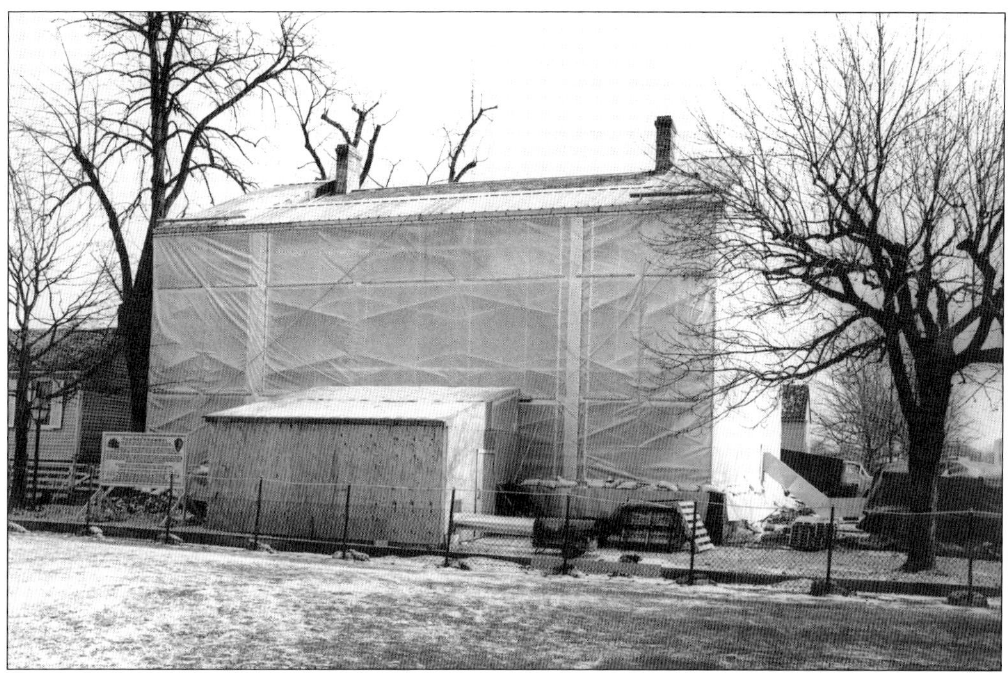

A giant plastic tent was placed around the home during the renovation in 1987–1988 in order to protect the structure and help maintain comfortable temperatures for workers inside. The renovation cost $1.7 million. (SVC.)

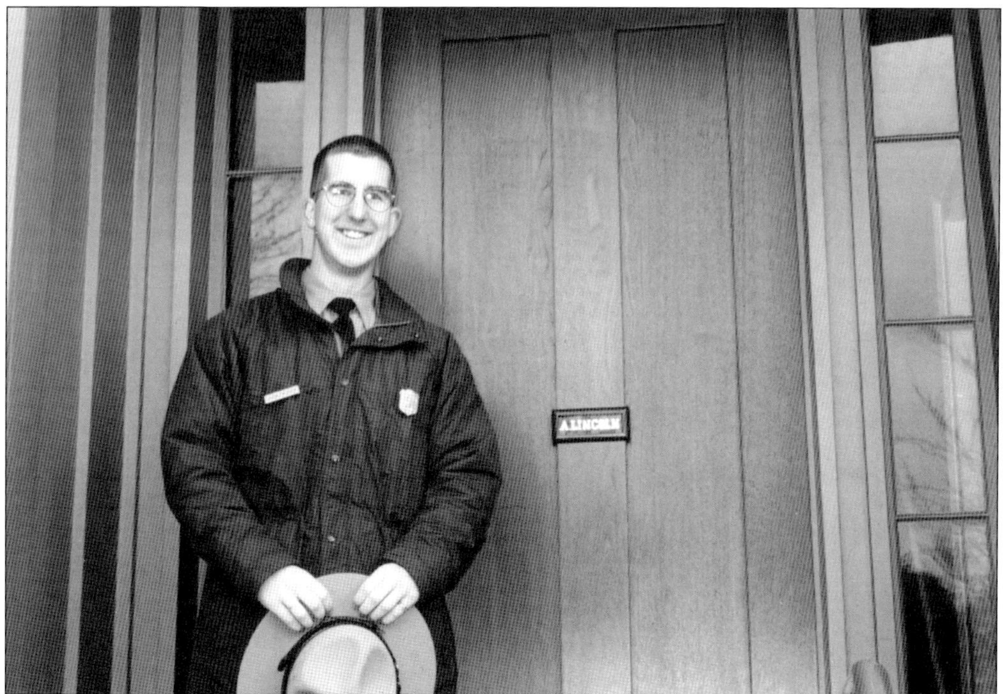

Early in his career, Jason Emerson worked as a seasonal ranger at the Lincoln Home (pictured here in 1997). Emerson went on to become the preeminent biographer of Robert Todd Lincoln, and the author of a half-dozen other books on Abraham and Mary Lincoln. (Jason Emerson.)

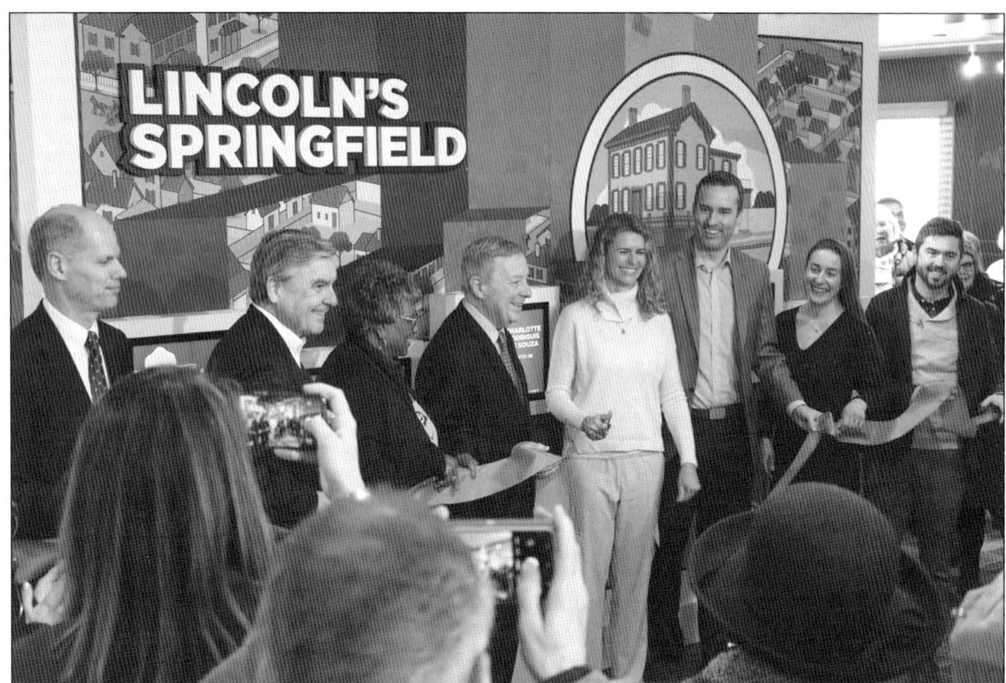

On February 12, 2024, the Lincoln Presidential Foundation opened the first-ever youth exhibit at the Lincoln Home National Historic Site. Located in the Corneau House, the exhibit brings to life the stories of six members of Lincoln's community, including Mariah Vance and Charlotte De Souza. Pictured here at the ribbon-cutting ceremony are Lincoln Home superintendent Tim Good, foundation board chair Satch Pecori, state senator Doris Turner, US senator Dick Durbin, MG Nelson Family Foundation representatives Tricia Becker and Mark Nelson, foundation president and CEO Erin Carlson Mast, and McCullough Creative president Patrick McCullough. (Above, photograph by Zach Adams; below, photograph by McCullough Creative; both, Lincoln Presidential Foundation.)

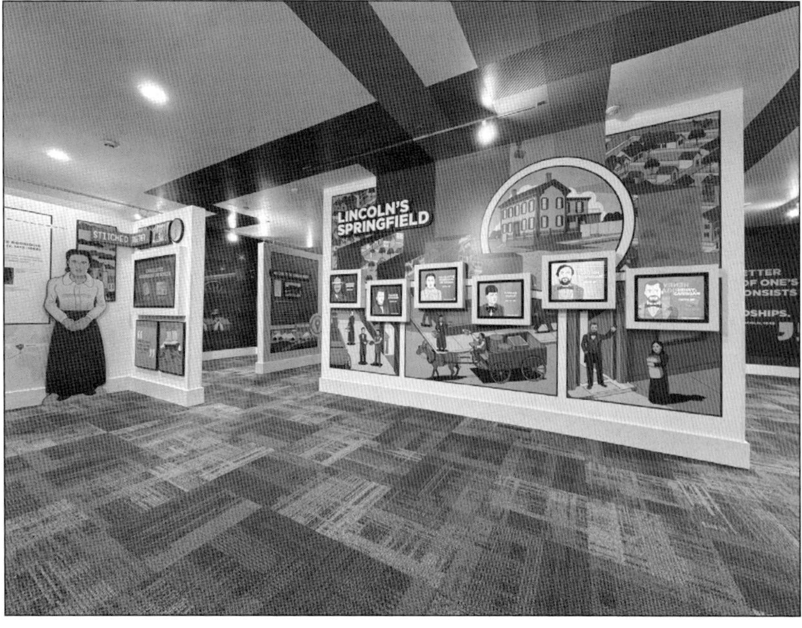

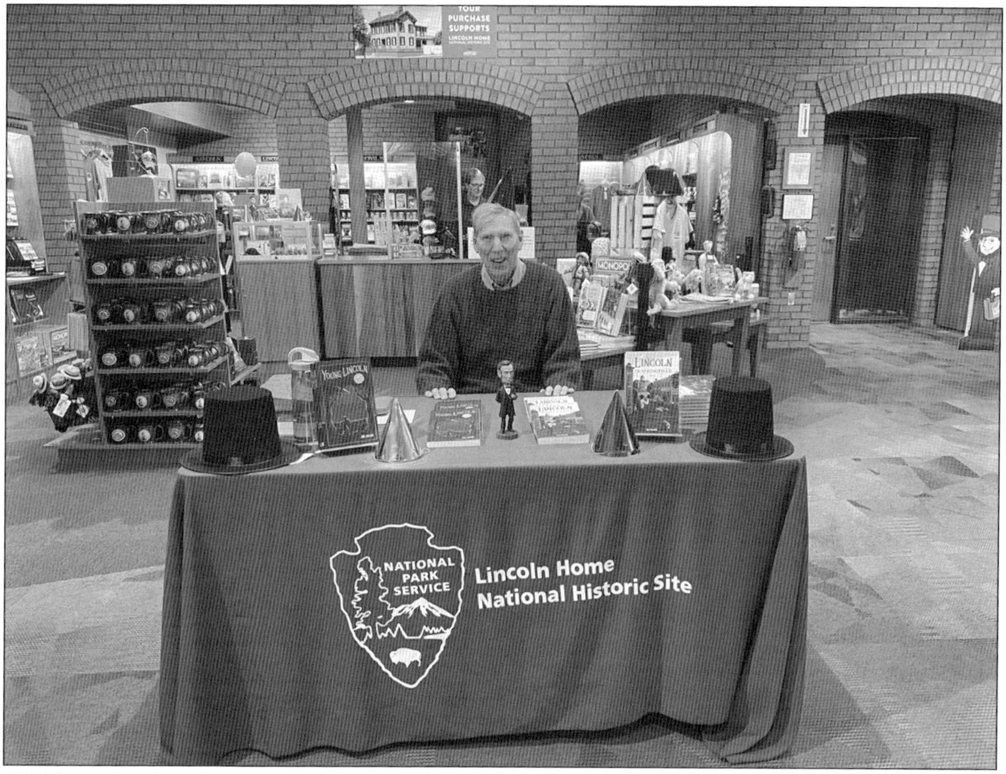

Children's book author Jan Jacobi is a regular at the Lincoln Home gift shop, signing copies of *Young Lincoln*, *Lincoln in Springfield*, and *Lincoln and Douglas* for visitors from around the country. A retired middle school English teacher from St. Louis, Jacobi plans two more volumes for his young adult series on Lincoln. Behind him, store manager Amy Devaisher works at the counter. (Jan Jacobi.)

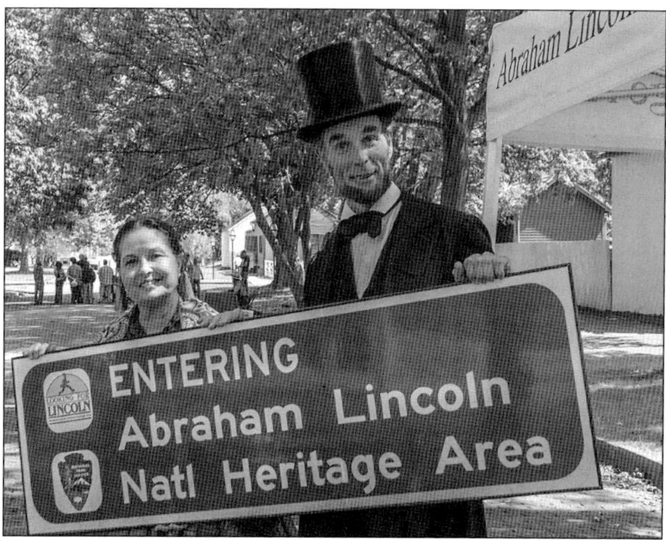

With offices located in the Lincoln Home National Historic Site, Looking for Lincoln is a nonprofit that promotes heritage tourism by working with communities throughout the 43-county Abraham Lincoln National Heritage Area to tell stories of Lincoln's life, times, and legacy. Pictured here are Fritz Klein and Pam Brown depicting Abraham and Mary Lincoln in honor of the National Park Service's 100th birthday in 2016. (Looking for Lincoln.)

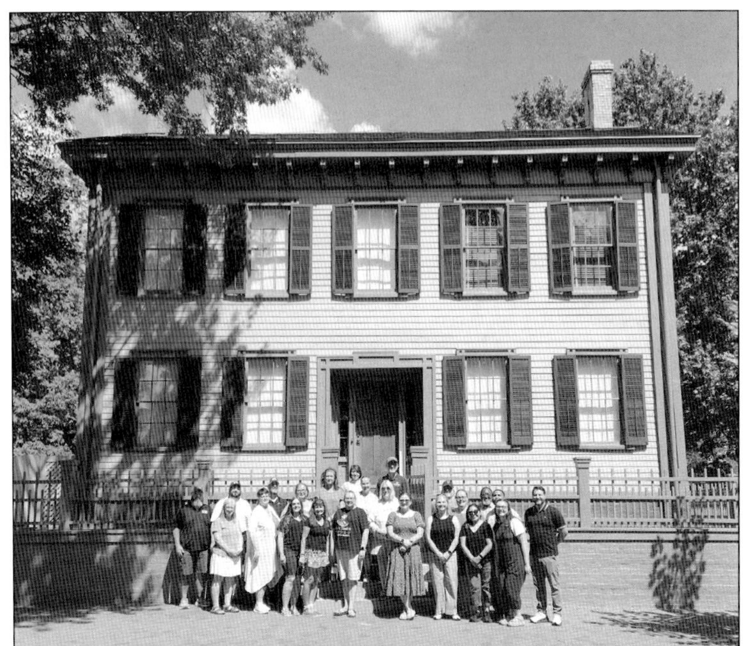

Every summer, the Gilder Lehrman Institute of American History hosts a weeklong workshop in Springfield. Teachers travel from around the United States to study the life of Abraham Lincoln so that they can take what they have learned back to their classrooms. Educators in this group in July 2025 came from as far away as Saipan in the Northern Mariana Islands. (JW.)

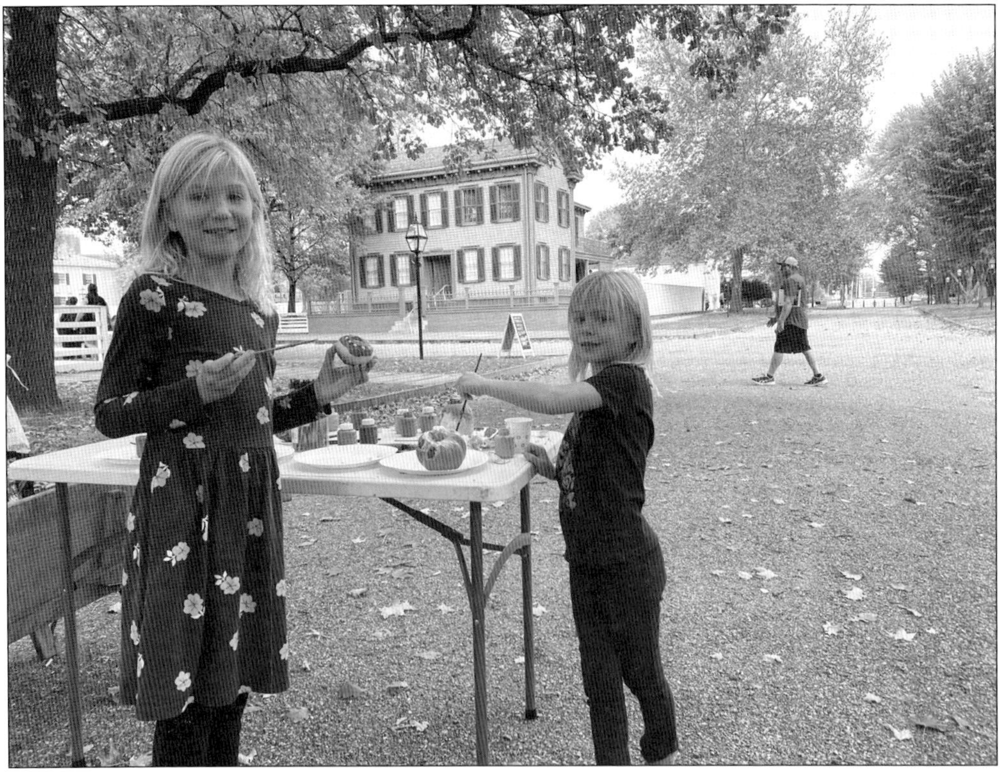

On October 22, 2022, the author of this book delivered a lecture at the University of Illinois Springfield on his book *A House Built By Slaves: African American Visitors to the Lincoln White House*. Earlier in the day, his family visited the Lincoln Home, where his daughters, Charlotte and Clara, did a fall-themed craft set up by National Park Service staff. (JW.)

Eight

The Disappearing Act
Isaac Diller's Special Memory

It was a moment Isaac R. Diller would never forget. He was at his aunt's house on the southwest corner of Eighth and Jackson Streets (the Corneau House), diagonally across the intersection from the Lincolns' home, when Boston photographer John Adams Whipple asked permission to set up on his aunt's stoop to take a photograph. Excitedly, Diller ran across the street to pose in a "free picture" with the Republican nominee and his two little sons. But just as Whipple was removing his lens cover to capture the scene, the six-year-old Diller heard a farm wagon clanking by. He turned his head, and, in the process, his entire upper body blurred. Only his feet and ankles appear sharp in Whipple's image.

It was the summer of 1860, and Abraham Lincoln was on the verge of making history. He posed perfectly still, along with Willie and Tad, knowing, perhaps, that this photograph would circulate among potential voters back east.

For the rest of his life, Diller loved to recount the story of "why my head did the 'disappearing act.' " On Lincoln's birthday in 1932, he addressed the 900 students at the state teachers college in Slippery Rock, Pennsylvania, about "the four times I remembered seeing Mr. Lincoln." Defending the veracity of his memories, he wrote in a letter in 1938, "Some people question a six year old boy remembering such things, but our minds were not kept in a whirl with moving pictures, etc, as children of today have, and events made a deeper impression, I contend."

Whipple took two photographs that day. The other image is reproduced on the back of the Lincoln Home National Historic Site tour tickets, enabling visitors to compare what they see with the image made in 1860.

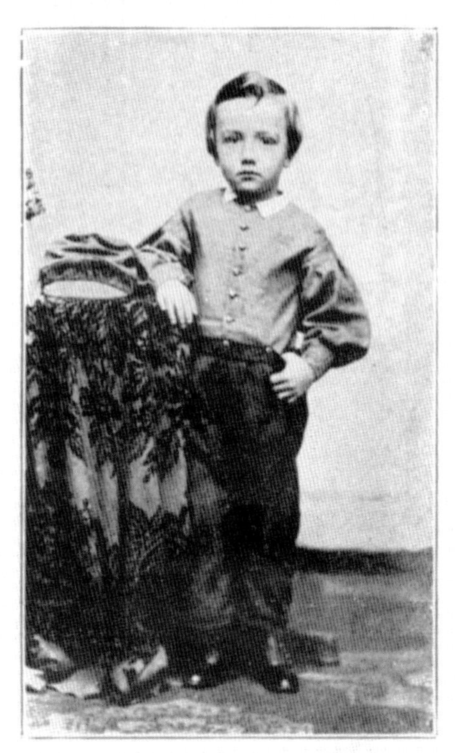

Born one block west of the Lincolns' home on July 14, 1854, young Isaac R. Diller was a regular playmate of Willie and Tad's. (His invitation to Willie's birthday party appears on page 50.) Diller is pictured here at about the time of his "disappearing act." (LFFC.)

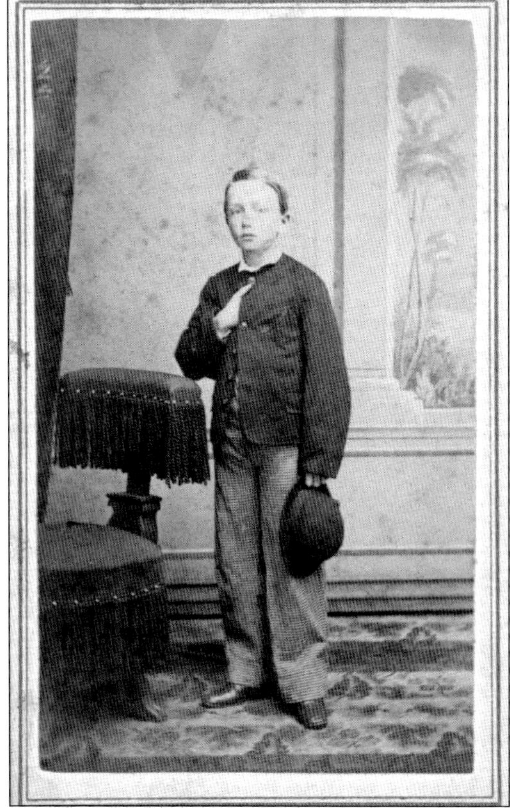

Diller was "born again" on April 3, 1866. As an adult, he always used the story of the Whipple photograph as an opportunity to share the Gospel. For instance, he concluded a 1938 letter about the picture by stating that the "most important" event in his life was being " 'Born Again,' and I am glad Mr. Lincoln also had that experience, and hope you have had also, as that makes all who have, brothers in Jesus." (Yale University.)

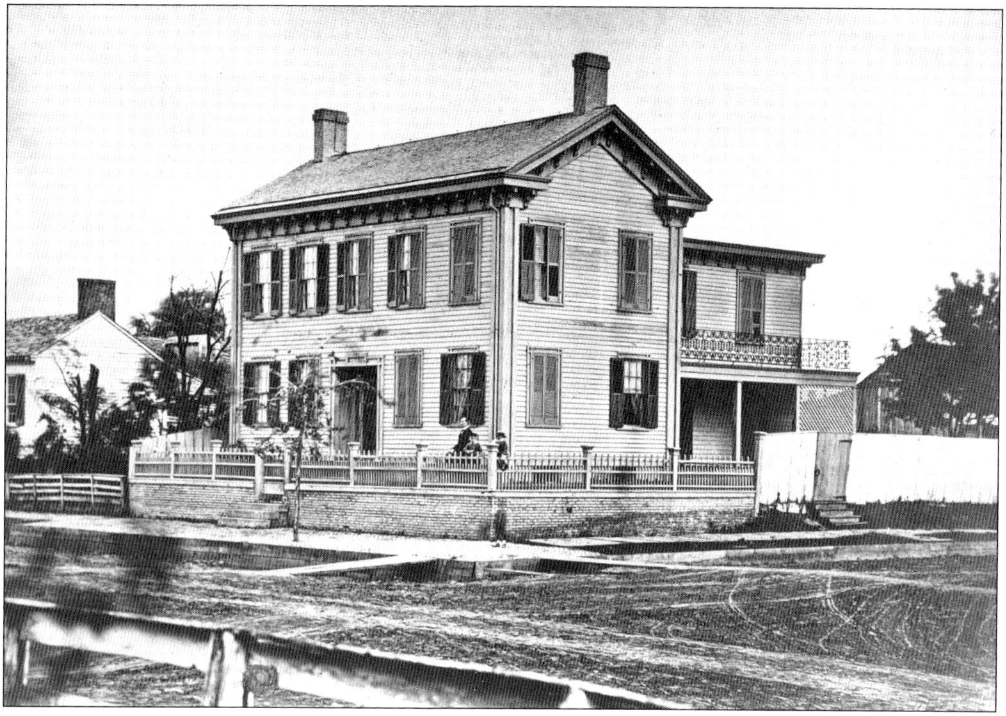

In John Adams Whipple's photograph, Diller's blurry figure can be seen just beneath Tad Lincoln, who sits perched upon the fence. In the 1930s, Diller produced a single-page flier telling the story of the photograph and sharing his Christian testimony. By 1940, he had printed five editions and distributed 12,500 copies. Seen here are the complete photograph and a close-up detail of Diller's blurry body. (Both, LOC.)

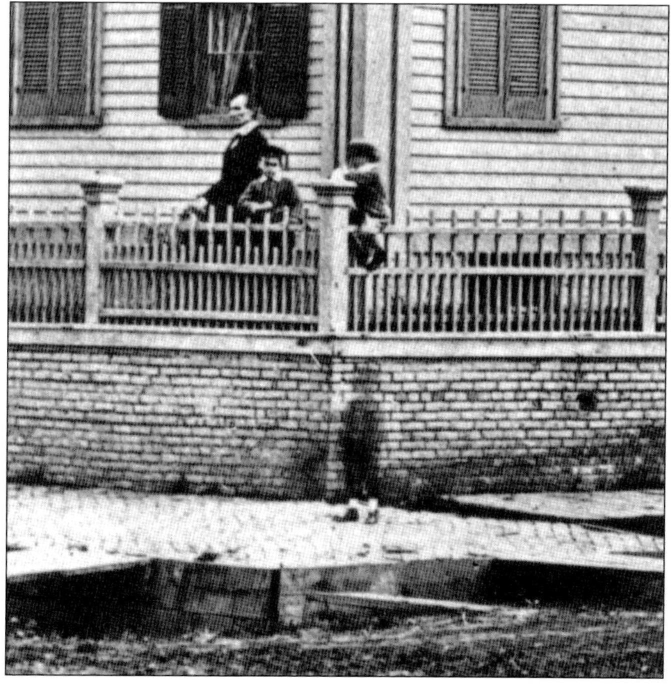

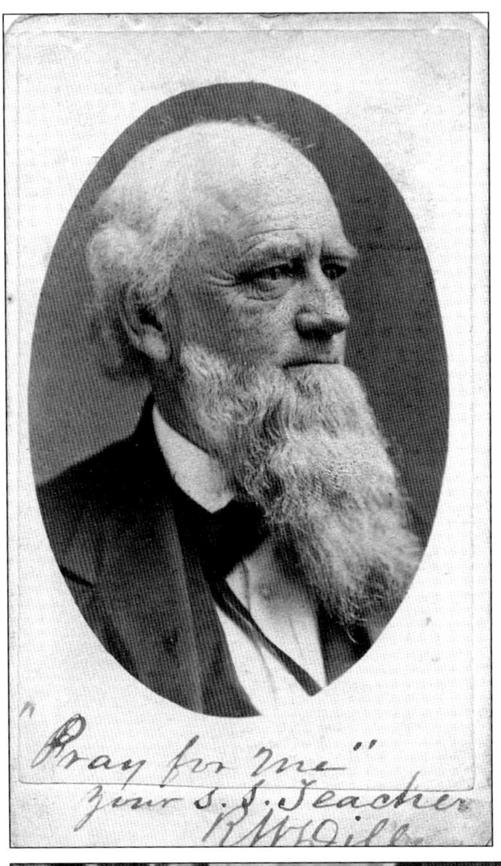

Diller's father, Roland W. Diller, was a local druggist in partnership with Charles S. Corneau, whom Lincoln regularly patronized. In February 1858, when a fire ripped through several buildings on the east side of the public square in Springfield, Lincoln tried to help save some of the items in the store. As he went out the door "with his long arms full of shelf bottles," someone bumped into him and "they all crashed to the sidewalk and broke." (LFA.)

Diller was the last living person to have been photographed with Lincoln. As an adult, he kept a copy of the 1860 Whipple photograph hanging above his desk. In this December 3, 1941, image, he holds that copy of the picture. Diller reflected, "Mine is only reflected glory, but I am glad to have had a slight contact with true greatness." Diller died in 1943 at the age of 89. (ALPLM.)

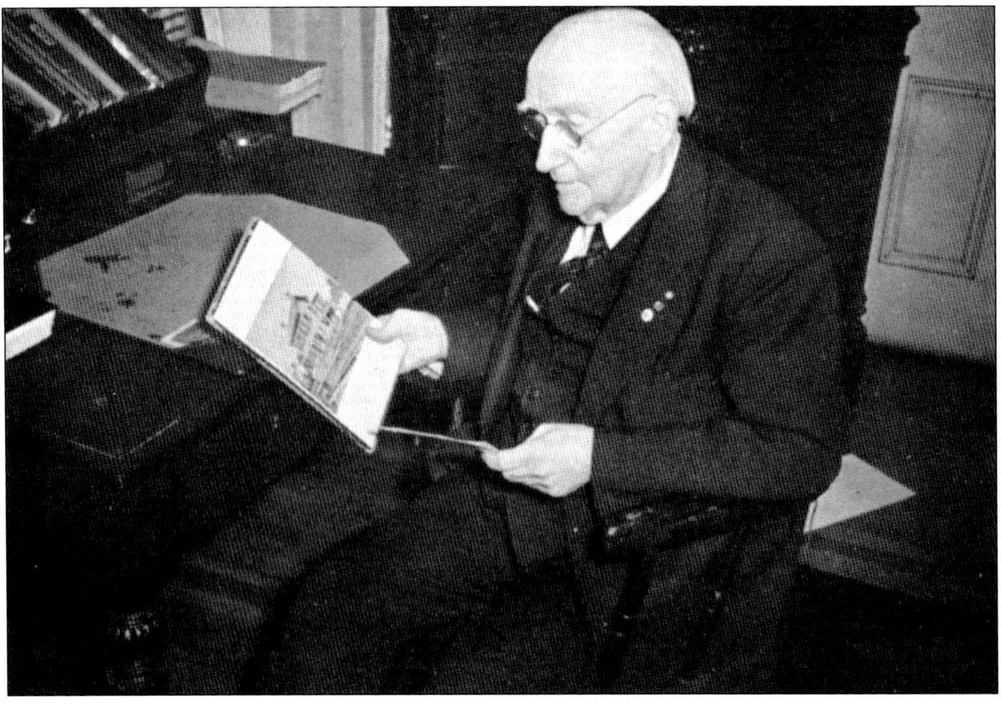

Bibliography

Andreasen, Bryon C. *Looking for Lincoln in Illinois: Lincoln's Springfield*. Southern Illinois University Press, 2015.

Bearss, Edwin C. *Historic Structure Report: Lincoln Home National Historic Site, Illinois*. National Park Service, 1973.

Bowen, A.L. "A. Lincoln: His House." In *Lincoln Centennial Association Papers*, pp. 17–75. Lincoln Centennial Association, 1925.

Burlingame, Michael. *Abraham Lincoln: A Life*. 2 vols. Johns Hopkins University Press, 2008.

Burlingame, Michael, ed. *Sixteenth President-in-Waiting: Abraham Lincoln and the Springfield Dispatches of Henry Villard, 1860–1861*. Southern Illinois University Press, 2018.

Emerson, Jason. *Giant in the Shadows: The Life of Robert T. Lincoln*. Southern Illinois University Press, 2012.

Helm, Katherine. *The True Story of Mary, Wife of Lincoln*. Harper and Brothers, 1928.

Hickey, James T. " 'Own the House till It Ruins Me': Robert Todd Lincoln and His Parents' Home in Springfield." *Journal of the Illinois State Historical Society* 74 (Winter 1981): 279–296.

Holzer, Harold. *Lincoln President-Elect: Abraham Lincoln and the Great Secession Winter 1860–1861*. Simon and Schuster, 2008.

National Park Service. *Historic Structure Report: Lincoln Home National Historic Site*. National Park Service, 2023.

Neely, Mark E., Jr., and Harold Holzer. *The Lincoln Family Album: Photographs from the Personal Collection of a Historic American Family*. Doubleday, 1990.

Paull, Bonnie E., and Richard E. Hart. *Lincoln's Springfield Neighborhood*. The History Press, 2015.

Sangamon Valley Collection, Lincoln Library, Springfield, IL.

Temple, Wayne C. *By Square and Compass: Saga of the Lincoln Home*, rev. ed. Mayhaven, 2002.

Turner, Justin G., and Linda Levitt Turner, eds. *Mary Todd Lincoln: Her Life and Letters*. Alfred A. Knopf, 1987.